Protest, Movements, and Dissent in the Social Sciences

T0316052

Drawing on a wide range of social science disciplines and approaches, each chapter in this book offers a comprehensive analysis of social protest, political dissent and collective action. The distinguished scholars contributing to the book discuss some of the key theoretical and methodological issues in social protest research, and analyse recent instances of collective dissent around the globe, ranging from the 15M movement in Spain, to the 2011 Salford riots in the UK, to Pro-Palestinian activism in Jerusalem. The result of these contributions is a sophisticated and multifaceted collection that enriches our understanding of why, when, and how groups of people decide to act collectively in order to pursue political change. The book is a timely testament to the vitality of the field. This book was originally published as a special issue of *Contemporary Social Science*.

Giovanni A. Travaglino, PhD, is a Research Associate in the School of Psychology at the University of Kent, Canterbury, UK. His research interests include leadership and deviance, collective opposition to organised crime, and protest. He is editor of *Contention: The Multidisciplinary Journal of Social Protest*, and founder of the *Interdisciplinary Network for Social Protest Research*.

Contemporary Issues in Social Science

Series editor: David Canter, *University of Huddersfield, UK*

Contemporary Social Science, the journal of the **Academy of Social Sciences**, is an interdisciplinary, cross-national journal which provides a forum for disseminating and enhancing theoretical, empirical and/or pragmatic research across the social sciences and related disciplines. Reflecting the objectives of the Academy of Social Sciences, it emphasises the publication of work that engages with issues of major public interest and concern across the world, and highlights the implications of that work for policy and professional practice.

The *Contemporary Issues in Social Science* book series contains the journal's most cutting-edge special issues. Leading scholars compile thematic collections of articles that are linked to the broad intellectual concerns of *Contemporary Social Science,* and as such these special issues are an important contribution to the work of the journal. The series editor works closely with the guest editor(s) of each special issue to ensure they meet the journal's high standards. The main aim of publishing these special issues as a series of books is to allow a wider audience of both scholars and students from across multiple disciplines to engage with the work of *Contemporary Social Science* and the Academy of Social Sciences.

Titles in the series:

Protest, Movements, and Dissent in the Social Sciences

A multidisciplinary perspective

Edited by
Giovanni A. Travaglino

Routledge
Taylor & Francis Group
LONDON AND NEW YORK

ACADEMY
of SOCIAL SCIENCES

First published 2016
by Routledge

2 Park Square, Milton Park, Abingdon, Oxon OX14 4RN
711 Third Avenue, New York, NY 10017, USA

Routledge is an imprint of the Taylor & Francis Group, an informa business

First issued in paperback 2017

British Library Cataloguing in Publication Data
A catalogue record for this book is available from the British Library

ISBN 13: 978-1-138-92454-3 (hbk)
ISBN 13: 978-1-138-09905-0 (pbk)

Typeset in Times New Roman
by RefineCatch Limited, Bungay, Suffolk

Publisher's Note
The publisher accepts responsibility for any inconsistencies that may have
arisen during the conversion of this book from journal articles to book chapters,
namely the possible inclusion of journal terminology.

Disclaimer
Every effort has been made to contact copyright holders for their permission to
reprint material in this book. The publishers would be grateful to hear from any
copyright holder who is not here acknowledged and will undertake to rectify
any errors or omissions in future editions of this book.

Contents

Citation Information

The chapters in this book were originally published in *Contemporary Social Science*, volume 9, issue 1 (March 2014). When citing this material, please use the original page numbering for each article, as follows:

Chapter 1
Social sciences and social movements: the theoretical context
Giovanni A. Travaglino
Contemporary Social Science, volume 9, issue 1 (March 2014) pp. 1–14

Chapter 2
Unity within diversity: a social psychological analysis of the internal diversity of the Indignados movement
Tiina Likki
Contemporary Social Science, volume 9, issue 1 (March 2014) pp. 15–30

Chapter 3
The political economy of Israel's 'social justice' protests: a class and generational analysis
Zeev Rosenhek and Michael Shalev
Contemporary Social Science, volume 9, issue 1 (March 2014) pp. 31–48

Chapter 4
Hashtags, ruling relations and the everyday: institutional ethnography insights on social movements
Bram Meuleman and Corra Boushel
Contemporary Social Science, volume 9, issue 1 (March 2014) pp. 49–62

Chapter 5
A matter of law and order: reporting the Salford riots in local news webpages
Sharon Coen and Caroline Jones
Contemporary Social Science, volume 9, issue 1 (March 2014) pp. 63–78

Chapter 6
The moral economy of the UK student protest movement 2010–2011
Joseph Ibrahim
Contemporary Social Science, volume 9, issue 1 (March 2014) pp. 79–91

Chapter 7

Networks, counter-networks and political socialisation – paths and barriers to high-cost/risk activism in the 2010/11 student protests against fees and cuts
Alexander Hensby
Contemporary Social Science, volume 9, issue 1 (March 2014) pp. 92–105

Chapter 8

Something's wrong here: transnational dissent and the unimagined community
Brian Callan
Contemporary Social Science, volume 9, issue 1 (March 2014) pp. 106–120

Chapter 9

Why the psychology of collective action requires qualitative transformation as well as quantitative change
Andrew G. Livingstone
Contemporary Social Science, volume 9, issue 1 (March 2014) pp. 121–134

For any permission-related enquiries please
visit: http://www.tandfonline.com/page/help/permissions

Notes on Contributors

Corra Boushel is currently completing her PhD in Science and Technology Studies at the University of Edinburgh, UK, looking at standards in carbon offset markets. She has previously worked with environmental organizations in the UK, Spain, and Switzerland.

Brian Callan is a doctoral candidate in the Department of Social Sciences at Loughborough University, UK. His thesis is titled 'Transnational Dissent: Embodied Social Processes in Activism in Israel and Palestine'.

Sharon Coen is a senior lecturer in Psychology at the University of Salford, UK. She has research and teaching experience in the areas of social and media psychology. Her main interests concern the way in which the media portray and respond to social and political issues and how these in turn inform public perceptions of the same issues.

Alexander Hensby is an ESRC-funded doctoral researcher at University of Edinburgh, UK. He previously taught sociology and education at the University of Roehampton, London, UK, and was a research fellow at its Social Research Centre. He is the co-author (with Darren O'Byrne) of *Theorizing Global Studies* (2011).

Joseph Ibrahim is Senior Lecturer in Sociology at Sheffield Hallam University, UK. His research interests are in social movements and political mobilizations, social and political theory, ideology, and social networks. He has published widely in these areas and is currently writing a monograph on the 21st century British anti-capitalist movement.

Caroline Jones is a lecturer in Social Policy at the University of Salford, UK. She teaches social policy and academic writing with a particular interest in sociology and feminism. Her research focuses on representations of the city, particularly in literature and the media.

Tiina Likki has recently obtained her PhD in Social Psychology from the University of Lausanne, Switzerland. Her research focuses on political opinion, in particular issues of social justice, power relations between advantaged and subordinate groups, and social protest. Her PhD thesis was a comparative study of attitudes towards the welfare state in Europe.

Andrew G. Livingstone is Senior Lecturer in Social Psychology at the University of Exeter, UK, having previously held positions at the University of Stirling, UK and Cardiff University, UK. His research interests focus on social identity, intergroup relations and emotion. He is currently an Associate Editor of the *British Journal of Social Psychology*.

Bram Meuleman is currently working towards his PhD in Sociology at the University of Edinburgh, UK, with a focus on the role of values in the internal and external communications of social movement organizations.

NOTES ON CONTRIBUTORS

Zeev Rosenhek is Associate Professor and Chair of the Department of Sociology, Political Science and Communication at the Open University of Israel. His fields of interest include state–economy relations, institutional change and the political economy of neo-liberalisation. He is currently conducting research on the ways in which central banks have diagnosed and explained the current global crisis and their effects on institutional change.

Michael Shalev is Professor of Sociology and Political Science at the Hebrew University of Jerusalem, Israel. He is currently Visiting Professor at the University of the Basque Country, Bilbao, Spain, conducting research comparing the social politics of mass mobilisation and consensus formation in the Spanish and Israeli protest movements of 2011. He has published on the comparative political economy of the advanced OECD countries and the politics and political economy of Israel.

Giovanni A. Travaglino, PhD, is a Research Associate in the School of Psychology at the University of Kent, Canterbury, UK. His research interests include leadership and deviance, collective opposition to organised crime, and protest. He is editor of *Contention: The Multidisciplinary Journal of Social Protest*, and founder of the *Interdisciplinary Network for Social Protest Research*.

Foreword: What Promotes Protests?

Television news now makes us aware of protests wherever they occur, whenever they occur, showing how many and varied they are. Indeed, over the last quarter of a century there has been hardly a country anywhere that has avoided some significant form of social protest. This makes me wonder whether the 21st Century could reasonably be called the Age of Social Protest. After all, even police officers protested on the streets of London not long after they had to manage similar protests in similar locations carried out by the more usual form of protesters: students. The present volume is therefore a timely contribution to consideration of how, why and when protests occur.

The power of social protests has been made clear by the actions in Kiev, not very long ago. A president was ousted and Russian war planes scrambled on the Ukraine border, with subsequent troop movements, because people took to the streets. The much gentler protest of Pussy Riot in neighbouring Russia also caused a stir far beyond its ironic activity. The ill-fated Arab Spring was set in motion by public protests as well.

Of course, there have always been social protests. They were even satirised 2000 years ago in Classical Greek comedies such as Aristophanes' *Lysistrata* in which women protest against the Peloponnesian war by withholding their sexual privileges. But I think the real change in the nature and prevalence of social movements happened in the mid-1980's when the world watched on television the mass demonstrations in the Phillipines which ousted President Ferdinand Marcos. This was the first time that mass protests reached a world-wide audience because of the emergent availability of almost instant television news.

Political and economic considerations are the usual sources for explanations of the emergence of social protests. But, as social protest has become more of a topic for social scientists, other perspectives are emerging that elucidate how these protests come about. In particular, three questions are emerging that are not often asked, but are central to understanding how protest movements gain momentum and sustain it.

One is that when some people take to the streets others stay at home. What causes some to join the protests and others not to? A related but possibly even more challenging question is why these social events occur when they do and what maintains them? Their apparently often sudden outburst is a further aspect requiring explanation. These puzzles are highlighted by the playwright David Hare. In a recent interview he asks why the British were not on the streets to protest against the omnipresent power of the security services, which have been so widely revealed. Hare does not make the point, but it is worth noting, that a ban on foxhunting generated more demonstrations than any outcry against the state of the NHS or other daily concerns of people, despite foxhunting's much more limited impact on most people's daily lives.

The early explanations of who protests, particularly when they erupted into crowds on the streets, proposed that the people involved were bizarre, from the fringes of society or at least displaced from their normal human state by being part of a crowd. The most influential of these viewpoints, still promulgated today, was LeBon's 19th Century use of Darwinian arguments to propose that people *en masse* become more like their animal origins. Half a century later Freudian suggestions that protesters were less open to control by their superegos was an only slightly more exotic framing of a similar idea.

The people putting forward these views of protesters as aberrant individuals were taking the standpoint of the authorities. They were really making moral judgements about those who challenged the existing social order. It was when social scientists themselves got caught up in protest movements in the 1960's, campaigning against the war in Vietnam and for Civil Liberties in the human rights movement, that protesters began to be thought of as rational individuals. The research questions then moved from whom the protesters were to consider what processes encouraged or enabled them to join protest movements.

A start at answering these questions is given in the current volume, guest edited by Giovanni Travaglino, a young academic from the University of Kent. The studies reported do show that this area of research demands a rather more courageous approach to data collection than many other areas of social science. A notable example is the study by Tiina Likki from the University of Lausanne. She explored participation in the Spanish *Indignados* movement by getting people to complete a seven page questionnaire while they were occupying the Hotel Madrid and waiting on the street for a demonstration to begin. The movement, *Indignados* being the Spanish for outrage, takes its name from the anger against apparently impotent politicians, felt by those experiencing the effects of the financial collapse in 2011.

Likki's bold approach to data collection paid dividends because it enabled her to reveal what a mixture of participants such mass movements are made of. The responses she obtained show that for some people it is commitment to the protest movement itself that is dominant, derived from their outrage with what people are suffering. For others it is a more personal concern about their own material insecurity that moves them onto the streets. There is no necessary correlation between these two motivators for protest.

This 'unity in diversity', as Likki calls it, is a recurring finding across the studies of social protest. A particularly interesting illustration of such diversity comes from Brian Callan's chapter examining pro-Palestininan protests in Israel. Although based at the University of Loughborough he spent time with different protest groups around Israel. As he points out, the protestors include "everyone from the Palestinian waiting at the checkpoint, to a Rabbi for Human Rights, the Anarchist blocking a bulldozer, the UN report compiler, the fact finding Christian, or Fasel who wants his house back". No religious or ideological viewpoints unite these people. It is more a feeling that things are not right. An emotional response brings them together rather than an intellectual one.

Where a community is more homogeneous, as when students protest, there is a similar set of central concerns, but these are more obviously facilitated by social networks. This was examined when protests against the increase in tuition fees erupted in the winter of 2010. Psychologists are rightly criticised for focusing too much on readily available students as subjects for their experiments, but when students participated in tuition fee protests they became an unusually appropriate topic for the study. In the present book, Joseph Ibrahim, Senior Lecturer in Sociology at Sheffield Hallam University, reports on the opportunity he took to interview 53 students actively involved in the protests. Alexander Hensby from the University of Edinburgh, in another chapter, also describes how he took advantage of the student protests to explore the paths and barriers to active participation in what he characterises as high risk activities.

These interviews revealed that it was the moral, or ethical, disquiet with the increased fees which motivated protest rather than the actual financial values that the fees were set at. Social networks and prior experience of political activism can energise this moral stance. But it is a shared emotional outrage, as in Spain, that supports the action rather than reasoned argument.

One further challenge in explaining the emergence of social protest is that it does usually seem to flare up. One moment there is a grumbling disquiet, the next there are hundreds or thousands of people on the streets. What creates this qualitative change from words to action? This is explored in the chapter by Andrew Livingstone. He argues that sometimes it is the media awareness of the protest which emerges suddenly rather than the protest itself. It has been going on unnoticed until it reaches a level that the media cannot ignore. But there are other processes that can encourage concerns to explode into active protest. These days they include the use of social media, which may well speed things up. Perhaps more importantly it is the build up of frustration that spills over into anger. The feeling that there is no redress by daily mechanisms that gives rise to action, rather than just talk of action.

Social protest has brought the Ukraine to the brink of war, much as anarchist protests sparked the First World War. The studies in this volume make clear that trying to find a simple reason for such protests is misguided. There will be a variety of motivations from a mixture of people. But what they all share is anger and frustration; a strongly emotional response that defies cold logic.

Professor David Canter
Editor, *Contemporary Social Science*

Social sciences and social movements: the theoretical context

Giovanni A. Travaglino

Centre for the Study of Group Processes, School of Psychology, University of Kent, Canterbury, UK

This manuscript situates the papers of this special issue within the broader context of social movement research. It discusses the historical and theoretical significance of the four main perspectives in the field of social movement, namely the collective behaviour paradigm, the resource mobilisation approach, the political opportunity model and the cultural turn in social movement studies. Each of these perspectives has highlighted the importance of different units and levels of analysis pertaining to the study of social movements, including the role of grievances, organisational and political structures and meanings associated with participation. As a result, the field is highly receptive to multidisciplinary dialogue and to relations of mutual influences among different disciplines. The next step in social movement studies consists in the elaboration of a coherent framework of research which links the different levels of analysis and dimensions.

Of what is a revolt composed? Of nothing and everything. (Victor Hugo, *Les Misérables*)

Introduction

On 5 June 1832, in France, Parisian students rose in rebellion against the king. The revolt, which was described by Victor Hugo in *Les Misérables*, was an unsuccessful attempt to overthrow the monarchy. In the years between 1960 and 1970, waves of protest swept across Europe and the USA, leading to important historical and political changes. More recently, in 2010, over 130,000 British students took part in protests against Parliament's decision to increase university fees. A few weeks later, a series of insurgencies spread through the Middle Eastern countries, the so-called 'Arab Spring'. During 2013, other major political actions have taken place in Brazil and Turkey, whereby thousands of people took to the streets demonstrating against their governments. As this very limited list suggests, protest, riots and social movements are ubiquitous across history and locations and their occurrence is becoming increasingly frequent (Snow, Soule, & Kriesi, 2004).

The scientific study of social protest and social movements has a long and rich history. In order to explain individuals' engagement in collective actions, several theories, models and approaches have been formulated across a wide range of disciplines (Klandermans & Roggeband, 2007; McAdam, McGarty, & Zald, 1996). These conceptualisations have emphasised different themes related to collective actions, including the role of *grievances*, the *structural features* conducive to participation and the *meanings* generating and generated by political action.

The emergence of different conceptualisations has also highlighted that protest is a highly multifaceted phenomenon, which can be approached from multiple levels of analysis and from a variety of different angles (Klandermans & Staggenborg, 2002). Indeed, protest and social movements are objects of study that fall at the intersection of different disciplinary fields (Klandermans & Roggeband, 2007; Klandermans & Staggenborg, 2002; Travaglino & Nulman, 2012). While these fields have developed very different languages, standards of evidence and methodologies, they also share a similar degree of ontological commitment to some core assumptions, which has promoted relations of mutual influence across disciplinary boundaries (Roggeband & Klandermans, 2007, p. 6).

The variety of frameworks and perspectives pertaining to the study of social movements and protest calls for greater dialogue between neighbouring disciplines. However, it is important that this variety is contextualised in the wider landscape of social movement studies. The present paper briefly reviews the historical and scientific context of research in social movement. Specifically, the most influential research programmes in the field and their contribution to the scientific understanding of protest are analysed and discussed.

Theoretical approaches in social movement research

Social movement studies span the entire social scientific spectrum. Organisational and political structures, grievances, identity, emotions, culture, media influence and frames are some of the many elements related to social movements. They are also objects of study in the many disciplines that have contributed to, and enhanced, our understanding of the field.

Sociology, however, is the discipline from which most of the more prominent and influential theories about social movements and protest have developed. Indeed, as discussed by Roggeband and Klandermans (2007), sociology has been the 'home front of social movement studies' (p. 6), the theoretical place where concepts imported from other disciplines have been re-elaborated and systematically integrated into formal models. Four main approaches have emerged, namely the collective behaviour paradigm, the resource mobilisation approach, the political opportunity model and the cultural framework. In this section, the basic propositions of these different approaches are reviewed and contextualised in their broader historical frame

Collective behaviour, mobilising structures and political opportunities

As early as 493 BC, whilst trying to prevent the plebs revolting, Agrippa metaphorically compared the Roman social order to a living organism. At first sight, it might have seemed convenient to the hardworking limbs (the plebs) to revolt against the apparently lethargic stomach (the patricians) and to stop carrying food within the organism. However, in so doing, the limbs would soon discover that, without nutrients, the whole body would weaken and perish. In his speech to the insurgent crowd, Agrippa was advancing a very simple yet powerful idea. That is, collective interest may only be achieved through the coordinated work of all organs or, bodily allegories aside, through harmonious relationships between social groups.

A similar emphasis on the value of social harmony informed early work on protest and social movements (e.g. Goodwin & Jasper, 2003; Jenkins, 1985, pp. 1–2). These early theories were anchored in intellectual traditions that underlined the value of functional integration in society. In these traditions, the social sphere was characterised as a structured whole in which stability and consensus were the main cornerstones of society. Challenging social norms was thus seen as a symptom of personal pathology or as a consequence of social disorganisation.

Along with his others contemporaries, Le Bon (1895/1968) famously hypothesised that masses and crowds were a danger to civilisation. His influential volume *Psychologie des Foule* was grounded in the view that a small aristocratic elite was necessary for ensuring a civil social life (cf. Reicher, 2011). Without any form of hierarchical control, society would have fallen prey to the irrationality and violence of the individual absorbed by the masses. Indeed, according to Le Bon's account, revolutionary masses were responsible for weakening the will of predisposed individuals and inducing them to violence (cf. Drury & Stott, 2011; Killan, 1964; Oberschall, 1973).

This emphasis on irrationality and violence of the masses (and by the extension of social movements; see Killian, 1964) endured in different forms and shapes up to the years successive to the Second World War. In the writings of these years, collective behaviour was contrasted to conventional behaviour and seen as ontologically different from individual action (cf. Marx & Wood, 1975). Acting collectivities were deprived of any political meaning and motive. Lacking rationality, as attributed to the individual, masses were unable to engage in authentic political action (cf. also Freud, 1930).

Explanations of collective behaviour were thus confined and reduced to abnormal psychology (cf. McAdam, 2002). These explanations were anchored in the idea that masses could only attract social outcasts or deviants. For instance, Kornhauser (1959) conceptualised the masses as 'large numbers of people who are not integrated into any broad social groupings, including classes' (p. 14). He argued that the elites' loss of political control, the electoral structure of the political system and the increasing atomisation of society were responsible for what he labelled as the 'mass society' – that is a society where mass movements would lead to anti-democratic 'violation' of the state. On a similar note, but at a socio-psychological level of analysis, Hoffer (1951) contended in his volume, *The True Believer*, that traits such as self-esteem and life satisfaction where negatively associated with participation in mass movement. In contrast, personality attributes such as impotence, selfishness and boredom characterised the 'potential converts', that is individuals prone to join mass movements.

This aversion towards the masses was not a characteristic of the entirety of the collective behaviour tradition (Buechler, 2004). However, also in its more structural accounts of protest activities, dissent was still perceived as being induced by social or psychological disorganisation, a reactionary symptom that something was wrong in society (Park & Burgess, 1921; Turner & Killian, 1957; see Buechler, 2004). Individuals' discontent and grievances would materialise in protest as a form of tension release due to social (e.g. Smelser, 1962) or psychological (e.g. Gurr, 1970) strains (for a review see Buechler, 2004; Marx & Wood, 1975).

These assumptions of irrationality and disorganisation were challenged by a new generation of theorists, in a significant paradigmatic shift in the field of social movement studies (cf. Gamson, 1975; McAdam, 2002; Stryker, Owens, & White, 2000). Historical and intellectual elements were contributed to this shift. New waves of contention, such as the struggle for black civil rights in America and the student protests against the Vietnam War, began to expand and gain public support. Many social scientists were themselves engaged in these political struggles and could easily notice the mismatch between scholarly explanations and the reality of the movements (cf. McAdam, 2002). Moreover, new social scientific approaches emerged which stressed conflict, rather than social integration (cf. Buechler, 2004).

In this new climate, explanations of social movements and protest turned on the institutional and structural elements related to participation. Scholars paid greater attention to the role of social movements in the broader political arena. The question of 'why do people protest?' was replaced by the question 'when do people engage in collective actions?' (cf. Klandermans & Staggenborg, 2002).

An important theoretical contribution came from Olson's (1965) theory of collective action (cf. McAdam, Tarrow, & Tilly, 2007). This work called into question a widespread assumption in previous models, the idea that 'groups of individuals with common interests are expected to act on behalf of their common interests much as single individuals are often expected to act on behalf of their personal interests' (Olson, 1965, p. 1). More specifically, Olson contended that, despite shared discontent, it does not *logically* follow that individuals would be willing to engage in collective participation to further their interests, due to the nature of a *collective good*. A collective good is by definition public and it is not possible (or feasible) to exclude selected individuals from its fruition. In addition, Olson emphasised that participation is a high-cost activity because it requires investment of time and resources. Thus, a *rational* individual would be more inclined towards non-participation, given that she will still be able to benefit from the collective good, while avoiding the costs related to engagement (i.e. the free-rider problem).

Olson's model had a great impact on the field of social movement studies because it forced scholars to take into account the 'free-rider problem'. Their explanations needed to specify under which circumstances individuals would engage in collective actions. Scientists' attention turned to the study of the benefits and cost reduction mechanisms related to participation (Oberschall, 1973). Thus, the analysis of the social processes and the organisational structures that enable mobilisation of resources and prompt participation in collective actions acquired theoretical and empirical centrality (Edwards & McCarthy, 2004; Jenkins, 1983; McCarthy & Zald, 1977).

Two influential perspectives emerged in the field of social movement studies. The first focused on the organisational elements conducive to protest (Jenkins & Perrow, 1977; McCarthy & Zald, 1977), while the other centred on the broader political context of collective actions (e.g. Tilly, 1978). These two new perspectives shared the core assumption that discontent, strains and grievances are ubiquitous in society and could not thus *in themselves* account for the variability in emergence and development of social movements.

The *Resource Mobilisation* approach stressed the importance of social movements' formal institutions (*social movement organisations*), micro-structural processes, material resources and tactics as preconditions to the emergence and development of a movement (McCarthy & Zald, 1977). For instance, resource mobilisation scholars demonstrated that sponsorships and resources from established organisations were needed in order to overcome the free-rider problem and induce political participation (Jenkins, 1985; Jenkins & Perrow, 1977). Those movements which were able to mobilise resources from external sources and offer incentives to their members were more likely to succeed (Gamson, 1975). Thus, in contrast to previous models that characterised protest as stemming from social disorder, this approach demonstrated that structural stability is a necessary condition for protest.

At a more macro level, the *Political Opportunities* approach emphasised the role of the opportunities afforded by the political context on emergence and development of social movements and their outcomes (Eisinger, 1973; Giugni, 2004; Tarrow, 1983; Tilly, 1978). Although the notion of political opportunity has proved to be a challenge to define (Kriesi, 2004), there is a certain consensus that encompasses the relative openness of the political system, the formal and informal set of power relations among potential allies and the degree of state repression (Giugni, 2004; McAdam, 1996, p. 27). For instance, in his investigation of the anti-nuclear movements across four different countries, Kitschelt (1986) showed that while the movements themselves had common attributes, differences in state structure impacted on mobilisation, strategies and outcomes. Specifically, the degree of openness of the political structure and its capacity to implement policies were shown to affect the outcomes of the movements (Kitschelt, 1986).

The theoretical shift from the irrationalism inherent in the first conceptualisations to the rationalism of later formulations had important consequences. This new theoretical scenario restituted political dignity to phenomena previously relegated to mere psychological abnormality or disorganised spasms (cf. Buechler, 2004; McAdam, 2002). Moreover, these approaches refuted the reductionism of earlier explanations grounded in individuals' personality and focused upon structural elements that shaped the emergence and development of social movements.

In so doing, however, they also narrowed the focus of the theories and substituted the reductionism of psychopathology with the reductionism of hyper-rationality (Gamson, 1992). Building on Olson's model, the unit of analysis implicit in these models was an individual intent upon sophisticated calculations of costs and benefits (Stryker et al., 2000). Many elements became absent from the theoretical vocabulary of these approaches. As Cohen (1985, p. 688) puts it, in their haste to distance themselves from the collective behaviour paradigm, these approaches threw 'out the baby with the bathwater by excluding the analysis of values, norms ideologies, projects, culture and identity in other than instrumental terms'. However, these elements play an important role in shaping, constraining and facilitating individuals' perception of the social conditions that trigger discontent and, ultimately, mobilisation (Snow, Cress, Downey, & Jones, 1998). Scientists needed theoretically plausible ways to re-introduce these concepts in the analysis of social movements.

Identity, culture, frame and emotions in the study of social movements

The resource mobilisation and the political opportunity models stressed the importance of organisations and political structure for the formation of social movements. One of the most important contributions of these new approaches has been the departure from classic views of masses and crowds as irrational and disorganised (Gamson, 1975; Jenkins, 1985). In contrast, scholars working in these paradigms stressed that social movements were not a marginal phenomenon in society. Indeed, they showed that social movements were more likely to emerge under conditions of structural stability, social connectedness and favourable mobilisation of resources. Importantly, protesters were redeemed by their image of alienated deviants. Quite on the contrary, they came to be characterised as rational actors, intent upon weighting costs and benefits of participation.

In spite of these important theoretical and social merits, these approaches were subject to criticisms from a number of different standpoints. In particular, the economic language used to describe social movements typical of the resource mobilisation approach and the almost exclusive focus upon structural and organisational elements left many students of social movements dissatisfied (Cohen, 1985; McAdam et al., 2007). Probably in their desire to neatly distance themselves from the collective behaviour tradition (cf. Gamson, 1975, p. 130), social scientists obliterated elements pertaining to the sphere of subjectivity from theorising on social movements (Gamson, 1992; Stryker et al., 2000).

In an important turn for social psychological accounts of social protest, Klandermans (1984a, 1984b) reintroduced the question of individualised perception in the resource mobilisation paradigm. Klandermans pointed out that this theory underestimated (indeed ignored) the role of social-cognitive variables in protest participation. Specifically, he emphasised that there are individual differences in the way in which people perceive and weigh the costs and benefits of participation and in how they define problems and resources. According to this author, these processes do not take place in an objective reality, but in a constructed one, which is in turn subjected to attempts of persuasion and influence from other significant figures (e.g. leaders of the movement, adversaries, etc.) (see also Klandermans, 1992).

Klandermans' (1984b) introduced the expectancy-value framework (Feather, 1982) to the study of mobilisation. According to this socio-psychological expansion of the resource mobilisation model, individuals' willingness to take part in social movements depends upon a set of different motives (i.e. social, material and goal-oriented motives). Each motive is further articulated in expectations regarding the outcome of a particular action, and cognitive attitudes towards these expectations.

Klandermans' model added important dimensions to the resource mobilisation approach and successfully reintroduced (or perhaps more correctly explicitly reinvented) a social psychological level of analysis in the study of social movements (see also Klandermans, 1997). This model shared, with the resource mobilisation approach, the emphasis on the role of instrumental rationality to bring about participation. However, although grievances, feelings of frustration and other psychological states were not considered sufficient for motivating participation, cognitive expectations and attitudes were attributed a more determinant role in triggering engagement in political action and social movements (Klandermans, 1984b).

This new development became part of a more general critique of the structural determinism implied in the resource mobilisation and political process approaches (Klandermans, 1992). This critique may be seen as part of a 'cultural turn' in social research (cf. Friedland & Mohr, 2004), in general, and social movement studies (Jasper, 2007), in particular. An important assumption of this 'cultural turn' is that individuals are active constructors of meanings and not merely recipients of stimuli (Klandermans, 1992; McAdam et al., 2007; Melucci, 1988). Thus, resources and opportunities cannot themselves account for individual participation (McAdam et al., 1996). Such structural features must pass through the filter of cultural, ideological and moral beliefs before they can trigger mobilisation (see Jasper, 2011; cf. also Melucci, 1988; Touraine, 1981; Zald, 1996).

In the European context, scholars were inspired by the analysis of the so-called *new social movements*. According to these scholars, these new movements differed from previous expressions of dissent because they were not only concerned with claims of economic redistribution (Cohen, 1985; Offe, 1985). Rather, 'the overall system of meaning which sets dominant rules in a given society' (Touraine, 1981, p. 81) was the authentic (although implicit) nexus of their political struggle. The analysis of the new social movements was thus accompanied by renewed attention to concepts such as identity (Klandermans & De Weerd, 2000; Melucci, 1988), morality and ideology (Cohen, 1985)

In particular, the notion of identity had a prominent theoretical role in the analyses of the new social movements (Melucci, 1989, 1996; Touraine, 1981; cf. McAdam et al., 2007). Melucci (1996) defined collective identity as 'an interactive and shared definition produced by several individuals (or groups at a more complex level) and concerned with the orientations of action and the field of opportunities and constraints in which the action takes place' (p. 44). The formation of a collective identity was seen as essential to the assignation of common meanings to events. Only by sharing the same interpretation of reality, participants are able to enter a process of symbolic negotiation, where grievances are assessed and framed, a collective conscience formed and opponents and allies of the social movements defined (Melucci, 1988; see also Gamson, Fireman, & Rytina, 1982; Klandermans & de Weerd, 2000).

In the American context, Snow, Benford and associates introduced the notion of framing processes to the study of social movements (Benford, 1997; Benford & Snow, 2000; Snow & Benford, 1988; Snow, Rochford, Worden, & Benford, 1986; see also Zald, 1996). This line of work was built on Goffman's (1974) *frame analysis*. According to Goffman (1974), individuals organise social experience through schemata of interpretation or frames. Frames are sets of beliefs, perspectives and mental structures which guide individuals' perception and action.

The framing approach to the study of social movements is aimed at examining the 'struggle over the production of mobilizing and countermobilizing ideas and meanings' (Benford & Snow, 2000, p. 613), by placing social movements as active agents in the formation of these ideas and meanings. This approach focused on how participants in social movements actively and interactively construct shared frames that filter and organise information about the social world. Frames are 'intended to mobilize potential adherents and constituents, to garner bystander support, and to demobilize antagonists' (Snow & Benford, 1988, p. 198).

The framing perspective revaluated the role played by grievances in triggering involvement, by examining how social movement participants negotiate shared understanding of victimisation and injustice. Thus, this perspective bridges structural, psychological and cultural elements that lead to mobilisation (Snow et al., 1986). Indeed, *collective action frames* may be applied instrumentally by organisational structures of social movements (Reese & Newcombe, 2003). That is, social movement organisations may strategically shape meanings and understandings of social problems in order to maximise the potential for mobilisation (e.g. Gerhards & Rucht, 1992). Nonetheless, culture, ideology and political structures may constrain, shape and define the types of frames adopted by movement activists (Reese & Newcombe, 2003; Benford & Snow, 2000).

Finally, the new cultural turn in social movement studies is also linked to a renewed interest in the emotional processes implied in collective and political actions (Jasper, 2007, 2011). Before the 1960s, theorising about emotions was associated with claims of irrationality and deviance. Individuals in an insurgent crowd were seen as prey of instinctual and destructive emotions. Thus, emotions were expunged from successive theories of social movements. More recently, however, sociologists (e.g. Jasper, 2007) and social psychologists (e.g. van Zomeren, Spears, Fischer, & Leach, 2004) have stressed the importance of the role played by emotions and group-based emotional appraisal in motivating or inhibiting political actions.

Social sciences and social movement research

As it has been sketched above, the field of social movements has seen the emergence of different research traditions. From the collective behaviour tradition to the emphasis on resources and political opportunities, followed by a renewed attention to issues of identity, meanings and emotions, social movement scholars have developed an impressive theoretical and methodological artillery for facing the epistemic challenges related to the study of social movements. The succession of approaches in social movement studies has also bequeathed the field with a diverse range of units and levels of analysis (see for instance Klamdermans & Staggenborg, 2002). Indeed, these different approaches are not necessarily incompatible and can be seen as highlighting different dimensions of social movements (McAdam et al., 1996).

This high level of multidimensionality within the field resonates also with the nature of the object of study under investigation. A key, fundamental problem in social movement studies consists of how to reconcile two apparently distinct theoretical levels of analysis, the individual (i.e. the psychological) and the collective (i.e. the social) (cf. Klandermans, 1992, 1997; for a general discussion of this problem in social sciences, see Farr, 1996, chap. 3). This problem is also often framed in terms of agency-structure (cf. Passy, 2001).

The fundamental status of this theoretical nexus is the reason why there is always a strict, although undetermined, mutual relation of influence between social psychological models of collective actions and broader conceptualisations of the social sphere. On the one side, in all the formulations reviewed above, there is nested a social psychological model of human behaviour (Stryker et al., 2000). This model was explicit in the collective behaviour paradigm, with its claims of irrationality in the crowd. It became more implicit in successive theoretical formulations, which were based on the idea of rational actors and on the economic model of human behaviour (e.g. Olson, 1965; cf. Stryker et al., 2000). On the other side, as discussed above, theories of social movements are informed by macro conceptions of the social sphere, which either privilege organic harmony or conflict in the way in which society is conceived (e.g. Jenkins, 1985).

Thus, to the extent that different disciplines tend to privilege different levels of analyses (e.g. van Stekelenburg & Klandermans, 2007), the study of social movement is also characterised by an extraordinary predisposition to cross-disciplinary fertilisation (see Meyer & Lupo, 2007; Roggeband & Klandermans, 2007). Consider the following examples. Gurr's (1970) (a political scientist) analysis of the role of relative deprivation in revolts was rooted in the psychological frustration-aggression model. The concept of relative deprivation was elaborated in the collective behaviour tradition in social movement studies (Buechler, 2004). Opportunely modified, it has returned to the socio-psychology of protest (for a recent example see Abrams & Grant, 2012). Similarly, identity and emotions have a prominent role both in sociological (Jasper, 2011; Melucci, 1988) and socio-psychological (Tajfel, 1981; van Zomeren et al., 2004; see Klander- mans & de Weerd, 2000; van Zomeren & Spears, 2011) explanations of political actions. More- over, culture is a fundamental object of study both in sociology and anthropology, and indeed the cultural turn in the sociology of social movement has been preceded by a sociological turn in the study of culture (Friedland & Mohr, 2004; Jasper, 2007).

This volume builds on the multidimensionality and cross-disciplinarity inherent in the study of social movements. It aims to further and increase dialogue among different disciplines. There- fore, the different papers presented here tackle social protest and social movements from different levels of analyses and with different methodologies. They do so by analysing a varied number of social movements and protest events.

An important question in social movement studies concern individuals' motivation to engage in movement participation. This question is approachable at different levels of analyses. More- over, this question is of particular interest in the instances of social movements recently emerged following the severe global recession of the 2008, such as the *Indignados* movement in Spain and the *Social Justice* movement in Israel. Indeed, these movements appear to appeal to a highly variegate constituency, composed of different background and classes.

Likki (2013) reports a case study about the Indignados movement in Spain. Adopting a socio- psychological perspective, Likki investigates the role played by instrumental motives and identi- fication in explaining individuals' motivations for participation. Drawing on the dual-pathway model of Sturmer and Simon (2004), which contends that both extrinsic (e.g. material incentives) and intrinsic (e.g. identification with the movements) factors conjunctly contribute to predict movement participation, Likki shows that subjective concerns about material needs and identifi- cation with the social movements distinctly and independently predict two fundamental motiv- ations to engage in collective actions in the Indignados movement, namely group-based emotions and beliefs about social problems. Interestingly, her results show that concerns about social problems and intensity of group-based emotions were more strongly related to the partici- pation among individuals who expressed both high degree of identification and high concern about material needs. In contrast, material needs played a more prominent role only among those individuals with lower levels of identification. This manuscript points at the importance of analysing differences in social identity content within the same movement.

The Israeli Social Justice movement examined by Rosenhek and Shalev (2013) also aims at a broad inclusiveness. However, its core is formed of the young sector of the middle class, the social group more deeply affected by Israeli neoliberal policies. As discussed by the authors, the emer- gence of this movement in the Israeli society has taken by surprise many commentators. Indeed, the economic circumstances contributing to the emergence of European (e.g. Indignados) and American (e.g. Occupy) movements were less accentuated within Israeli society. Moreover, the centrality of the economic claims in this movement is somehow in contrast with strategic reper- tories and collective identities of existing Israeli movements, more attuned to issues of intergroup/ interstate relations (e.g. Arab–Palestinian relations). As the authors write, these elements 'should have narrowed the structure of political opportunities for the emergence of a mass social protest in Israel' (p. 34). Their analysis questions the sharp distinction between economic-based and iden- tity-based movements postulated by the 'new social movements' theorists (cf. also Cohen, 1985). The authors contend that the new wave of mobilisation is characterised by a re-politicisation of issues of class and redistribution. At the same time, these movements adopt strategies and reper-toires of post-materialist (i.e. new) social movements.

Among the strategies adopted by the so-called new social movements, there is a strong reliance on digital technologies and new media. Academic debate on the role of social media in social movements has framed the question in terms of whether their use should be considered as a form of political action or not. This issue is analysed by Boushel and Meuleman (2013). Specifically, the authors draw on the work of the Canadian sociologist Dorothy E. Smith, and her method of Institutional Ethnography, in order to analyse the current debate on social media activities in the context of political participation.

Smith's (2005) Institutional Ethnography approach focuses on the concreteness of individ-uals' social relations and activities with the aim of highlighting how these shape the broader organisational settings and institutions in which they take place. In keeping with the principles of this method, Boushel and Meuleman show the difficulties of distinguishing the political from the non-political in the use of social media, while at the same time emphasising the impor-tance of focusing on the concrete and historically situated experience of the individuals who use these technologies. Their analysis calls for a greater attention to the everyday practices and dis-courses surrounding individuals' expressions of political ideas in social movements.

Another important function of social media in relation to social movements refers to their role in shaping the public perception of protest activities (Reicher & Stott, 2011). As discussed in the pre-vious section, public perception of protest may oscillate between two opposite poles (Turner, 1969). Protest may be construed either as deviant or criminal or as a legitimate way of expressing dissent and pursuing social change. In turn, public perception has important consequences on the 'bargain-ing potential' (cf. Lipsky, 1968) of social movements, which generally need to appeal to wider con-stituencies and win their sympathies in order to gain important resources. The way in which media frame the public image of a protest has thus important social and political consequences.

Coen and Jones (2013) examine the local media coverage of the August 2011 riots in Salford. These riots followed the death of Mark Duggan at the hands of the police and were part of a larger set of riots that took place in England in the course of four days (cf. Reicher & Stott, 2011). Specifically, the authors focus on how online local newspapers framed the riots in Salford, a city afflicted by a long story of animosity between police and local communities. Their analysis shows that, despite being more ingrained in their local cultural texture, local media portray the riots in a way very similar to national sources, framing the issue as one pertaining to the sphere of deviance and criminality. The authors discuss the consequences of this representation in terms of a missed opportunity for local media to contribute to the community to which they belong.

Indeed, social movements do not take place in a social vacuum. Their actions may originate from and have an impact on whole communities. Two manuscripts examine the UK 2010/2011 student protests against the new policies concerning British higher education, in relation to the broader student community in which they took place. In the course of the 2010/2011, following the publication of the Browne Review into higher education, British students engaged in a series of protests against the proposals to raise the university tuition fees and substantially reduce the public spending for higher education. These acts of protests were extremely widespread.

Ibrahim (2013) explains students' engagement in protests in terms of Thompson's framework of moral economy. According to Thompson (1971), economic practices are legitimised by moral feelings, traditions and norms. Thus, protests may be a consequence of sentiments of moral outrage due to the transgression of economic practices perceived to be legitimate or fair within a given community. In line with this argument, Ibrahim contends and provides initial empirical evidence for the fact that, students' mobilisation is at least partially the result of the perceived vio-lation of a tradition of entitlement embedded within the student community, namely the right to affordable higher education. Specifically, from a sociological standpoint, Ibrahim argues that the recent steps towards commodification of higher education violates students' expectations of what should be fair and just with regard the economic management of higher education. As a consequence, the student community expressed its moral outrage and dissatisfaction through protests. Interestingly, this sociological framework concurs with recent socio-psychological research concerning the centrality of morality for groups (see Leach, Ellemers, & Barreto, 2007).

Hensby (2013) complements Ibrahim's papers by exploring sociological determinants of non-participation in high-risk/cost activities (e.g. occupations; cf. also Toupin, 2013), in the same context of the student movement. In spite of similar levels of grievances and sympathy and regardless of the similarity of opportunities to get involved, individuals' participation in high-cost–risk activities shows a notable degree of variability. Hensby stresses that participation is fundamentally a social activity. His analysis shows that elements such as the degree of political socialisation and the networks in which individuals are embedded play an important role in determining political (in)action in high cost forms of participation.

Similarly, but from an anthropological standpoint, Callan (2013) emphasises the notion of sociality in the context of the transnational Pro-Palestinian activism and advocacy. The Pro-Palestinian phenomenon is an international amalgamation of practices in support of the Palestinians' rights, which coalesces on the Gaza Strip and West Bank. The sense that something is wrong gathers activists from around the world and invokes their participation in acts of non-violent protest against the Israeli hegemony. Callan calls our attention on the way in which the actors 'make the movement' (cf. Salman & Assies, 2007, p. 258) and contends that Pro-Palestinian dissenters shape their sense of belonging around the emotional significance of the idea of wrongness. Through a shared feeling of injustice, dissenters produce collective interpretations of reality, shared values and visions, but also intimacy, friendship and animosity of concrete relationships. In other words, the Pro-Palestinian movement similar to other transnational movements may be conceptualised as a heterogeneous community of practices and purposes. In turn, the notion and practice of community can, in this case, be said to stem from an unspoken and even uncertain affective judgement that Israel is not doing right by the Palestinian people.

As these contributions show and as argued by McAdam (2002, p. 6), social movement scholars show a high degree of commitment to empirical research. Indeed, scholars working from different disciplines have been able to establish certain regularities and facts about social movements and protest events of great applied value. For instance, in the course of the last two decades, social psychology has identified several important factors implied in the emergence of collective and political action, such as group identification, perception of legitimacy, efficacy and the impact of different group-based emotions (anger and moral outrage). Several statistical models have been proposed within the field, which enable researchers to test hypotheses on the relations between different variables and the magnitude of their explanatory contribution.

In his critique of social psychological models of collective actions, however, Livingstone (2013) acutely notices that in spite of their theoretical and methodological sophistication, these models have overlooked an important point. That is, they do not adequately explain when collective behaviour emerges and at which point in time psychological changes trigger the transition from inaction to action. According to Livingstone, future research on collective actions should take into account the dynamic nature of participants' shared representations and find way to theoretically conceptualise and empirically capture their impact on different courses of (in)action. While this critique specifically addresses social psychological models, its message might be extended to more structural accounts of social movements which also need to better specify the processes and 'dynamic variables' that link structure to the ongoing mobilisation processes (McAdam, 2002).

Conclusion: towards an interdisciplinary dialogue in social movement research

Social movements and protest are objects of study that cross the conventional boundaries of academic disciplines. Our comprehension of these phenomena is thus dependent on our ability to take into account the different levels and units of analysis inherent in their phenomenology (Klandermans & Staggenborg, 2002). In line with this idea, the articles which contribute to this volume stress the importance of different motives, factors and structures related to participation. They employ a variety of methodologies and points of view. Moreover, they examine different social movements and protest events around the globe.

This variety is a testimony to the complexity inherent to the field of social movements. It is also a clear sign of the lively and healthy status of research in this area. New approaches and themes continuously emerge, which enrich our understanding of social movements and stimulate theoretical and methodological debate.

Multidisciplinarity is indeed a fundamental first stage and provides researchers with the opportunity of acquainting themselves with different languages and standpoints. The next step consists in delineating the theoretical paths among disciplines and specifying processes and connectors among different levels of analysis, in order to increase collaboration, stimulate dialogue and produce coherent, and more complete, frameworks of research.

Acknowledgements

The author wishes to thank Professor David Canter for his suggestions during the preparation of this special issue and of this article and Ruth Lamont and Abigail Player for their comments on this article. Finally, the author would like to thank Professor Dominic Abrams and Dr Georgina Randsley de Moura for their guidance and support.

References

Abrams, D., & Grant, P. R. (2012). Testing the social identity relative deprivation (SIRD) model of social change: The political rise of Scottish nationalism. *British Journal of Social Psychology, 51*, 674–689.

Benford, R. D. (1997). An insider's critique of the social movement framing perspective. *Sociological Inquiry, 67*, 409–430.

Benford, R. D., & Snow, D. (2000). Framing processes and social movements: An overview and assessment. *Annual Review of Sociology, 26*, 611–639.

Boushel, C., & Meuleman, B. (2013). Hash tags, ruling relations and the everyday: Institutional ethnography insights on social movements. *Contemporary Social Science, 9*, 49–62.

Buechler, S. M. (2004). The strange career of strain and breakdown theories. In D. A. Snow, S. A. Soule, & H. Kriesi (Eds.), *The Blackwell companion to social movements* (pp. 47–66). Malden, MA: Blackwell.

Callan, B. (2013). Something's wrong here: Transnational dissent and the unimagined community. *Contemporary Social Science, 9*, 106–120.

Coen, S., & Jones, C. (2013). A matter of law and order: Reporting the Salford riots in local news webpages. *Contemporary Social Science, 9*, 63–78.

Cohen, J. L. (1985). Strategy or identity: New theoretical paradigms and contemporary social movements. *Social Research, 52*, 663–716.

Drury, J., & Stott, C. (2011). Contextualising the crowd in contemporary social science. *Contemporary Social Science, 6*, 275–288.

Edwards, B., & McCarthy, D. J. (2004). Resources and social movement mobilization. In D. A. Snow, S. A. Soule, & H. Kriesi (Eds.), *The Blackwell companion to social movements* (pp. 116–152). Malden, MA: Blackwell.

Eisinger, P. K. (1973). The conditions of protest behavior in American cities. *American Political Science Review, 67*, 11–28.

Farr, R. (1996). *The roots of modern social psychology*. Oxford: Blackwell.

Feather, N. T. (1982). *Expecations and actions: Expectancy-value models in psychology*. Hillsdale, NJ: Erlbaum.

Freud, S. (1930). *Civilization and its discontents*. London: Hogarth.

Friedland, R., & Mohr, J. (2004). The cultural turn in American sociology. In R. Friedland & J. Mohr (Eds.), *Matters of culture: Cultural sociology in practice* (pp. 1–70). Cambridge: Cambridge University Press.

Gamson, W. A. (1975). *The strategy of social protest*. Belmont, CA: Wadsworth.

Gamson, W. A. (1992). The social psychology of collective action. In A. D. Morris & C. M. Mueller (Eds.), *Frontiers in social movement theory* (pp. 53–76). New Haven, CT: Yale University Press.

Gamson, W. A., Fireman, B., & Rytina, S. (1982). *Encounters with unjust authority*. Homewood, IL: Dorsey Press.

Gerhards, J., & Rucht, D. (1992). Mesomobilization: Organizing and framing in two protest campaigns in West Germany. *American Journal of Sociology, 98*, 555–595.

Giugni, M. (2004). *Social protest and policy change: Ecology, antinuclear, and peace movements in comparative perspective*. Lanham, MD: Rowman and Littlefield.

Goffman, E. (1974). *Frame analysis: An essay on the organization of experience*. Cambridge, MA: Harvard University Press.

Goodwin, J., & Jasper, J. M. (Eds.). (2003). *The social movements reader: Cases and concepts*. Malden, MA: Blackwell.

Gurr, T. R. (1970). *Why men rebel*. Princeton, NJ: Princeton University Press.

Hensby, A. (2013). Networks, counter-networks and political socialisation – paths and barriers to high-cost/risk activism in the 2010/11 student protests against fees and cuts. *Contemporary Social Science, 9*, 92–105.

Hoffer, E. (1951). *The true believer*. New York, NY: HarperCollins.

Ibrahim, J. (2013). The moral economy of the UK student protest movement 2010-2011. *Contemporary Social Science, 9*, 79–91.

Jasper, J. M. (2007). Cultural approaches in the sociology of social movements. In B. Klandermans & C. Roggeband (Eds.), *Handbook of social movements across disciplines* (pp. 59–109). New York, NY: Springer.

Jasper, J. M. (2011). Emotions and social movements: Twenty years of theory and research. *Annual Review of Sociology, 37*, 285–303.

Jenkins, J. C. (1983). Resource mobilization theory and the study of social movements. *Annual Review of Sociology, 9*, 527–553.

Jenkins, J. C. (1985). *The politics of insurgency: The farm workers movement in the 1960s*. New York, NY: Columbia University Press.

Jenkins, J. C., & Perrow, C. (1977). Insurgency of the powerless farm worker movements (1946–1972). *American Sociological Review, 42*, 249–268.

Killian, L. M. (1964). Social movements. In R. E. L. Faris (Ed.), *Handbook of modern sociology* (pp. 426–455). Chicago, IL: Rand McNally.

Kitschelt, H. P. (1986). Political opportunity structures and political protest: Anti-nuclear movements in four democracies. *British Journal of Political Science, 16*, 57–85.

Klandermans, B. (1984a). Mobilization and participation: Social psychological expansions of resource mobilization theory. *American Sociological Review, 49*, 583–600.

Klandermans, B. (1984b). Mobilization and participation in trade union action: An expectancy-value approach. *Journal of Occupational Psychology, 57*, 107–120.

Klandermans, B. (1992). The social construction of protest and multiorganizational fields. In A. D. Morris & C. M. Mueller (Eds.), *Frontiers in social movement theory* (pp. 77–103). New Haven, CT: Yale University Press.

Klandermans, B. (1997). *The social psychology of protest*. Oxford: Blackwell.

Klandermans, B., & De Weerd, M. (2000). Group identification and political protest. In S. Stryker, T. J. Owens, & R. W. White (Eds.), *Self, identity, and social movements* (pp. 68–92). Minneapolis: University of Minnesota Press.

Klandermans, B., & Roggeband, C. (Eds.). (2007). *Handbook of social movements across disciplines*. New York, NY: Springer Science & Business Media.

Klandermans, B., & Staggenborg, S. (Eds.). (2002). *Methods of social movement research*. Minneapolis: University of Minnesota Press.

Kornhauser, W. (1959). *The politics of mass society*. Glencoe, IL: Free Press.

Kriesi, H. (2004). Political context and opportunity. In D. A. Snow, S. A. Soule, & H. Kriesi (Eds.), *The Blackwell companion to social movements* (pp. 67–90). Malden: Blackwell.

Leach, C. W., Ellemers, N., & Barreto, M. (2007). Group virtue: The importance of morality (vs. competence and sociability) in the positive evaluation of in-groups. *Journal of Personality and Social Psychology, 93*, 234–249.

Le Bon, G. (1968). *The crowd: A study of the popular mind* (Original work published 1895). Dunwoody, GA: Norman S. Berg.

Likki, T. (2013). Unity within diversity: A social psychological analysis of the internal diversity of the Indignados movement. *Contemporary Social Science, 9*, 15–30.

Lipsky, M. (1968). Protest as a political resource. *American Political Science Review, 62*, 1144–1158.

Livingstone, A. (2013). Why the psychology of collective action requires qualitative transformation as well as quantitative change. *Contemporary Social Science, 9*, 121–134.

Marx, G. T., & Wood, J. L. (1975). Strands of theory and research in collective behavior. *Annual Review of Sociology, 1*, 363–428.

McAdam, D. (1996). Conceptual origins, current problems, future directions. In D. McAdam, J. D. McCarthy, & M. N. Zald (Eds.), *Comparative perspectives on social movements: Political opportunities, mobilizing structures, and cultural framings* (pp. 23–40). Cambridge: Cambridge University Press.

McAdam, D. (2002). Beyond structural analysis: Toward a more dynamic understanding of social movements. In M. Diani, & D. McAdam (Eds.), *Social movements and networks: Relational approaches to collective action* (pp. 281–298). Oxford: Oxford University Press.

McAdam, D., McCarthy, J. D., & Zald, M. N. (1996). Introduction: Opportunities, mobilizing structures, and framing processes – toward a synthetic, comparative perspective on social movements. In D. McAdam, J. D. McCarthy, & M. N. Zald (Eds.), *Comparative perspectives on social movements: Political opportunities, mobilizing structures, and cultural framings* (pp. 1–22). Cambridge: Cambridge University Press.

McAdam, D., Tarrow, S., & Tilly, C. (2007). Comparative perspectives on contentious politics. In M. Lichbach & A. Zuckerman (Eds.), *Comparative politics. Rationality, culture and structure* (pp. 260–290). Cambridge: Cambridge University Press.

McCarthy, J. D., & Zald, M. N. (1977). Resource mobilization and social movements: A partial theory. *American Journal of Sociology, 82*, 1212–1241.

Melucci, A. (1988). Getting involved: Identity and mobilization in social movements. In B. Klandermans, H. Kriesi, & S. Tarrow (Eds.), *International social movements – from structure to action: Comparing social movements across cultures* (pp. 329–348). Greenwich, CT: JAI.

Melucci, A. (1989). *Nomads of the present: Social movements and individual needs in contemporary society*. London: Hutchinson Radius.

Melucci, A. (1996). *Challenging codes. Collective action in the information age*. Cambridge: Cambridge University Press.

Meyer, D. S., & Lupo, L. (2007). Assessing the politics of protest: Political science and the study of social movements. In B. Klandermans & C. Roggeband (Eds.), *Handbook of social movements across disciplines* (pp. 111–156). New York, NY: Springer.

Oberschall, A. R. (1973). *Social conflicts and social movements*. Englewood Cliffs, NJ: Prentice-Hall.

Offe, C. (1985). New social movements: Challenging the boundaries of institutional politics. *Social Research, 52*, 817–868.

Olson, M. (1965). *The logic of collective action: Public goods and the theory of groups*. Cambridge, MA: Harvard University Press.

Park, R. E., & Burgess, E. W. (1921). *Introduction to the science of sociology*. Chicago, IL: University of Chicago Press.

Passy, F. (2001). Socialization, connection, and the structure/agency gap: A specification of the impact of networks on participation in social movements. *Mobilization: An International Journal, 6*, 173–192.

Reese, E., & Newcombe, G. (2003). Income rights, mothers' rights, or workers' rights? Collective action frames, organizational ideologies, and the American welfare rights movement. *Social Problems, 50*, 294–318.

Reicher, S. (2011). Mass action and mundane reality: An argument for putting crowd analysis at the centre of the social sciences. *Contemporary Social Science, 6*, 433–449.

Reicher, S., & Stott, C. (2011). *Mad mobs and Englishmen? Myths and realities of the 2011 riots.* Constable Robinson. Kindle Edition. Retrieved from http://www.madmobsandenglishmen.com/

Roggeband, C., & Klandermans, B. (2007). Introduction. In B. Klandermans & C. Roggeband (Eds.), *Handbook of social movements across disciplines* (pp. 1–12). New York, NY: Springer.

Rosenhek, Z., & Shalev, M. (2013). The political economy of Israel's "social justice" protests: A class and generational analysis. *Contemporary Social Science, 9,* 31–48.

Salman, T., & Assies, W. (2007). Anthropology and the study of social movements. In B. Klandermans & C. Roggeband (Eds.), *Handbook of social movements across disciplines* (pp. 205–266). New York, NY: Springer.

Smelser, N. J. (1962). *Theory of collective behavior.* New York, NY: The Free Press.

Smith, D. E. (2005). *Institutional ethnography: A sociology for people.* Oxford: AltaMira Press.

Snow, D. A., & Benford, R. D. (1988). Ideology, frame resonance, and participant. *Mobilization: An International Journal, 1,* 197–192.

Snow, D. A., Cress, D. M., Downey, L., & Jones, A. W. (1998). Disrupting the 'quotidian': Reconceptualizing the relationship between breakdown and the emergence of collective action. *Mobilization: An International Journal, 3,* 1–22.

Snow, D. A., Rochford, E. B., Worden, S. K., & Benford, R. D. (1986). Frame alignment processes, micro-mobilzation, and movement participation. *Annual Sociological Review, 51,* 464–481.

Snow, D. A., Soule, S. A., & Kriesi, H. (2004). Mapping the terrain. In D. A. Snow, S. A. Soule, & H. Kriesi (Eds.), *The Blackwell companion to social movements* (pp. 3–16). Malden, MA: Blackwell.

Stryker, S., Owens, T. J., & White, R. W. (2000). Social psychology and social movements: Cloudy past and bright future. In S. Stryker, T. J. Owens, & R. W. White (Eds.), *Self, identity, and social movements* (pp. 1–17). Minneapolis: University of Minnesota Press.

Stürmer, S., & Simon, B. (2004). Collective action: Towards a dual-pathway model. *European Review of Social Psychology, 15,* 59–99.

Tajfel, H. (1981). *Human groups and social categories.* Cambridge: Cambridge University Press.

Tarrow, S. (1983). *Struggling to reform: Social movements and policy change during cycles of protest.* Ithaca, NY: Cornell University Press.

Thompson, E. P. (1971). The moral economy of the English crowd in the 18th Century. *Past & Present, 50,* 76–136.

Tilly, C. (1978). *From mobilization to revolution.* Boston, MA: Addison-Wesley.

Toupin, S. (2013). An open-air self-managed social center called occupy. *Contention: The Multidisciplinary Journal of Social Protest, 1,* 17–30.

Touraine, A. (1981). *The voice and the eye: An analysis of social movements.* New York, NY: Cambridge University Press.

Travaglino, G. A., & Nulman, E. (Eds.). (2012). *Theory, action and impact of social protest: An interdisciplinary conference. Contention: The Multidisciplinary Journal of Social Protest, 0.* New York: Punctum Books.

Turner, R. H. (1969). The public perception of protest. *American Sociological Review, 34,* 815–831.

Turner, R. H., & Killian, L. M. (1957). *Collective behavior.* Englewood Cliffs, NJ: Prentice-Hall.

Zald, M. N. (1996). Culture, ideology and strategic framing. In D. McAdam, J. D. McCarthy, & M. N. Zald (Eds.), *Comparative perspectives on social movements: Political opportunities, mobilizing structures, and cultural framings* (pp. 261–275). Cambridge: Cambridge University Press.

van Stekelenburg, J., & Klandermans, B. (2007). Individuals in movements: A social psychology of contention. In B. Klandermans & C. Roggeband (Eds.), *Handbook of social movements across disciplines* (pp. 157–204). New York: Springer.

van Zomeren, M., & Spears, R. (2011). The crowd as a psychological cue to in-group support for collective action against collective disadvantage. *Contemporary Social Sciences, 6,* 325–341.

van Zomeren, M., Spears, R., Fischer, A. H., & Leach, C. W. (2004). Put your money where your mouth is! Explaining collective action tendencies through group-based anger and group efficacy. *Journal of Personality and Social Psychology, 87,* 649–664.

Unity within diversity: a social psychological analysis of the internal diversity of the Indignados movement

Tiina Likki

Institute of Social Sciences, University of Lausanne, Lausanne, Switzerland

This article examines the relationships between four categories of motivational characteristics among social movement activists: grievances, identification, beliefs about social problems and group-based emotions. Using data from the Spanish Indignados movement ($N = 230$), a typology was constructed based on the dimensions of subjective material insecurity and identification with the protests, yielding three different activist profiles (insecure identifiers, secure identifiers and non-identifiers). In linear and typological analyses grievances and identification had independent and additive effects on beliefs about social problems and group-based emotions. Interactive effects also showed that high levels of identification may at times render grievances redundant in predicting concern for social problems and group emotions. Overall, the findings demonstrate a pattern of diversity in terms of grievances and identification coupled with unity regarding social identity content. The implications of different motivational patterns for collective action are discussed.

I think, therefore I resist. (Indignados woman, 45 years old)

The Spanish Indignados movement has attracted unparalleled support and participation in recent Spanish history and surprised observers by its tenacity. However, the movement is often depicted in the media as a movement of marginalised youth (so-called 'perroflautas').[1] The starting point for the present study was this seeming contradiction between the wide support base of the Indignados movement,[2] on the one hand, and the common media image of the movement, portrayed as consisting of the young and the marginalised lacking any concrete or realistic solutions to the problems. This paper argues that the movement is, in fact, highly diverse and that uncovering the different motivational constellations within the movement will further our understanding of the internal dynamics of social movement participation.

Social movement studies is by nature a multidisciplinary field (cf. Klandermans & Roggeband, 2010; Travaglino & Nulman, 2012) and any full understanding of a movement will require inclusive models that focus on factors both at the individual level (such as grievances, identities or attitudes) and at the structural level (such as resources and political opportunities) (Goodwin & Jasper, 2009; Klandermans, Kriesi, & Tarrow, 1988; see also Tajfel, 1981). While acknowledging the importance of structural factors, this paper takes a social psychological approach, focusing on the individual level and on variables related to subjective perceptions, identity, motivation and group-based emotion (Van Stekelenburg & Klandermans, 2010). The task is to analyse the internal diversity of the movement, as opposed to studying why some people participate while others do not (Snow & Oliver, 1995, p. 577). From a social identity perspective, mapping the shared views and emotions among activists informs us about the meaning and content of that social identity (Turner, Hogg, Oakes, Reicher, & Wetherell, 1987) which, in turn, predicts how the group acts (Livingstone & Haslam, 2008; Stott & Drury, 2004).

Focusing on a singe movement in a specific city at a given time point, the research can be considered a case study (see Snow & Trom, 2002, for a critical discussion of the characteristics of a case). In line with Snow and Trom (2002), I argue that a focus on a particular movement does not exclude the possibility of theoretical generalisability. Taken together, this paper hopes to complement existing theoretical models by studying the internal diversity of social movements.

Motivations for collective action

Social psychological literature on collective action participation has identified four main categories of motivations for participation. These include instrumental motives, identity motives, group-based anger motives and ideology motives. Van Stekelenburg and Klandermans (2011) have shown that rather than being competing paradigms, these four factors complement each other. Following calls for research on the different motivational configurations (e.g. Van Stekelenburg & Klandermans, 2011), this paper examines such constellations in the context of the Indignados movement.

Grievances and instrumental motivations

Classical theories of protest participation considered protest as a reaction to grievances, with the aim of improving one's situation (Gurr, 1970). According to relative deprivation theory, a sense of deprivation arises when people compare themselves to some standard of reference: to their own situation in the past or to the outcomes of other individuals or groups (Crosby, 1976; Major, 1994; Runciman, 1966). The resulting assessment of illegitimate inequality is a central factor that gives rise to protest. To take the Indignados as an example, a movement like the Indignados would arise as a reaction to feeling unjustly deprived compared to the ruling political and financial elites.

Resource mobilisation theory, with its focus on organisational characteristics of social movements, grew to criticise the view of grievances (and social psychological factors more generally) as the main source of protest mobilisation (Stryker, Owens, & White, 2000). Resource mobilisation theorists pointed out that not only did highly aggrieved groups often not contest their conditions but that there were also many instances where individuals who were not directly touched by the problems decided to stand up (so-called 'conscience constituents') (McCarthy & Zald, 1977). Complementing explanations based on material interests or relative deprivation, the concept of conflicting principles refers to the idea that sometimes merely the view that one's principles or values have been violated is enough to spur protest as an expression of moral indignation (Van Stekelenburg & Klandermans, 2009). This was the outcome of research on the so-called New Social Movements, focused on a new generation of materially secure movement participants who drew their motivation from post-material values (Inglehart, 1977). In the case of the Indignados, we are also likely to find different types of participants based on the different weights they give to conflicts of material interests and conflicting principles. Those directly touched by economic adversities in the country would be acting based on subjective grievances while those who morally disagree with the direction of politics would be acting based on principled motivations.

Identification

From a social psychological perspective, an individual's identification with different aggrieved or activist groups emerges as a central answer to the question of what drives people to engage in collective action. According to social identity theory (SIT), people acquire part of their identity from belonging to different groups, together with the value and emotional significance attached to those memberships (Tajfel, 1981; Tajfel & Turner, 1979). Studies on collective action partici- pation show that the more individuals identify with a group, the more likely they are to participate in collective action on behalf of that group (Klandermans, Sabucedo, Rodriguez, & De Weerd, 2002; Simon et al., 1998; Van Zomeren, Postmes, & Spears, 2008). In the case of social move- ments, the groups individuals identify with are often based on shared opinions (e.g. anti-war and pro-life). Identification with such opinion-based groups (as opposed to general social categories) has been argued to be a particularly potent predictor of commitment to social action (Bliuc, McGarty, Reynolds, & Muntele, 2007; Simon & Klandermans, 2001; Thomas, Mavor, & McGarty, 2012).

In addition to studying individuals' subjective degree of identification with the group, it is central to study the socially shared understandings of the *content* of the identity (Livingstone & Haslam, 2008; Postmes, Haslam, & Swaab, 2005). Social identity content consists of the differ- ent norms, conventions, ideology, stereotypes or behaviours that individuals attach to their group membership (Turner et al., 1987). Identifying with a group that is valued and central to one's self- concept is related to behaviours that are consistent with the group's norms (Abrams & Hogg, 1990; Terry & Hogg, 1996; Turner et al., 1987). It is, however, the content of a social identity, not identification per se, that predicts group members' behaviour (Livingstone & Haslam, 2008). For example, in field studies of the 1980 riots in St. Paul in Bristol, Reicher (1984, 1987) explained patterns of crown behaviour and violence through the shared sense of alienation and exploitation as a part of social identity.

While the degree of identification is commonly used to predict collective action participation, few studies have looked at the content of social identity. The present study goes beyond measur- ing the degree of identification by looking at whether social identity content is consensual or diverse. The focus is on how subjective grievances and identification with the movement are related to differences in beliefs about social problems and group-based emotions – two possible elements included in the social identity of the Indignados.

Beliefs about social problems

A key starting point for a social psychological approach to social movements is that people live in a perceived world where collectively elaborated and shared knowledge of social reality deter- mines how people think and act (Moscovici, 1984; Van Stekelenburg & Klandermans, 2009). According to SIT, individuals' beliefs regarding the nature of relations between social groups affect whether they will consider collective action as a possible way towards social change. When members of disadvantaged groups perceive the social situation as (a) illegitimate and (b) unstable they are more likely to engage in protest than if the situation is perceived as either legit- imate or stable (Mummendey, Kessler, Klink, & Mielke, 1999; Tajfel & Turner, 1979). In Spain, perceived lack of democracy, political corruption, media partiality, cuts in social spending and mortgage issues were among the many problems that the Indignados consider as unjust.

Furthermore, there is evidence that consensus around social identity content increases collective protest against unfair treatment, in particular when individual social mobility is not possible (Stott & Drury, 2004). In the case of the Indignados, consensus regarding social problems could be a factor explaining the relative success of the movement.

Group-based emotions

Emotions play a crucial role in collective action participation, as illustrated by the name of the Indignados movement (referring to moral outrage). Although absent for a long time, emotions have made their way back to explanations of social movement participation (Goodwin, Jasper, & Polletta, 2001, 2004; Jasper, 1998; Van Zomeren, Spears, Fischer, & Leach, 2004). Out of specific group-based emotions that predict collective action, moral outrage and anger have probably received the most attention (Mackie, Devos, & Smith, 2000; Montada & Schneider, 1989; Van Zomeren et al., 2004). Although conceptually similar, moral outrage is 'anger provoked by the perception that a moral standard – usually a standard of fairness of justice – has been violated' (Batson et al., 2007, p. 1272). The role of anger in motivating participation has been found to vary depending on the type of protest activity and it may be that anger plays the most important part through increasing identification with the protests (Stürmer & Simon, 2009). Sadness, in turn, has received less attention but was found to be less effective in preparing for action than anger (Nerb & Spada, 2001; Smith, Cronin, & Kessler, 2008). Group-based guilt is an emotion experienced by members of an advantaged group regarding current injustice or past wrongdoings towards a disadvantaged group (Doosje, Branscombe, Spears, & Manstead, 1998). Research has shown that guilt is unlikely to motivate action for social change (Iyer, Schmader, & Lickel, 2007; Leach, Iyer, & Pedersen, 2006). Instead, guilt should motivate either avoidance or symbolic attempts to reduce inequality (Thomas, McGarty, & Mavor, 2009b). Finally, hope is an understudied emotion in the field of protest participation. Calls have been made to consider the role of positive emotions in motivating social action (Thomas et al., 2009b) but so far no empirical research has investigated hope in the context of collective action.

Studies on the role of identification as a precursor of group-based emotions have shown that the higher the group identification, the more people experience group-based emotions because when a social identity is salient, people evaluate situations in terms of their consequences for the ingroup (Mackie et al., 2000; Van Zomeren, Spears, & Leach, 2008; Yzerbyt, Dumont, Wigboldus, & Gordijn, 2003). Recently, a reverse causal ordering has been evoked where awareness of shared emotions gives rise to social identity, a view more in line with the importance of social identity content (Kessler & Hollbach, 2005; Peters & Kashima, 2007; Thomas et al., 2009b). However, to our knowledge, no studies have compared whether identification relates more strongly to specific emotions. That is, whether certain emotions are emblematic and normative to highly identified movement members, thereby reflecting central social identity content.

Analytical approach

Several social psychological models have focused on the relationships between different predictors of collective action. With the aim of complementing earlier cost–benefit approaches to protest participation (Klandermans, 1984, 1997), most of these models place social identity processes in a central role. Simon and Stürmer's (Simon et al., 1998; Stürmer & Simon, 2004; Stürmer, Simon, Loewy, & Jörger, 2003) dual-pathway model of collective action proposes two pathways to collective action that seem to operate independently. The instrumental pathway concerns the calculation of costs and benefits of movement participation, whereas the identity pathway explains collective action participation as a function of an inner obligation to enact a collective identity. Other integrative frameworks include the social identity model of collective action (Van Zomeren, Postmes et al., 2008) and the encapsulated model of social identity in collective action (Thomas et al., 2012; Thomas, McGarty, & Mavor, 2009a) which focus on perceived injustice, efficacy and identification as three key predictors of collective action.

Although the focus in this paper is not on predicting collective action participation, the integrative frameworks are useful in guiding an analysis focused on the diversity and richness of different combinations of grievances, identity, emotions and cognitions among activists. In the approach adopted in this paper, grievances and identification were used as two fundamental organising dimensions for delineating a typology of movement participants. Distinguishing groups with different profiles on these dimensions allows investigating possible variations in the meaning of the movement among activists.

First, in line with the dual-pathway hypothesis, subjective grievances and identification with the movement were expected to independently contribute to beliefs about social problems and group-based emotions, in particular the emotions of moral outrage and anger that have previously been found to predict collective action participation. Interactions between subjective grievances and identification were also tested in order to see whether subjective grievances matter less at high levels of identification (such interactions were hypothesised, but rarely found, by Stürmer & Simon, 2004). Second, the internal diversity of the movement was analysed through constructing a typology of activist profiles that emerged from crossing the dimensions of grievances and identification. This was followed by a comparison of typology groups regarding beliefs about social problems and group-based emotions.

The context for the present analysis reflects the 2008 financial crisis, followed by a global recession and the implementation of severe austerity measures in many countries. Throughout the world, several new protest movements emerged such as the global Occupy movement, the Greek protests and the Spanish Indignados movement. The movements were opposed to spending cuts in social, education and health sectors, increased unemployment, as well as the underlying political corruption and global financial system that had contributed to the crisis. The Indignados movement allows studying different sub-groups of participants in the context of economic crisis and austerity.

Method

Procedure

Data were collected during two large demonstrations organised by the Indignados movement (also known as the '15M' referring to 15 May 2011 when the movement first emerged), during various street assemblies and in an occupied building ('Hotel Madrid') over a week in Madrid in November 2011, a week before parliamentary elections. The participants were sampled on the spot and most filled in the seven-page questionnaire while sitting down and listening to public speeches at the demonstrations or while waiting for an assembly to begin.

Participants

Out of the 249 participants who filled in the questionnaire, 230 were retained for final analyses. Since our interest was to study the internal diversity of the movement, we wanted to ensure that our sample consisted of people who could be considered active in the movement. To do so, we kept only participants who had participated in at least one of the four main activities related to the 15M movement: demonstration on 15 May 2011, demonstration on

Table 1.   Participation in 15M-related activities ($N=230$).

	Demonstration on 15 May 2011	Demonstration on 15 October 2011	Encampment	Participation in assemblies
Percentage of participants (%)	79.6	79.6	43.5	88.7

15 October 2011, encampment and assemblies. As we can see from Table 1, most participants had participated in several of the activities. One hundred and eleven participants were male, 113 female and 6 did not indicate their gender. Mean age was 33.04 ($SD=12.77$), and the level of education was high, with 66% of the participants having finished university education or currently studying at university.

Measures

The measures concerned grievances, identification with the protests, beliefs about social problems and emotions. Table 2 presents means, standard deviations as well as alphas for all measures.

Subjective grievances

Subjective material insecurity (SMI) was measured with three items: 'Compared to other people in Spain, what is your economic situation?' where responses ranged from 1 = *poor* to 6 = *wealthy*; 'Thinking about what might happen in the next 12 months, how likely is it that there will be some periods when you don't have enough money to cover your household necessities?/how likely is it that you will not receive the health-care you really need if you become ill?' Responses for the last two questions ranged from 1 = *not at all likely* to 7 = *very likely*. Since not all three items had the same response scale, standardised scores were used to create a measure of SMI ($\alpha=.63$).

Table 2.   Sample descriptive statistics.

	No. of items	Range	M	SD	α
Grievances					
SMI	3	1–7	3.83	1.29	.63
Identification					
Identification with protests	3	1–7	5.64	1.13	.79
Beliefs about social problems					
Concern over public services	5	1–7	6.42	.83	.85
Concern over inequality and democracy	4	1–7	6.33	.78	.73
Concern over markets and corruption	3	1–7	6.56	.64	.59
Emotions					
Outraged	1	1–7	6.55	.89	–
Angry	1	1–7	6.01	1.36	–
Guilty	1	1–7	3.50	1.94	–
Hopeful	1	1–7	3.18	2.05	–
Sad	1	1–7	5.41	1.73	–

Note: The SMI scale used in the analyses is based on standardised items but was re-scaled to range from 1 to 7 in this table to facilitate comparison with other measures.

Identification with the protests

Identification with the protest movement was measured with three items: 'I feel strong ties to other protesters', 'Participating in the protests is an important reflection of who I am' and 'Generally I feel good about myself when I think about being part of the protests' The response scales ranged from 1 = *completely disagree* to 7 = *completely agree*. The three items were averaged to form a scale with adequate reliability ($\alpha = .79$).

Beliefs about social problems

Participants were presented a list of twelve issues and asked 'How important are the following issues for you personally in deciding to join the protests?' The participants rated the issues on a scale from 1 = not at all important to 7 = very important. A factor analysis with orthogonal rotation was performed on the twelve items, yielding three factors. The percentage of explained variance by the three factors was 61.4%. Items loading on each factor were used to create summary scores that were named as follows: (1) *Concern over public services* (5 items, $\alpha = .85$), (2) *Concern over inequality and democracy* (4 items, $\alpha = .73$), (3) *Concern over markets and corruption* (3 items, $\alpha = .59$). (List of items for each factor can be found in Appendix 1.)

Group-based emotions

Five emotions were measured each with a single item asking 'When I think of people who are economically disadvantaged in Spain, I feel: morally outraged / angry / guilty / hopeful / sad'. Responses ranged from 1 = *completely disagree* to 7 = *completely agree*.

Results

Identification and grievances as independent dimensions[3]

Identification with the movement was uncorrelated with SMI, $r = .07$, $p = .29$, indicating that one's level of SMI was not uniformly related to the degree of identification with the movement. Next, to examine how identification and grievances relate to other participation motives, a series of linear regressions were run with three beliefs about social problems and five group-based emotions as dependent variables, and SMI and identification as independent variables, as well as an interaction term between SMI and identification.

Both SMI and identification independently predicted beliefs about social problems, with the exception of concern over public services which was not related to SMI (see Table 3). The interaction between SMI and identification was non-significant for concern over inequality and democracy, and concern over markets and corruption, indicating that the two factors are truly independent. Regarding concern over public services, however, the interaction term was significant: SMI was related to higher concern over public services only among those with low identification with the protests (see Figure 1). Among highly identified participants, concern over public services was independent of their level of SMI.

Table 4 displays results from linear regression models predicting five group-based emotions. SMI and identification were related to negative emotions of moral outrage, anger and sadness, but unrelated to guilt and hope. Furthermore, the interaction between SMI and identification was significant for outrage and anger. In other words, among highly identified participants, SMI was unrelated to how morally outraged or angry individuals were.

Table 3. Linear regressions predicting beliefs about social problems.

	(1) Concern over public services		(2) Concern over inequality and democracy		(3) Concern over markets and corruption	
	B	SE	B	SE	B	SE
Material insecurity	.15	.09	.35***	.09	.26**	.09
Identification	.17*	.06	.20**	.06	.13*	.06
Insecurity *Identification	−.21**	.07	−.10	.07	.04	.07
R^2	.10		.14		.07	

Note: All models are controlled for age and gender.
*p < .05.
**p < .01.
***p < .001.

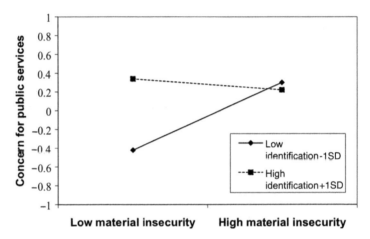

Figure 1. Identification moderates the effect of SMI on concern for public services.

Table 4. Linear regressions predicting group-based emotions.

	Moral outrage		Anger		Guilt		Hope		Sadness	
	B	SE	B	SE	B	SE	B	SE	B	SE
Material insecurity	.26**	.08	.38**	.12	−.19	.18	.03	.19	.53**	.15
Identification	.18***	.05	.19*	.08	.04	.12	.21	.12	.26*	.10
Insecurity*Identification	−.17**	.06	−.24*	.10	−.08	.15	−.05	.15	−.14	.13
R^2	.14		.09		.01		0.4		.09	

Note: All models are controlled for age and gender.
*p < .05.
**p < .01.
***p < .001.

Typology of Indignados participants

In order to depict and analyse the internal diversity of the movement, SMI and identification with the protests were used to construct a typology of motivational constellations. K-means clustering was chosen as it is a method adapted for grouping together similar cases in large samples (Aldenderfer & Blashfield, 1984; Everitt, Landau, Leese, & Stahl, 2011). This procedure classifies participants by maximising dissimilarity between categories and similarity within categories. A solution with three clusters yielded the clearest differentiation on the two dimensions. The groups were named *insecure identifiers* ($n = 102$), *non-identifiers* ($n = 34$) and *secure identifiers* ($n = 94$), where the first part of the label refers to the participants' level of SMI and the second part to their score on the identification with the movement scale (see Table 5). As expected, the groups differed significantly on both SMI, $F(2, 227) = 41.69$, $p < .001$, $\eta_p^2 = .269$ and identification, *Welch's F* $(2, 79.42) = 216.01$, $p < .001$, *est.* $\omega^2 = .65$.[4] The groups were named *relative* to each other, meaning that even non-identifiers were not at the lowest end of the identification scale ($M = 3.65$, $SD = .87$, on a scale from 1 to 7).

Overall, we see that the two largest groups are insecure identifiers and secure identifiers meaning that the majority of participants felt identified with the movement. Differing levels of SMI further indicate that many individuals who were active in the movement did not feel materially insecure.

To gain a fuller picture of the different motivational configurations among the Indignados, the three groups were compared regarding beliefs about social problems and group-based emotions. One-Way ANOVAs showed that the groups differed significantly on all three beliefs: concern over public services, *Welch's F* $(2, 82.06) = 11.83$, $p < .001$, *est.* $\omega^2 = .09$, concern over inequality and democracy, *Welch's F* $(2, 82.56) = 13.62$, $p < .001$, *est.* $\omega^2 = .10$, and concern over markets and corruption, *Welch's F* $(2, 79.68) = 15.43$, $p < .001$, *est.* $\omega^2 = .11$. A similar pattern emerged for all three beliefs: insecure identifiers were significantly more concerned about social problems than secure identifiers and non-identifiers (see Table 6 for the results from post hoc tests). This

Table 5. Typology of Indignados participants with three profiles on SMI and identification with the movement.

	Insecure identifiers		Non-identifiers		Secure identifiers	
	M	SD	M	SD	M	SD
Material insecurity	4.50[a]	1.21	3.97[a]	1.14	3.06[b]	.97
Identification	6.50[a]	.52	3.65[b]	.87	5.40[c]	.55

Note: Values that do not share a superscript are significantly different based on ANOVAs with Games–Howell post hoc tests.

Table 6. Beliefs about social problems across three participant profiles.

	Insecure identifiers		Non-identifiers		Secure identifiers	
	M	SD	M	SD	M	SD
Concern over public services	6.69[a]	.60	6.10[b]	.97	6.24[b]	.91
Concern over inequality and democracy	6.61[a]	.59	6.08[b]	.95	6.12[b]	.81
Concern over markets and corruption	6.79[a]	.43	6.38[b]	.79	6.37[b]	.69

Note: Values that do not share a superscript are significantly different based on ANOVAs with Games–Howell post hoc tests.

Table 7. Group-based emotions across three participant profiles.

	Insecure identifiers		Non-identifiers		Secure identifiers	
	M	SD	M	SD	M	SD
Outraged	6.82[a]	.57	6.24[b]	1.03	6.37[b]	1.03
Angry	6.38[a]	1.27	5.58[b]	1.68	5.77[b]	1.23
Guilty	3.45[a]	2.01	3.24[a]	2.09	3.65[a]	1.81
Hopeful	3.47[a]	2.31	2.84[a]	1.97	2.98[a]	1.74
Sad	5.78[a]	1.72	5.09[ab]	2.04	5.12[b]	1.56

Note: Values that do not share a superscript are significantly different based on ANOVAs with Games–Howell post hoc tests.

pattern is in line with the regression models above, where SMI and identification had additive rather than interactive effects on beliefs about social problems. Since insecure identifiers were high on both dimensions, they could be expected to display higher concern about social problems than either non-identifiers or secure identifiers.

The three groups of participants also differed on the emotions of moral outrage, Welch's F (2, 77.10) = 10.43, $p < .001$, est. $\omega^2 = .08$, anger Welch's F (2, 82.59) = 7.03, $p = .002$, est. $\omega^2 = .05$ and sadness, F (2, 221) = 4.23, $p = .016$, $\eta_p^2 = .037$, but not on guilt, F (2, 221) = .59, $p = .557$, $\eta_p^2 = .005$, or hope, Welch's F (2, 87.01) = 1.75, $p = .180$, est. $\omega^2 = .01$. Post hoc tests presented in Table 7 show that, again, insecure identifiers displayed a pattern that was different from non-identifiers and secure identifiers who, in turn, resembled each other. Insecure identifiers were higher on the emotions of moral outrage, anger and sadness compared to the two other groups. This is in line with an additive model where grievances and identification independently contribute to higher levels of concerns and group emotions.

Although the differences are statistically significant, the means of the three groups regarding concerns about social problems and emotions are all at the higher end of the scale (about 6 on a scale from 1 to 7). This is a sign of what I call unity within diversity, where the meaning and content attached to the three subgroups does not differ greatly. Participants in the Indignados movement differ in terms of how materially aggrieved they are and how much they identify with the protests, yet they still very much agree on the main social problems as well as share emotional reactions.

Discussion

Based on the present analysis, the Indignados movement emerges as a diverse and inclusive group of individuals with varying degrees of SMI and identification with the protests. The finding that grievances and identification have independent and additive effects on beliefs about social problems and emotions is in line with work on the dual-pathway model of collective action (Stürmer & Simon, 2004). Highest levels of social concern and group emotions occur when grievances and identification co-exist: insecure identifiers (high SMI and high identification) consistently displayed higher levels of beliefs about social problems and group emotions compared to non-identifiers (high SMI and low identification) and secure identifiers (low SMI and high identification).

The moderating effects of identification further show that when identification is high, subjective grievances become less important for determining beliefs and emotions, suggesting that individually experienced grievances are not always a necessary condition for contestation to arise. These findings are in line with the proposition by Van Zomeren and Spears (2009) that low identifiers may have different motivations for collective action compared to high identifiers: low identifiers may be primarily motivated by individual-based (instrumental) motivations, while high identifiers would be motivated by the maintenance of positive identities towards important constituencies and by the defence of important norms and values. From the perspective of social movement organisers, this may mean finding ways of appealing to different participants by focusing on both subjective interest and on values and principles.

Among secure identifiers, identification with the movement seemed to be the key factor behind beliefs about social problems and emotional reactions. This underlines the importance of social identity content, that is, what it *means* to be a member of a group (Turner et al., 1987). Social identity content defines the norms, values and behaviours that are typical of the group, predicting action tendencies and forms of protest (Livingstone & Haslam, 2008; Reicher, 1984). Furthermore, the greater the consensus regarding the meaning of the group, the greater the likelihood for collective action (Stott & Drury, 2004). For the Indignados, their unity regarding the criticism of prevailing political and economic arrangements coupled with strong emotions of moral outrage and anger may explain the dynamism and longevity of the movement. Future work on collective action could benefit from linking the consensuality of social identity content to group efficacy by analysing whether participants perceive the internal diversity of a movement as strength or weakness, as a factor that increases or decreases a sense of efficacy (cf. Van Zomeren et al., 2004). Diversity is likely to explain the movement's appeal and ability to draw in large numbers of participants but it may also represent a weakness, as activists try to reconcile many different demands and priorities within the movement.

While the current study conceptualised beliefs and emotions related to the protest movement as relating to social identity content, future research should focus more explicitly on the effects of shared understandings of social identity content on collective action. Furthermore, the dynamic and changing aspect of social identity content should also be taken into account. Namely, research has shown that the meaning of a social identity can change as a result of interaction with other groups, such as when protests change from peaceful to violent in response to police action (Drury & Reicher, 1999, 2000). Changes in the meaning of an activist identity may partly explain the evolution of strategies and even the success or failure of social movements.

The results regarding group-based emotions merit also some reflection. Overall, the participants displayed high levels of moral outrage, anger and sadness (with small differences between the groups for the first two). The overall levels of hope and guilt were clearly lower and did not show differences as a function of material insecurity and identification. The low levels of hope were somewhat surprising, as one might consider hope to be similar to 'cognitive liberation' (McAdam, 1982) or an affective antecedent for feeling efficacious. Considering the work on the effects of group efficacy on mobilisation (Van Zomeren, Postmes et al., 2008; Van Zomeren et al., 2004), we would not expect people active in a movement to be so pessimistic. That said, the question wording referred to emotions felt when thinking of 'people who are economically disadvantaged' and may simply reflect a realistic assessment of how likely Spain is to eradicate inequality at a time of dire economic crisis. That hope was not related to identification shows us that hope is not emblematic to the Indignados, which is an 'angry' rather than a 'hopeful' movement. Guilt, despite high variation in the sample, was not predicted by grievances or identification, suggesting that other processes might best explain this emotion. Overall, the emotional portrait of the Indignados emerges as one dominated by negative, externally oriented emotions of moral outrage, anger and sadness. The more general implication seems to be that feeling hopeful is not a necessary condition for contestation.

The present study suffers from a number of limitations. The first one is a limitation shared with many case studies of social movements regarding the statistical generalisation of the findings. The sample consisted of Indignados participants from Madrid, and it is unclear whether the motivation profiles would have been different had the study been conducted for example in Barcelona or Valencia or in a different country. Statistical generalisation of the findings is further affected by the sampling method, which is not a random sample of all individuals involved in the movement in Madrid. Future work should therefore address how the motivational constellations converge across protest movements. The lack of statistical generalisation that plagues many case studies does not, however, exclude analytic, or theoretical, generalisation (see Snow & Trom, 2002). While the sample does not statistically represent the whole movement, the findings can still extend existing theory by showing that the selected individual-level variables can be differentially related to each other among protesters.

The second limitation concerns the lack of comparison with non-participants. We do not know how different the current activist sample is from the rest of the population in terms of grievances, emotions or concerns. Without a comparison group, the study does not allow explaining how we get from perception to emotion or action, or gauging how far others are from mobilising. Furthermore, the participation measures available in the data (see Table 1) proved not to differentiate between varying degrees of participation within the movement. Indeed, SMI and identification did not significantly predict any of the four movement activities (analyses not shown). This was probably due to the fact that the overall participation rates were very high, thus leaving little variance to be explained.

Conclusion

Social psychological approaches to social movement participation study the social, cognitive and emotional processes of mobilisation. This paper focused on different constellations of grievances, identification, cognition and emotion showing that, in the case of Indignados, the four motives combine and a give rise to a pattern of unity within diversity. The three subgroups of movement participants varied in levels of subjective grievances and identification with the protests, but showed striking unity in their perceptions of social problems as well as emotional reactions to economic disadvantage. The practical implication of this pattern is that social movements may be more successful in attracting supporters through inclusive frames that do not provide restrictive or prototypical images of activists.

Theoretically, I have argued that the shared understandings of what it means to belong to a social movement can be central to the strategies participants choose and even to the success of the movement. Future work should address whether such unity is always necessary for a movement's success or whether diversity can be used to appeal to different constituencies and to gain wider support. Undoubtedly, to arrive at a fuller understanding of the dynamic and contextual variation in motivational patterns as well as behaviours we need to study the socio-structural, political and organisational factors related to social movement participation. To achieve this, research needs to combine case studies of social movements with a comparative analysis of how social psychological factors of identification, perception and emotions are influenced by contextual factors.

Notes

1. An article in the online edition of the main Catalan daily, La Vanguardia, notes the common and strategic use of the term 'perroflautas' (used to describe dishevelled young people with dogs) to undermine the credibility and diversity of the Indignados movement (Lladó, 2011).
2. According to a 2011 poll, 81% of respondents from the general population in Spain felt the Indignados were right, and 91% agreed that current parties should change their way of functioning – a central demand of the movement (Metroscopia, 2011).
3. Some results should be interpreted with caution due to the low alpha coefficients of some of the scales.
4. Due to violation of the homogeneity of variance assumption for some of the variables the more robust Welch's F-ratio was used.

References

Abrams, D., & Hogg, M. A. (1990). Social identification, self-categorization and social influence. *European Review of Social Psychology, 1*, 195–228. doi: 10.1080/14792779108401862

Aldenderfer, M. S., & Blashfield, R. K. (1984). *Cluster analysis*. Thousand Oaks, CA: Sage.

Batson, C. D., Kennedy, C. L., Nord, L. A., Stocks, E., Fleming, D. Y. A., & Marzette, C. M. (2007). Anger at unfairness: Is it moral outrage? *European Journal of Social Psychology, 37*, 1272–1285. doi: 10.1002/ejsp.434

Bliuc, A.-M., McGarty, C., Reynolds, K., & Muntele, D. (2007). Opinion-based group membership as a predictor of commitment to political action. *European Journal of Social Psychology, 37*, 19–32. doi: 10.1002/ejsp.334

Crosby, F. (1976). A model of egoistical relative deprivation. *Psychological Review, 83*, 85–113. doi: 10.1037/0033–295X.83.2.85

Doosje, B., Branscombe, N. R., Spears, R., & Manstead, A. S. R. (1998). Guilty by association: When one's group has a negative history. *Journal of Personality and Social Psychology, 75*, 872–886.

Drury, J., & Reicher, S. (1999). The intergroup dynamics of collective empowerment: Substantiating the social identity model of crowd behavior. *Group Processes & Intergroup Relations, 2*, 381–402. doi: 10.1177/1368430299024005

Drury, J., & Reicher, S. (2000). Collective action and psychological change: The emergence of new social identities. *British Journal of Social Psychology, 39*, 579–604. doi: 10.1348/014466600164642

Everitt, B. S., Landau, S., Leese, M., & Stahl, D. (2011). *Cluster analysis* (5th ed.). Chichester: Wiley.

Goodwin, J., & Jasper, J. J. (Eds.). (2009). *The social movements reader. Cases and concepts*. Chichester: Wiley-Blackwell.

Goodwin, J., Jasper, J. M., & Polletta, F. (2001). *Passionate politics: Emotions and social movements*. Chicago: University of Chicago Press.

Goodwin, J., Jasper, J. M., & Polletta, F. (2004). Emotional dimensions of social movements. In D. A. Snow, S. A. Soule & H. Kriesi (Eds.), *The Blackwell companion to social movements* (pp. 413–432). Oxford: Blackwell Publishing.

Gurr, T. R. (1970). *Why men rebel*. Princeton, NJ: Princeton University Press.

Inglehart, R. (1977). *The silent revolution: Changing values and political styles among Western publics*. Princeton, NJ: Princeton University Press.

Iyer, A., Schmader, T., & Lickel, B. (2007). Why individuals protest the perceived transgressions of their country: The role of anger, shame and guilt. *Personality and Social Psychology Bulletin, 33*, 572–587. doi: 10.1177/0146167206297402

Jasper, J. M. (1998). The emotions of protest: Affective and reactive emotions in and around social movements. *Sociological Forum, 13*, 397–424. doi: 10.1023/A:1022175308081

Kessler, T., & Hollbach, S. (2005). Group-based emotions as determinants of ingroup identification. *Journal of Experimental Social Psychology, 41*, 677–685. doi: 10.1016/j.jesp.2005.01.001

Klandermans, B. (1984). Mobilization and participation: Social-psychological expansions of resource mobilization theory. *American Sociological Review, 49*, 583–600.

Klandermans, B. (1997). *The social psychology of protest*. Oxford: Blackwell.

Klandermans, B., Kriesi, H., & Tarrow, S. (Eds.). (1988). *From structure to action: Comparing social movement research across cultures* (Vol. 1). Greenwich, CT: JAI Press.

Klandermans, B., & Roggeband, C. (Eds.). (2010). *Handbook of social movements across disciplines*. New York, NY: Springer.

Klandermans, B., Sabucedo, J. M., Rodriguez, M., & De Weerd, M. (2002). Identity processes in collective action participation: Farmers' identity and farmers' protest in the Netherlands and Spain. *Political Psychology, 23*, 235–251. doi: 10.1111/0162-895X.00280

Leach, C. W., Iyer, A., & Pedersen, A. (2006). Anger and guilt about ingroup advantage explain the willingness for political action. *Personality and Social Psychology Bulletin, 32*, 1232–1245. doi: 10.1177/0146167206289729

Livingstone, A., & Haslam, S. A. (2008). The importance of social identity content in a setting of chronic social conflict: Understanding intergroup relations in Northern Ireland. *British Journal of Social Psychology, 47*, 1–21. doi: 10.1348/014466607×200419

Lladó, A. (2011, May 25). *¿Eres un perroflauta?* Lavanguardia.com. Retrieved March 5, 2013, from http://www.lavanguardia.com/cultura/20110525/54161274942/eres-un-perroflauta.html

Mackie, D. M., Devos, T., & Smith, E. R. (2000). Intergroup emotions: Explaining offensive action tendencies in an intergroup context. *Journal of Personality and Social Psychology, 79*, 602–616.

Major, B. (1994). From social inequality to personal entitlement: The role of social comparisons, legitimacy appraisals, and group membership. In M. P. Zanna (Ed.), *Advances in experimental social psychology* (Vol. 26, pp. 293–335). San Diego, CA: Academic Press.

McAdam, D. (1982). *Political process and the development of black insurgency, 1930–1970.* Chicago: University of Chicago Press.

McCarthy, J. D., & Zald, M. N. (1977). Resource mobilization and social movements: A partial theory. *American Journal of Sociology, 82*, 1212–1241.

Montada, L., & Schneider, A. (1989). Justice and emotional reactions to the disadvantaged. *Social Justice Research, 3*, 313–344. doi: 10.1007/BF01048081

Moscovici, S. (1984). The phenomenon of social representations. In R. M. Farr & S. Moscovici (Eds.), *Social representations* (pp. 3–70). Cambridge: Cambridge University Press.

Mummendey, A., Kessler, T., Klink, A., & Mielke, R. (1999). Strategies to cope with negative social identity: Predictions by social identity theory and relative deprivation theory. *Journal of Personality and Social Psychology, 76*, 229–245.

Nerb, J., & Spada, H. (2001). Evaluation of environmental problems: A coherence model of cognition and emotion. *Cognition & Emotion, 15*, 521–551. doi: 10.1080/02699930126254

Peters, K., & Kashima, Y. (2007). From social talk to social action: Shaping the social triad with emotion sharing. *Journal of Personality and Social Psychology, 93*, 780–797.

Postmes, T., Haslam, S. A., & Swaab, R. I. (2005). Social influence in small groups: An interactive model of social identity formation. *European Review of Social Psychology, 16*, 1–42. doi: 10.1080/10463280440000062

Reicher, S. (1984). The St. Paul's riot: An explanation of the limits of crowd action in terms of a social identity model. *European Journal of Social Psychology, 14*, 1–21. doi: 10.1002/ejsp.2420140102

Reicher, S. (1987). Crowd behavior as social action. In J. C. Turner, M. A. Hogg, P. J. Oakes, S. Reicher & M. S. Wetherell (Eds.), *Rediscovering the social group: A self-categorization theory* (pp. 171–202). New York, NY: Basil Blackwell.

Runciman, W. G. (1966). *Relative deprivation and social justice.* London: Routledge & Kegan Paul.

Simon, B., & Klandermans, B. (2001). Politicized collective identity: A social psychological analysis. *American Psychologist, 56*, 319–331. doi: 10.1037/0003–066X.56.4.319

Simon, B., Loewy, M., Stürmer, S., Weber, U., Freytag, P., & Habig, C. (1998). Collective identification and social movement participation. *Journal of Personality and Social Psychology, 74*, 646–658.

Smith, H. J., Cronin, T., & Kessler, T. (2008). Anger, fear, or sadness: Faculty members' emotional reactions to collective pay disadvantage. *Political Psychology, 29*, 221–246. doi: 10.1111/j.1467–9221.2008.00624.x

Snow, D. A., & Oliver, P. E. (1995). Social movements and collective behavior. In K. S. Cook, G. A. Fine & J. S. House (Eds.), *Sociological perspectives on social psychology* (pp. 571–599). Boston, MA: Allyn & Bacon.

Snow, D. A., & Trom, D. (2002). The case study and the study of social movements. In B. Klandermans & S. Staggenborg (Eds.), *Methods of social movement research* (pp. 146–172). Minneapolis, MN: University of Minnesota.

Stott, C., & Drury, J. (2004). The importance of social structure and social interaction in stereotype consensus and content: Is the whole greater than the sum of its parts? *European Journal of Social Psychology, 34*, 11–23. doi: 10.1002/ejsp.183

Stryker, S., Owens, T. J., & White, R. W. (2000). *Self, identity, and social movements.* Minneapolis, MN: University of Minnesota.

Stürmer, S., & Simon, B. (2004). Collective action: Towards a dual-pathway model. *European Review of Social Psychology, 15*, 59–99. doi: 10.1080/10463280340000117

Stürmer, S., & Simon, B. (2009). Pathways to collective protest: Calculation, identification, or emotion? A critical analysis of the role of group-based anger in social movement participation. *Journal of Social Issues, 65*, 681–705. doi: 10.1111/j.1540-4560.2009.01620.x

Stürmer, S., Simon, B., Loewy, M., & Jörger, H. (2003). The dual-pathway model of social movement participation: The case of the fat acceptance movement. *Social Psychology Quarterly, 66*, 71–82.

Tajfel, H. (1981). *Human groups and social categories: Studies in social psychology*. Cambridge: Cambridge University Press.

Tajfel, H., & Turner, J. C. (1979). An integrative theory of intergroup conflict. In W. G. Austin & S. Worchel (Eds.), *The social psychology of intergroup relations* (pp. 33–48). Monterey, CA: Brooks/Cole.

Terry, D. J., & Hogg, M. A. (1996). Group norms and the attitude-behavior relationship: A role for group identification. *Personality and Social Psychology Bulletin, 22*, 776–793. doi: 10.1177/01461 67296228002

Thomas, E. F., Mavor, K. I., & McGarty, C. (2012). Social identities facilitate and encapsulate action-relevant constructs: A test of the social identity model of collective action. *Group Processes & Intergroup Relations, 15*, 75–88. doi: 10.1177/1368430211413619

Thomas, E. F., McGarty, C., & Mavor, K. I. (2009a). Aligning identities, emotions, and beliefs to create commitment to sustainable social and political action. *Personality and Social Psychology Review, 13*, 194–218. doi: 10.1177/1088868309341563

Thomas, E. F., McGarty, C., & Mavor, K. I. (2009b). Transforming 'apathy into movement': The role of prosocial emotions in motivating action for social change. *Personality and Social Psychology Review, 13*, 310–333. doi: 10.1177/1088868309343290

Travaglino, G. A., & Nulman, E. (Eds.). (2012). *Theory, action and impact of social protest: An interdisciplinary conference. Contention. The Multidisciplinary Journal of Social Protest, 0*. New York: Punctum Books.

Turner, J. C., Hogg, M. A., Oakes, P. J., Reicher, S. D., & Wetherell, M. S. (1987). *Rediscovering the social group: A self-categorization theory*. Oxford: Blackwell.

Van Stekelenburg, J., & Klandermans, B. (2009). Social movement theory: Past, present and prospects. In I. Van Kessel & S. Ellis (Eds.), *Movers and shakers: Social movements in Africa* (pp. 17–43). Leiden: Brill.

Van Stekelenburg, J., & Klandermans, B. (2010). Individuals in movements: A social psychology of contention. In B. Klandermans & C. Roggeband (Eds.), *Handbook of social movements across disciplines* (pp. 157–204). New York, NY: Springer.

Van Stekelenburg, J., & Klandermans, B. (2011). Combining motivations and emotion: The motivational dynamics of protest participation. *Revista de Psicologia Social, 26*, 91–104. doi: 10.1174/ 021347411794078426

Van Zomeren, M., Postmes, T., & Spears, R. (2008). Toward an integrative social identity model of collective action: A quantitative research synthesis of three socio-psychological perspectives. *Psychological Bulletin, 134*, 504–535. doi: 10.1037/0033–2909.134.4.504

Van Zomeren, M., & Spears, R. (2009). Metaphors of protest: A classification of motivations for collective action. *Journal of Social Issues, 65*, 661–679. doi: 10.1111/j.1540-4560.2009.01619.x

Van Zomeren, M., Spears, R., Fischer, A. H., & Leach, C. W. (2004). Put your money where your mouth is! Explaining collective action tendencies through group-based anger and group efficacy. *Journal of Personality and Social Psychology, 87*, 649–664.

Van Zomeren, M., Spears, R., & Leach, C. W. (2008). Exploring psychological mechanisms of collective action: Does relevance of group identity influence how people cope with collective disadvantage? *British Journal of Social Psychology, 47*, 353–372. doi: 10.1348/014466607X231091

Yzerbyt, V., Dumont, M., Wigboldus, D., & Gordijn, E. (2003). I feel for us: The impact of categorization and identification on emotions and action tendencies. *British Journal of Social Psychology, 42*, 533–549. doi: 10.1348/014466603322595266

Appendix 1

Items comprising the three dimensions of beliefs about social problems

(1) Concern over public services
  - Concern about the health-care system
  - Concern about the education system
  - Concern about the pension system
  - High levels of unemployment
  - Weakening of the welfare state through spending cuts
(2) Concern over inequality and democracy
  - Inequality between different social classes

- Inequality between different ethnic groups
- Manipulation by medias
- Lack of democracy

(3) Concern over markets and corruption

- Frustration with global financial markets and banks
- Political corruption
- Housing and mortgage problem

The political economy of Israel's 'social justice' protests: a class and generational analysis

Zeev Rosenhek[a] and Michael Shalev[b]

[a]Sociology, Political Science and Communication, Open University of Israel, Raanana, Israel; [b]Sociology, Hebrew University, Jerusalem, Israel

In the summer of 2011, similar to and partly inspired by Spain's 15M (indignados) movement, Israel experienced an unprecedented wave of socio-economic protest featuring tent encampments and mass rallies. Headlined 'the people demand social justice', the protest was surprising since distributive conflicts and social policy issues are peripheral to Israeli politics, and Israel was not in the throes of an economic crisis. These were not anti-austerity protests, but reflected the eroding life chances of young adults. Specifically, liberalisation of Israel's political economy – which contributed to a substantial rise in the living standards of the parental generation of the middle class and improved their life chances in the 1990s – is now impeding inter-generational class reproduction for their children. We document significant changes in home ownership, relative incomes, and the value of higher education and other assets that were previously the key to middle class incomes and lifestyles. The impact of neo-liberal policies is evident, for instance, in the declining scope and generosity of the public sector's role in employment and housing. At the subjective level, on the eve of the protests young adults with higher education were less optimistic about their economic prospects than other groups. Finally, even though the protests appeared to be broadly consensual and inclusive, a closer look reveals that its core supporters and activists were drawn from social and political sectors closely associated with the middle class.

Similarly to other phenomena that are understood as global, the wave of mass protests in 2011 in many advanced capitalist societies has exhibited a combination of common supra-national features and idiosyncratic local traits (Pabst, 2011). The protest movements that emerged in Europe and North America have a number of characteristics in common: the initiators and leaders of these movements are educated young people with middle class backgrounds, protesting against their own reduced economic opportunities and the widening inequality between the wealthy and the rest of the population; their protests express deep alienation from institutionalised politics; they occupy public space in an attempt to imbue it with new meaning and instill alternative forms of political action; they hold mass demonstrations attended by broader audiences; and they make diffuse demands on the state for more or less radical changes to the economy and socio-economic policies – demands that are fundamentally redistributive (Tejerina & Perugorria, 2012). The movements in different countries also share specific practices of protest and collective action: the wide use of theatrical performativity; a reliance on digital technologies and new media to spread their message and mobilise activists; a network logic of action and organisation; and an effort to implement direct democracy and non-hierarchical coordination (Bennett & Segerberg, 2012; Castells, 2012; Mason, 2012).

These features were shared by the protests that unexpectedly broke out in Israel in the summer of 2011 under the banner 'the people demand social justice', and succeeded in dominating the public agenda for two tumultuous months. The global wave of protests doubtless expanded the structure of political opportunities for the Israeli movement by offering models for imitation and ideational frameworks for identification and legitimation. Similarly to the Spanish, Greek, Portuguese and Chilean cases, the Israeli protest successfully garnered support from far beyond the internal nucleus of activists, mobilising mass rallies with often unprecedented numbers of supporters who had not previously participated in this kind of protest activity over economic and social issues. Yet the protests in Israel emerged in unusual circumstances. As we show below, economic conditions differed profoundly from those that struck such a blow to Western Europe and the USA following the financial crisis that erupted in 2008. Furthermore, the legacy of protest politics in Israel – and politics in general – also differed from those in most established democracies. Since 1967, if not before, they have been dominated by Israel's protracted conflict with Arab states and the Palestinians, and by the future of the Occupied Territories – issues that are related to conflicts over competing definitions of collective identity in Israeli society. Distributive conflicts and issues have been marginalised and have failed to serve as a platform for mass political mobilisation.

Our objective in this article is to examine the relations between the underlying economic and political factors that led to the surprising emergence of Israel's social protest. To this end we shall offer a class and generational analysis that focuses on the protest's instigators and leaders – young adults from the middle class – examining changes in their life chances and their relationship to the dynamics of Israel's political economy. Our argument is that political-economic dynamics in Israel (and perhaps in other countries as well) have created a situation in which this class-generational unit is struggling to maintain the lifestyle and living standards enjoyed by the previous generation of the middle class and to which they grew accustomed during the formative years when they lived in their parents' home. The comprehensive liberalisation of Israel's political economy in recent decades – which contributed to a substantial rise in the living standards of the parental generation and improved their life chances in the 1990s – is now impeding inter-generational class reproduction for a significant segment of the middle class, leading to growing discontent based on relative deprivation (Runciman, 1966; Wolbring, Keuschnigg, & Negele, 2013). Together with political dynamics, we argue, this class-generational dynamic is foundational to the growth of the protest movement and its broad demands for 'social justice'.

The relevance of this analysis goes beyond the Israeli case, and it can shed light on one of the key theoretical questions posed to the study of social movements by the current wave of protests in western societies. While in a number of important ways Occupy-type protests have followed a pattern familiar from earlier 'new' and 'post-materialist' social movements, the socio-economic injustice frames animating these protests and their central demands are unmistakably materialistic. They seek to alter the distribution of resources and the structure of inequality, and they challenge key elements of the prevailing model of state–economy relations. In a dialectical process, the class and generational dynamic that has accompanied the institutionalisation of the neoliberal regime and its crisis led to the emergence of a protest movement that seeks to repoliticise distributive and economic issues.

The empirical puzzle – a thoroughly unexpected protest

The Israeli protests began in the wake of Internet campaigns by disgruntled consumers during the first half of 2011 (Alimi, 2012; Grinberg, 2013; Monterescu & Shaindlinger, 2013). The opening step was an encampment in the heart of the Tel Aviv financial district, inspired by the Spanish model, which was designed to draw attention to the housing problems faced by young students.[1] Enthusiastically publicised by most of the mainstream media as well as via social media and other informal channels, the protest quickly expanded in three directions: establishment of parallel tent camps in other locations around the country; support by and collaboration with diverse cause groups and lobbying groups, most importantly the national union of students; and a series of half a dozen mass rallies that peaked on September 3 with an unprecedented turnout of 300,000 in Tel Aviv and 100,00 in other areas of the country. Both the demands and the collective identity adopted by the protest broadened as it developed, from an initial emphasis on housing and other consumer issues to a redefinition as a middle class protest with aspirations to represent 'the people' in a struggle for 'social justice'. In addition to students and young people, the protest leaders embraced other publics including striking medical residents and parents complaining about the cost of childcare, and made efforts to reach out to marginalised groups, primarily Jewish residents of poor neighborhoods and the geographical periphery.

In retrospect, it is tempting to see the Israeli protest as the inevitable consequence of more than two decades of radical neoliberal policies that undermined the economic and social security of large segments of the Israeli population. But at the time, the remarkable success of the movement in mobilising wide public support took all observers of Israeli society and politics utterly by surprise. It was hard to believe that 400,000 Israelis would take to the streets over issues such as the distribution of wealth in society, and social and economic policy. First, as noted, the protest in Israel emerged in entirely different economic circumstances from those prevalent in the USA and much of Europe. The protests there were the result of a deep and ongoing economic crisis that hit a large part of the population extremely hard, including the middle class, and particularly its younger generation. Unemployment soared, reaching 10% in the USA and the Eurozone in 2010, and 20% in Spain. Unemployment among the young was, and remains, especially high – 18% in the USA; 21% in the Eurozone; and 41% in Spain in 2010.[2] Moreover, in countries where the financial crisis turned into a public debt crisis, states adopted austerity policies that involved deep cutbacks in public expenditure, which seriously harmed both social rights and the employment opportunities of young adults from the middle class. Given that those states were simultaneously channeling trillions of taxpayers' dollars into failing banks and financial institutions, one of the central motifs of the protests was that massive public resources were being diverted to save the very financial capitalists and their lackeys who had caused the crisis, while as a consequence, the remainder of the population was obliged to suffer contraction of the welfare state.

In Israel, by contrast, on the eve of the protests the global crisis had not significantly harmed domestic economic performance. The financial market remained relatively stable, no bailouts and massive monetary injection were necessary and there was no real threat of a debt crisis. From the second half of 2009 Israel enjoyed favorable growth rates by international standards, and unemployment declined in 2010 to less than 7% (twice that among the young), one of the lowest levels experienced since 1985. Furthermore, in 2010 and 2011 no severe cutbacks to public budgets were on the agenda. Nevertheless, as we explain below, these aggregate indicators conceal a far more complex socio-economic reality characterised not only by ever-widening gaps in the distribution of economic resources, but also by relative deterioration in the economic opportunities of the younger generation as a whole, and that of the middle class in particular. Be that as it may, in the summer of 2011 Israel was exempt from either the socio-economic distress or the atmosphere of a deep crisis demanding radical change in the political economy which were the basis for the protest movements in other countries.

The Israeli protest was also surprising because of the striking contrast it posed to the cleavages and identities that had characterised the political field and contentious mobilisation in Israel since

1967. These were all primarily organised around issues of war and peace, including relations with the Palestinians and the region's Arab states, and the future of the Occupied Territories. These issues had been central in both institutional and non-institutional politics, and had largely defined the socio-political identities of different groups, voting patterns, and the demands of most of the country's protest movements. The main extra-parliamentary movements that had successfully positioned themselves at the top of the political agenda and were responsible for the largest mass mobilisations emerged around these issues, such as the opposing movements regarding the future of the Occupied Territories (Peace Now and *Gush Emunim*), and those targeted to support of or opposition to either ceding territory for peace (first with Egypt, later with the Palestinians) or controversial actions by the Israeli military (Hermann, 2009). Additional political conflicts that sometimes occupied the center of the public stage – and especially the conflict between Israel's religious and secular populations – were closely related to competing views concerning war and peace issues and to the wider political question of the ethno-national definition of the Israeli state and society. Consequently, the main political conflicts in Israel were perceived and interpreted as enacting a fundamental struggle between contradictory political and cultural collective identities. While the 1970s and 1980s saw instances of protest over issues of distribution, they reached nothing like the scale of mass mobilisation seen in the protest of 2011 (Lehman-Wilzig, 1990). A partial exception was a protest in 1971 led by young residents of slum neighborhoods who styled themselves as Israeli Black Panthers. Though the protest spread throughout the country, it did not reach massive dimensions and continued to be viewed as the particularistic outcry of the second generation of disadvantaged Jewish immigrants from Arab countries (Bernstein, 1984).

Given this type of politics, in which social conflicts were understood and formulated in terms of clashes between fundamental cultural identities, distributive issues and class interests played a marginal role in electoral politics, serving as only a muted or implicit political cleavage. Even when the material interests of different groups formed the basis for their organisation and political action, they were understood and portrayed in terms of cultural identities – mainly religious and/ or ethnic – or in terms of an effort at attaining peace and democratisation (Filc, 2006; Peled, 1998; Shalev & Levy, 2005). Although public support for the welfare state and expressions of concern about the increasing economic inequality were more pronounced in Israel than in most other countries (Shalev, 2007), until the summer of 2011 those issues did not produce large protest movements or mass political mobilisation, and they were certainly not the grounds for the construction of socio-political identities.

The third factor that should have narrowed the structure of political opportunities for the emergence of a mass social protest in Israel is related to the rise in recent decades of alienation and mistrust toward politics and politicians, often described as anti-politics (Arian & Shamir, 2005; Hermann, 2012a). It would seem that most Israelis became indifferent, antithetical even, to politics (Filc, 2012). This atmosphere of anti-politics was felt not only in declining turnouts at election time, but also in what would seem to be a reduced propensity to take part in protest activities (Yishai, 2012). In the context of the accelerated liberalisation of Israel's political economy and the penetration of individualistic and consumerist principles into many spheres of life, the neoliberal project of depoliticising economic policy, and indeed economics in general, and its definition as the preserve of 'apolitical' experts, was remarkably successful in Israel (Maman & Rosenhek, 2011).

It appeared that most Israelis, especially among the middle class, were not at all interested in taking part in collective action with political objectives, particularly when those objectives were related to the politics of the distribution of resources. Moreover, rising apathy toward and revulsion from politics were viewed as particularly notable among the younger members of the middle class – a generation that was portrayed in public discourse as hedonistic, radically individualistic, and indifferent to matters of public import, particularly those of a socio-economic nature. However, it was precisely this class-generational unit that launched and led a protest that raised the banner of solidarity and social justice.

Before presenting our explanation for the surprising emergence of Israel's social protest, we shall position it within the broader context of the theoretical challenges posed by the current wave of protests in advanced capitalist countries to the study of social movements, and especially to the new social movements approach.

The theoretical puzzle – new social movements and the current wave of protests

For three decades sociologists have been discussing the 'death of class' and its decline as an organising principle for the articulation of interests, identities, and collective action (Pakulski & Waters, 1996). Their discussions have raised questions about the relevance of material life chances, class identities, distributive demands, and socio-economic issues in general for collective action in both institutionalised and non-institutionalised politics (Clark & Lipset, 2001; Evans, 1999). Scholars have highlighted the increasing importance of post-materialist socio-cultural issues and conflicts as the primary bases for political mobilisation at the expense of the class identities and distributive demands that used to play such an important role in the political dynamics of capitalist societies until the final quarter of the twentieth century (Kitschelt, 1994). According to this approach, political struggles in contemporary societies are more likely to form around questions of values and lifestyle than around the unequal distribution of economic resources. The conceptualisation of post-industrial societies as founded on post-materialist identities and values (Inglehart, 1990) is also embodied in the 'new social movements' paradigm, which has dominated the study of social movements for decades (Larana, Johnston, & Gusfield, 1994).

This approach sharply distinguished between the classic protest movements of advanced capitalist societies and those that emerged since the student movement of the 1960s. These distinctions referred to the collective grievances and identities constructed and expressed by the movements, as well as to features of their activists and supporters and the political practices they used. The classic protest movements were strongly related to identities formed in the economic arena; they expressed material concerns and interests; put forward distributive demands; were led or supported by the organised working class; and deployed highly institutionalised practices, usually linked to hierarchically organised labor unions or left-wing parties (Piven & Cloward, 1977). The new social movements, by contrast, emerged tightly associated with identities that were formulated on the basis of cultural distinctions and lifestyle, and their demands were mainly related to post-materialist values and the recognition of those distinct identities (Kriesi, Koopmans, Duyvendak, & Giugni, 1995; Steinmetz, 1994). Even when some of the issues dealt with by certain of these movements had a clearly distributive aspect, their demands were primarily framed in terms of the recognition of the distinct culturally based identities of excluded and oppressed groups. Some of the more notable examples of these new social movements are the women's movements, student movements, the gay rights movement, the movements against nuclear arms and energy, and the environmental movement. The main support base of these movements is the educated middle and upper-middle classes, especially their younger members. They are also characterised by a principled rejection of institutionalised politics and by practices that aim to underscore this rejection: fluid and seemingly non-hierarchical organisational structures; participatory democracy and deliberative decision making; and creative and innovative protest activities in which humor, playfulness, and theatrical performativeness play a central part (for the Israeli case, see Katriel & Livio, 2012; Larana et al., 1994).

The recent wave of protest in advanced capitalist societies – from the Portuguese Geração à Rasca ('desperate generation') and Indignados in Spain, through the Occupy Wall Street movement in the USA to the social justice movement in Israel – poses a serious challenge to the dichotomous distinction between old materialistic social movements and new post-materialistic ones. On the one hand, the current wave of protest shares many characteristics with the new social movements: the instigators, leaders, and many of the supporters are youngsters with a middle class background, and they are generally university students or graduates. Moreover, following consolidation of these practices by the preceding anti-globalisation movement, the contemporary protests have further developed the fluid and participatory internal practices and forms of protest characteristic of new social movements. At the same time, however, the recent protest wave took shape around opposition to existing modes of resource distribution and demands for alternative socio-economic policies. Finally, in the process of repoliticising socio-economic issues, these movements have attempted to construct new collective identities based on quasi-class distinctions. While there is no longer talk of 'the working class' or 'the labor movement', these new identities are nonetheless constructed and formulated in relation to the structure of social inequality: 'the 99% vs. the 1%' in the USA; 'the people against bankers and politicians' in Spain; and 'the middle class versus the tycoons' in Israel. In this regard, the current protests rearticulate the relationship between identities and distributive conflicts as the basis for political action. Our analysis of the Israeli case suggests that the class dimension of the protests can be sharpened and clarified by focusing on the links between generational and class dynamics and their association to changes in the political economy.

Generational and class dynamics and the social protest in Israel

Building on the classic theory of 'sociological generations' laid out by Karl Mannheim (1952), we propose to examine the material origins of the social protest in Israel through the concept of 'class-generational unit'. Mannheim saw generation and class as two distinct categories that indicate different types of social location. A similar assumption underlies most contemporary analyses of political action in general, and protest activities in particular, which tend to focus on either class or age as the basis for the formation of social movements (see, for instance, Whittier, 1997). In contrast, our argument is that the intersection of class and generational locations may define a distinct social position that can serve as basis for collective political action, particularly when the process of inter-generational class reproduction is disrupted and it ceases to operate smoothly.

We define a class-generational unit as a set of individuals with shared formative experiences in the areas of consumption and life chances, experiences that derive primarily from their parents' class location. These experiences influence their economic outlook and expectations regarding their adult lives. This conceptualisation is anchored in a Weberian understanding of class, that is, one that focuses on individuals' positions in different markets, primarily the labor market, but also the housing market, and which assumes that these are the main fields in which the life chances of individuals and families are determined. Accordingly, the middle class is defined in terms of the economic, social, and cultural resources that enable integration in the labor market in positions that, in principle, ensure economic stability and levels of income that allow relatively high levels of consumption, including home ownership. In modern societies academic education has served as the central mechanism of social closure critical to enabling members of the middle class to attain advantageous jobs, as well as a form of cultural capital that marks and sharpens their privileged position and facilitates inter-generational class reproduction (Bourdieu, 1984). In the case of young adults, academic education is seen in society as the most important condition conducive to entry into the middle class, and it functions as an important factor shaping young adults' expectations regarding life chances, prestige, and other privileges. Accordingly, empirically we treat income and higher education as indicative of actual (or for young people, potential) member-ship in the middle class.

As we have already suggested, in generational terms the leaders of the 2011 protest were the children of the liberalisation of Israel's political economy. They grew up in middle and upper-middle class families in the 1990s and the early 2000s just as most members of those classes were enjoying a significant improvement in their standard of living and were adopting modes of conspicuous consumption that were quite novel in Israel. Their parents were the main benefi-ciaries of the liberalisation of the Israeli economy, and this shaped their experiences as a class-generational unit. However, when reaching early adulthood, they found themselves in a situation where the successful reproduction of their parents' life chances was in no way guaranteed, includ-ing the level and modes of consumption to which they had become accustomed during their for-mative years. As we explain below, the same features of the liberalised political economy that had formed the basis for their parents' significantly improved life chances since the 1990s, had become a hindrance to many of the younger generation seeking to reproduce their class position. In other words, many of the sons and daughters of the beneficiaries of the neoliberal regime became its losers.

Before examining the relationships between class-generational dynamics and changes in Israel's political economy, we shall present some figures that point to the diminished life chances of the younger middle class generation in the last decade that have contributed to the emergence and strengthening of a sense of relative deprivation. This erosion is documented by means of both objective indicators (home ownership and attainment of superior incomes) and individuals' subjective perception of their economic situation and prospects. The empirical data presented here, like our overall analysis, refer only to Israel's Jewish majority. While Pales-tinian-Arab citizens (one-fifth of the total Israeli citizenry) supported the objective of reducing inequality and rehabilitating the welfare state, they appear to have viewed the protest (quite accu-rately) as an internal Jewish matter, and their active participation was far more limited than among the Jewish population (Hermann, 2012b). Furthermore, because of the specific location of Pales-tinian citizens in Israel's political economy, its internal class-generational dynamics differ from those of the Jewish population. Their housing problems were quite different to those of Jews, and a growing segment of the younger generation succeeded in achieving inter-generational upward mobility by academic education or entrepreneurial initiative (Haidar, 2013).

Two other sectors of Israeli society – immigrants from the Former Soviet Union and *Haredim* (ultra-orthodox Jews) – are also either treated separately, or excluded from our analysis. Young *Haredi* families are a special case because of widespread poverty, the result of a combination of high fertility and low labor force participation (many male spouses are engaged in full-time religious studies). The younger members of the massive wave of 'Russian' immigration to Israel that began after 1989 are exceptional in having achieved high levels of upward mobility, in part because early arrivals were seriously disadvantaged. Finally, available data do not permit drawing a distinction between young Jewish adults of Ashkenazi (European) and Mizrahi (Middle Eastern) origins, since there is no information on their grandparents' country of birth. Still, there are indications that the classic ethnic divide among Israeli Jews is less relevant today than in the past in influencing the chances of young adults to enter the middle class. In this regard, recent research by Momi Dahan (2013) suggests that Israeli-born Mizrahim now enjoy the same weight in the Israeli middle class as they do in the population as a whole.

The protest was sparked by demands regarding the difficulties faced by young adults – especially those living in the Tel Aviv area – in attaining affordable housing. Even when the movement and its demands were broadened to include other issues, and more general critiques of inequality and neoliberal policy were articulated, the issue of the younger generation's limited access to housing continued to play a central role in the protests. Analysis of large-scale annual surveys carried out by the Israeli Central Bureau of Statistics (CBS) shows that in the course of the 2000s there was a decline in the rate of home ownership among young families. However, as detailed in Table 1, the decline occurred mainly among young Israeli-born Jews, especially those living in the central area of the country. Both Russian-speaking immigrants living outside of the Center and *Haredim* (ultra-orthodox Jews) also experienced falling rates of ownership, but they were much more moderate. Russian-speaking immigrants in the center of the country actually improved their rates of ownership, though they still trailed behind other groups, while among Arabs in Israel, home ownership was and is almost universal.

This raises the question of whether the decline in home ownership among the young Israeli-born Jewish population was particularly prominent among the middle class. This is addressed by distinguishing between different quintiles of household income.[3] Figure 1 shows that the decline in the probability that a young family owns the home in which they live has mainly affected the middle quintile and above, while we find the steepest decline (17 percentage points) in the highest

Table 1.   Home ownership among young working families by sector and period.

	2001–2004 (%)	2009–2010 (%)
Israeli-born Jews – Center	74	60
Israeli-born Jews – Other areas	73	63
Russian-speaking immigrants – Center	37	47
Russian-speaking immigrants – Other areas	65	61
Haredim (all areas)	73	68
Arabs (all areas)	90	93
Total – Center	69	61
Total – Other areas	76	71

Source: Authors' analysis of CBS Income Surveys. 'Center' refers to Tel Aviv and surrounding areas.

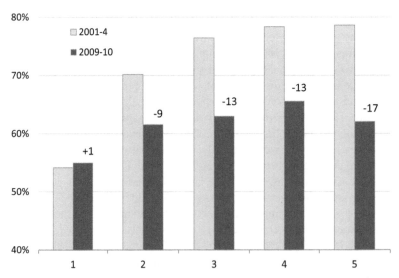

Figure 1.   Rate of home ownership among young working families (Israeli-born Jews) by income quintile and period.
Source: See Table 1.

Table 2. Percentage of Israeli-born Jewish families in the upper income quintile by age and education of household head.

	University graduates		Others	
	Ages 30–39 (%)	Ages 40–49 (%)	Ages 30–39 (%)	Ages 40–49 (%)
2000–2004	49	54	12	16
2009–2010	40	54	8	16

Source: Adapted from Shalev (2012, Fig. 12a).

quintile. We suspect that this is partly the result of exceptionally large increases in property prices at the high end of the market, and partly because lifestyle changes have led some privileged young families to delay buying a permanent home, possibly while purchasing another property as an investment or an option for the future. In any case, the data available to us do not contradict the protesters' argument that it has become harder for young adults from the middle class to buy an apartment.

The position occupied by the young individuals and families in the national hierarchies of earnings and income has deteriorated markedly over the last decade (Shalev, 2012). A salient indicator for our argument regarding shrinking access of young families to middle class lifestyles is the proportion of these families that succeed in attaining relatively high incomes. Table 2 shows shifts between the beginning and end of the decade preceding the protests in the percentage of families reaching the highest quintile of household income. The figures refer only to Israeli-born Jews and they are split by both age and education. Among families in which the head of the household[4] had an academic degree and was in his or her thirties, the proportion in the upper quintile declined from 49% in 2000–2004 to 40% in 2009–2010. In contrast, the other groups experienced little or no decline.

The evidence presented so far clearly suggests that the structure of opportunities facing the younger generation of Israeli-born Jews has contracted in recent years, in both labor and housing markets, and that this reduction has been especially felt among those with a university education. However, when examining processes of political mobilisation it is no less important – and perhaps even more so – to look at the way in which individuals perceive their economic situation. To shed light on this, we draw on the CBS annual Social Survey to evaluate changes in perceptions between 2006 and 2010 while distinguishing between four groups within the Jewish population defined by age (25–34 and 35–44) and whether or not they have academic education. It is worth noting that for the Jewish population as a whole, evaluations of personal economic circumstances in 2010 – the year before the protest erupted – were very positive, more so than in 2006. For instance, the proportion of respondents who expected their economic situation to improve in the future rose from 42% in 2006 to 47% in 2010, and the proportion of those satisfied with their current economic situation rose from 55% to 61% over the same period. Quite surprisingly, a similar pattern pertains in relation to housing, where the proportion of those satisfied rose from 83% in 2006 to 87% in 2010.

However, the picture becomes especially interesting when we compare rates of change between different segments of the population. The pattern that emerges is that the trend among university-educated young adults differed from that of the three other groups – young adults without an academic education and the two groups of older adults. This pattern can be clearly seen in Figure 2, which shows the relative change between the two points in time in relation to respondents' perception of their present economic situation. The only group with an increase (of 14%) in the proportion expressing dissatisfaction was that of the younger and university-

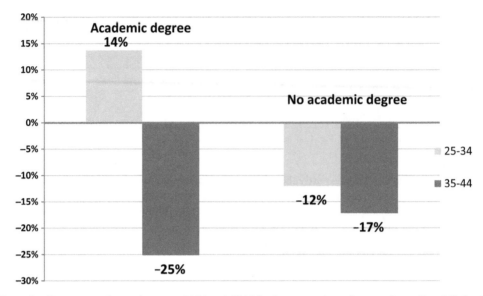

Figure 2. Percentage change between 2006 and 2010 in the proportion of respondents dissatisfied with their personal economic situation by education and age.
Source: Authors' analysis of CBS Social Survey 2006 and 2010.

educated Israelis, while the other three groups saw a significant decline. Similar trends emerged in responses to a question regarding concern about losing one's job. Younger and university-educated respondents were the only group in which the percentage saying they were not at all worried fell.

Table 3 presents a parallel analysis of a question asking about satisfaction with housing. Once more, the trend among the young and highly educated differed from that of the other groups. While among the older respondents and those without an academic education there was a notable decline in levels of dissatisfaction with housing, there was no change among the university-educated and younger respondents. This implies that, relative to the other groups, their perceived situation regarding housing had deteriorated. The same trends were identified in relation to respondents' satisfaction with their income.

To summarise, in the course of the last decade both the objective and perceived economic situation of young Jewish adults with an academic education (not including immigrants) suffered significant deterioration, leading to a growing sense of relative deprivation. These trends were reinforced as a basis for political mobilisation by the formative experiences of that class-generational unit as children of Israel's liberalisation, who grew up with a significant improvement in their families' standard of living. In the section that follows, we contend that the declining

Table 3. Percentage change between 2006 and 2010 in the proportion of respondents dissatisfied with their housing situation by education and age.

	Percentage change
25–34: Academic degree	0
35–44: Academic degree	−37
25–34: No academic degree	−22
35–44: No academic degree	−15

Source: Authors' analysis of CBS Social Survey 2006 and 2010.

ability of young middle class Israelis to reproduce their parents' life chances is inextricably related to the shift in relations between state and the economy in Israel.

Class-generational dynamics and Israel's political economy

Nearly four decades ago Henry Rosenfeld and Shulamit Carmi published a path-breaking analysis of the mechanisms through which the state created Israel's middle class during the first decades of its existence (Rosenfeld & Carmi, 1976). The Israeli developmental state produced a broad structure of opportunities for the veteran Ashkenazi population in both labor and housing markets, which enabled this group to accumulate significant amounts of financial and social capital. The establishment of a wide-ranging bureaucratic and professional state apparatus; the construction of public and private industrial sectors; the expansion of the banking system – all these gave this relatively privileged segment of society the opportunity to assume advantageous positions in the primary labor market and to advance down the path of resource accumulation. Heavily state-subsidised public housing programs – usually in collaboration with the *Histadrut* (peak labor organisation) and targeted at veteran residents – were a further mechanism for producing the middle class in the 1950s and 1960s (Rosenhek, 2007). Ownership of these housing assets – which was concentrated in the center of the country and whose value rose continuously – was critical to the inter-generational transfer of wealth and the reproduction of the class structure in Israel (Lewin-Epstein & Semyonov, 2000).

The process by which the middle class gained advantages deepened in the subsequent second generation of Israelis born in the 1940s and 1950s. This generation inherited considerable economic, social, political, and cultural capital from its predecessor and continued to benefit from preferential economic resources provided by the state. It profited from the expansion of the welfare state, which reached its peak in the 1970s, and a significant part of which was designed to assist the middle class. It was this class-generational unit that benefited from the first wave of the expansion of higher education in Israel in the 1970s, enabling its members to acquire academic degrees that were extremely valuable in the labor market almost without cost. It was also the primary beneficiary of very generous state subsidies for home purchase through entitlement-based mortgage programs that operated from the early 1970s to the early 1990s (Rosenhek, 2007).

Later on, upon reaching middle age in the 1980s and 1990s, the second generation of the middle class accumulated the economic, social, and cultural resources that enabled it to nurture a degree of autonomy from the state, thereby becoming an important supporter of the liberalisation of the Israeli political economy that was taking place at the time. This trend was given clear political expression in the support of the veteran middle and upper-middle class for the Oslo process, which combined decolonisation with liberalisation of the political economy and Israel's integration into the global economy (Shafir & Peled, 2002). Although the Oslo 'peace process' was a resounding failure, the liberalisation of the political economy has only deepened since 2000 (Maman & Rosenhek, 2012). This shift led to far-reaching changes in the structure of inequality in Israel, including the formation of a new class of capitalists with a controlling position in the Israeli economy, enormous widening of gaps in income and wealth, a decline in economic and social security among large parts of the lower middle class, and the marginalisation of disadvantaged groups (Kristal, 2013). As part of these changes, significant sections of the second generation of the veteran middle class managed to leverage the economic and social resources that they had inherited and accumulated to benefit from the new political-economic regime.

The neoliberal turn of the Israeli political economy contributed to expanding the opportunities of many members of this class-generational unit, improving their life chances both in labor and consumer markets. First, the expansion of the private sector brought about by privatisation and foreign investment provided them with opportunities to exploit their social and cultural capital in order to attain high-ranking professional and managerial positions. The proliferation of lawyers, accountants, and various types of consultants offering services to the business sector attested to this process. Enhanced integration of the local economy in the global economy – including the liberalisation of international trade and the growth of the high-tech industry – opened up new pathways for entrepreneurs and intermediaries between the local economy and global markets. In addition, financial liberalisation and the resulting explosive growth of the financial sector not only produced well-paid and attractive jobs, but in some periods also substantial capital gains for investors. Those who remained employed in the public sector managed to exploit existing institutional arrangements and their positions of power in order to preserve the advantages of the sheltered labor market in which they were employed. Processes such as the privatisation of public corporations (including in the arms industry) and outsourcing were typically implemented in ways that preserved existing privileges, and the sting of many neoliberal reforms in the public labor market was deferred in practice to future generations of employees.

These developments contributed to a significant rise in the relative income levels of those with advantageous jobs. One indication of this trend is that the share of the top two deciles in the overall gross income of salaried workers climbed from 39.3% in 1988 to 44.9% in 2009 (Swirski & Konor-Attias, 2007, p. 7; Swirski, Konor-Attias, & Abu-Khala, 2010, p. 13). At the same time, neoliberal tax reforms implemented since the early 2000s significantly reduced income tax levels for high earners, adding to their disposal income. It is fair to say that capitalism's ideological promise that each generation, at least those from the middle class, would have better life chances than their predecessors was realised in the case of the second generation of Israel's middle and upper-middle classes. In contrast, for many members of the third generation this is no longer the case. This turnaround is primarily due to the effects of liberalisation on young newcomers.

Current aspirants to middle class life chances and lifestyle enter a labor market bereft of many of the protections that used to be afforded to workers. The labor conditions, salaries, and employment security of young workers in a large swathe of the contemporary labor market – including many professionals – are far worse than they used to be, prior to processes of neoliberal 'flexibilisation' (Paz-Fuchs, 2009). Irregular forms of employment through manpower agencies or subcontractors that first appeared in non-professional fields have been spreading to several professions commonly taken up by young people with higher education, particularly women and especially in the public sector. Similar to what occurred in other countries, these processes have created a new *precariat* composed of educated young people from middle-class backgrounds (Standing, 2011).

The life chances of those young adults were also undermined by welfare state reforms. While the most drastic cutbacks, mainly since 2003, were made to programs that targeted the lower classes – such as unemployment insurance, guaranteed minimum income, and child benefits – the Israeli welfare state also contracted in areas that are important to the middle class. Reduced public spending on education and health and the heavy cost of childcare and quasi-private education for young children hurt young middle class families, who today have to pay for services that their parents were given for free, or at least were heavily subsidised. The drastic reduction in state support for the middle class in the realm of housing is particularly notable. During the 1990s, mortgage schemes for young couples that included a significant state subsidy that primarily benefited the middle class were almost entirely eliminated. In parallel, the difficulty of buying a home increased as a result of large price rises in real terms. Those who managed to buy a property had to make far higher mortgage repayments than their parents had in the 1970s when they bought their first apartment with substantial governmental subsidies.

To summarise this section, the generational dynamics of the economic situation of the Israeli middle class explain the unease which was at the root of the unexpected emergence of a mass protest movement around distributive issues and material interests. The children of Israel's liberal-isation found themselves in a situation where capitalism's promise of a constantly improving stan-dard of living failed to be met. In light of what appears to be a failure in the inter-generational reproduction of the life chances of a sizable segment of the middle class, this class-generational unit sought to position itself at the forefront of a broad movement issuing wide-ranging distribu-tive demands in the name of 'the people'. As we shall see in the following section, the protest movement embodied an effort to rearticulate material interests and demands while coping with divisions and conflicts formulated in terms of cultural identities – that is, to maneuver between a politics of redistribution and a politics of recognition.

Status politics and republicanism

So far we have focused our analysis on class-generational dynamics and their relation to the pol-itical economy, while emphasising what was novel about the protest as a mass mobilisation that emerged around distributive issues. However, this is not to say that the social protest of 2011 was detached from the principles that have organised the political field in Israel for the past four decades: political identities based on cultural distinctions and conflicts over non-economic issues. The complex relationship between the protest and pre-existing identities and conflicts in Israeli society was central to the public debate that emerged around it: the conflict between left and right (as they are defined in Israel), between the secular and the ultra-Orthodox, between the Ashkenazi (European origin) center and the Mizrahi (Middle Eastern origin) periph-ery, between rich and spoiled Tel Aviv and the rest of the country – all these conflicts and their associated identities were both simultaneously present in and absent from the protest and the dis-course surrounding it.

At the most overt level, the protest made broad and inclusive demands on the state. Alongside the demand to improve the life chances of the middle class, and especially its younger generation, demands were also made that the state aid the disadvantaged and ease their plight by expanding social protection. The combination of a wide range of specific demands with the all-inclusive demand for social justice and solidarity and the attribution of responsibility to the state for its citi-zens' welfare, created the impression that the protest movement was actually demanding the rebuilding of a universal welfare state that would advance a more egalitarian distribution of resources. Leaders of the protest movement apparently hoped that these demands would construct a 'pan-Israeli' socio-political identity that would rise above the old familiar political and cultural conflicts and identities, especially those related to the future of the Occupied Territories and secular-religious relations. The aim was to create an inclusive identity representing the general social interest, which would rise above the old divisions and quarrels – in the face of corrupt poli-ticians, of governments, past and present, which abrogated responsibility for their citizens, and 'tycoons' who were exploiting the people.

To be sure, in terms of public support and participation in mass demonstrations, the protest was remarkably successful in transcending entrenched social and cultural boundaries. For example, according to the 'Peace Index' survey carried out by the Israel Democracy Institute a few weeks after the protests began, 88% of all respondents said they were either very or quite supportive (Hermann, 2011). While launched by young, educated, left-wing and secular Tel Avi-vians, the protest was embraced by diverse segments of the population whom the former tried to construct as 'the Israelis'. In this regard, the Israeli protests were similar to the preceding 15M movement in Spain, where tent encampments in the main squares sparked mass demonstrations throughout the country with participants who were more diverse in terms of both generation and class.

However, if we look below the surface, it turns out that the protest was deeply embedded in the same identities and conflicts that have structured politics in Israel since the 1970s. Public support varied significantly between different sections of the Jewish population, mirroring the classic divisions of Israeli society and politics. Left-leaning Israelis supported and participated in the protest more than those on the right; the secular more than the religious; the educated more than the less educated; and middle to high-earners more than low-earners (Hermann, 2012b). These differences in support and participation reflect the tension between the effort to construct the protest as expressing the interests of all Israelis, and its class-related socio-political foundations. The core of the protest remained largely the domain of the secular, educated and 'left wing' middle class.

The tension between inclusiveness and privilege was also expressed in the republican motifs mobilised in the protests, which have always been a central basis for claims-making in Israeli politics (Shafir & Peled, 2002). The protesters' demands were often justified in relation to the contribution of the middle class to society, in terms of both military service and its contribution to the economy. In this way, protest leaders sought to constitute a collective socio-political identity which represented the middle class as a 'universal class', expressing and advancing the common good. The centrality of this motif was clearly manifested in the results of the 2013 elections, particularly in the remarkable success of the newly established party 'There is a future' (*Yesh Atid*), which won 19 seats in the Parliament (out of 120) and became the second largest party after the Likud. Established and led by Yair Lapid, a TV celebrity-turned-politician, the party capitalised on the protests and built its electoral campaign on the grievances and claims of the secular middle-class. It presented itself as the true and only representative of this 'universal class' – defined as those who contribute to the country by working, paying taxes and serving in the military but are neglected by the state, as opposed to those who gain resources without contributing, especially the Ultra-Orthodox population.

In more general terms, the call for social justice can be interpreted as an attempt by the middle class, including the parental generation, to reposition itself at the center of the political and social fields as the backbone of society. During the 1990s, the middle class in Israel had attempted to construct itself as a universal class that promoted the common good through the peace project. However, after the collapse of the Oslo process and in a political context in which a discourse based on peace-making was no longer accepted as representing the common good, but rather the opposite, the middle class turned instead to distributive issues and social justice, not only in order to improve its life chances but also in order to regain recognition and socio-political dominance. This aspiration was reinforced by the persistent political dominance of a coalition of the nationalist right wing and ultra-orthodox parties. Members of the secular middle class felt that they had been pushed to the margins by these dominant forces, which were orchestrating a full-frontal assault on the values and practices of liberal democracy. In response, the protest movement was also a way to rebuild the collective identity of the secular and 'left wing' middle class. Mass demonstrations were an opportunity for this group to take to the streets and celebrate solidarity, after a long absence from the public sphere as a collective. The protest thus not only embodied a politics of distribution, which formed its overt outer layer, but also an implicit inner layer driven by a politics of status and recognition managed by a social sector that sought to reclaim its dominance through a revised collective identity.

What emerges, therefore, is an interesting reversal in the relationship between material interests and socio-cultural identities. Israeli politics has long blurred material interests and class categories as bases for political action, and demands on the state have been couched in terms of the recognition of distinct social-cultural identities and amelioration of status inequalities. The protest of 2011 rearticulated the relations between these two dimensions. Its demands were explicitly formulated in distributive terms as opposition to economic inequality and to the state's withdrawal from responsibility for the welfare of its citizens. The protestors and their supporters portrayed their action as a new politics that would replace the old, Balkanized struggles between culturally defined 'sectors'. However, while the protest was undoubtedly innovative in comparison to traditional Israeli politics, this does not imply that the politics of status simply vanished; rather, it changed its location. The group which had insistently disowned the strategy of political mobilisation on the basis of an explicit 'sectoral' identity, implicitly did precisely that in the backstage of the protests.

Conclusions

Israel's 'social justice' movement was even more encompassing than the mass protests that preceded it in Spain, Portugal, and Greece. Yet it was an improbable candidate for such inclusivity, given that the Israeli movement had to contend with deeply institutionalised socio-political cleavages and lacked the unifying and motivating stimulus of radical state-imposed austerity. We have argued that the material foundation of the Israeli protest was embedded in a generational shift in the life chances of the middle class, shaped by Israel's transition to a neoliberal political-economic regime.

The institutionalisation of the neoliberal model in Israel in the early 2000s undermined the promise of inter-generational reproduction of middle class life chances for significant numbers of the younger generation of that class. However, alongside this class-generational dynamic, the protest was also closely linked to pre-existing social and cultural identities and the conflicts between them. In this sense, the subtext of the protest can be interpreted as a bid by the secular and 'left wing' middle class to reclaim its social dominance by reinventing itself as a universal class under the flag of inclusiveness and social justice. The tension between the material and cultural interests of the protest's instigators and their attempt to build an inclusive identity that would rise above societal cleavages and conflicts percolated through many aspects of the protest. In this regard, it remained deeply embedded in the distinguishing features of the Israeli political field for the last 40 years.

We opened this article by referring to other protest movements that emerged in advanced capitalist countries following the deep economic crisis that started in 2008, but with only cursory reference to the causal role of this protest wave for the Israeli case. Occupy-type protests in western countries and preceding popular uprisings in some Arab states certainly played a part in the Israeli protest, despite sharp differences in political and economic circumstances. Similar to other global phenomena, there were processes of diffusion through which ideas and practices crossed national boundaries. The global wave of protests in 2010 and 2011 expanded the structure of political opportunities for the protest in Israel by providing models for imitation and ideational frameworks for identification and legitimation.

That said, this article aims to contribute in a different way to our understanding of the 'networks of outrage and hope' (Castells, 2012) which emerged in Israel and other advanced capitalist societies, by focusing on domestic conditions. We believe that the class and generational analysis presented here for the Israeli case may be relevant to other recent protest movements as well, despite clear differences in specific circumstances (Mason, 2012). For the first time since World War II in Europe and North America, and since 1948 in Israel, it is far from clear that young adults from middle class backgrounds will enjoy a higher standard of living than their parents, or even succeed in maintaining the conditions that they grew up with. For many young adults, capitalism's basic promise to the middle class regarding the uninterrupted inter-generational reproduction of life chances and improvement in living standards has been broken. The global financial crisis has accentuated this turnaround in the hardest-hit countries, but it has not been solely responsible for it. Like the crisis itself, the threat facing young would-be managers, professionals, and entrepreneurs anticipating advantageous positions in labor and consumer markets fundamentally results from the uneven and contradictory effects of the neoliberal model of economic growth and the diminished role that it assigns to the state as an employer, regulator, and provider of social protection. The consequent economic threat to young people, which is new and unexpected for those who entered adulthood with middle-class advantages, explains the emergence of protest movements which on the one hand resemble the 'new' social movements of old, but on the other raise demands for redistribution and seek to construct identities based on quasi-class membership and economic inequality.

The most important outcome of this wave of contention – an outcome which the Israeli case shares with others – is the repoliticisation of economic issues in general, and socio-economic policy in particular. One of the most notable successes of the neoliberal project in recent decades was its depoliticisation of the economic sphere (Hay, 2007; Maman & Rosenhek, 2011). According to the ideology that rationalised this development, distributive processes should be determined by market forces and economic policy should be made primarily by experts. Very little political space was left between 'apolitical' market forces and 'apolitical' experts. The protests in advanced capitalist societies, including Israel, have sought to reopen this space. They succeeded for a time in bringing politics back into the economy, and the economy back into politics – but it is still too early to say whether this shift will contribute to significant changes in the political economy, or else will turn out to have been only a passing episode.

Notes

1. See activism.org.il, especially a post on 7 July 2011 under the pseudonym 'Amnon Hagibor'. The official protest website is j14.org.il.
2. Employment and Labour Markets: Key Tables from OECD (http://www.oecd-ilibrary.org/employment/employment-and-labour-markets-key-tables-from-oecd_20752342).
3. In both Figure 1 and Table 2 income has been adjusted for household size using the OECD equivalence scale.
4. Among married couples with children – our unit of analysis – the CBS normally defines the household head as the spouse with higher earnings.

References

Alimi, E. Y. (2012). 'Occupy Israel': A tale of startling success and hopeful failure. *Social Movement Studies*, *11*(3–4), 402–407.
Arian, A., & Shamir, M. (2005). On mistaking a dominant party in a dealigning system. In A. Arian & M. Shamir (Eds.), *The elections in Israel, 2003* (pp. 13–31). New Brunswick: Transaction Publishers.

Bennett, W. L., & Segerberg, A. (2012). The logic of connective action. *Information, Communication & Society, 15*, 739–768.

Bernstein, D. (1984). Conflict and protest in Israeli society: The case of the Black Panthers of Israel. *Youth and Society, 16*, 129–152.

Bourdieu, P. (1984). *Distinction: A social critique of the judgement of taste.* Cambridge MA: Harvard University Press.

Castells, M. (2012). *Networks of outrage and hope: Social movements in the internet age.* Cambridge, UK: Polity.

Clark, T. N., & Lipset, S. M. (2001). *The breakdown of class politics: A debate on post-industrial stratification.* Baltimore: Johns Hopkins University Press.

Dahan, M. (2013). Did the melting pot succeed in the economic field? Working paper, Federman School of Public Policy, The Hebrew University of Jerusalem (in Hebrew).

Evans, G. (Ed.). (1999). *The end of class politics? Class voting in comparative context.* Oxford: Oxford University Press.

Filc, D. (2006). *Populism and hegemony in Israel.* Tel-Aviv: Resling Publishing (in Hebrew).

Filc, D. (2012). Neo-Liberalism, sovereignty, and the crisis of representation in Israel. In T. Hermann (Ed.), *By the people, for the people, without the people? The emergence of (Anti)political sentiment in western democracies and in Israel* (pp. 226–246). Jerusalem: The Israel Democracy Institute.

Grinberg, L. L. (2013). The J14 resistance mo(ve)ment: The Israeli mix of Tahrir and Puerta Del Sol. *Current Sociology, 61*, 491–509.

Haidar, A. (2013). '*The emergence of an Arab middle-class in Israel*', *Opening plenary on Social Classes in Israel.* Paper presented at the 44th Annual Meeting of the Israeli Sociological Society, Ruppin Academic Center.

Hay, C. (2007). *Why we hate politics.* Cambridge: Polity Press.

Hermann, T. (2009). *The Israeli peace movement: A shattered dream.* Cambridge: Cambridge University Press.

Hermann, T. (2011). *The Israeli democracy index, 2011.* Jerusalem: The Israel Democracy Institute (in Hebrew).

Hermann, T. (2012a). Introduction. In T. Hermann (Ed.), *By the people, for the people, without the people? The emergence of (Anti)political sentiment in western democracies and in Israel* (pp. 9–39). Jerusalem: The Israel Democracy Institute.

Hermann, T. (2012b). *The Israeli democracy index, 2012.* Jerusalem: The Israel Democracy Institute (in Hebrew).

Inglehart, R. (1990). *Culture shift in advanced industrial society.* Princeton: Princeton University Press.

Katriel, T., & Livio, O. (2012). *The poetics of language and space in the Israeli 2011 protest.* Paper presented at the Annual Conference of the Association of Social Anthropologists of the UK and the Commonwealth, Jawaharlal Nehru University, New Delhi, India.

Kitschelt, H. (1994). *The transformation of European social democracy.* Cambridge: Cambridge University Press.

Kriesi, H., Koopmans, R., Duyvendak, J. W., & Giugni, M. G. (1995). *New social movements in Western Europe: A comparative analysis.* Minneapolis: University of Minnesota Press.

Kristal, T. (2013). Slicing the pie: State policy, class organization, class integration, and Labor's share of Israeli national income. *Social Problems, 60*, 100–127.

Larana, E., Johnston, H., & Gusfield, J. R. (1994). *New social movements: From ideology to identity.* Philadelphia: Temple University Press.

Lehman-Wilzig, S. N. (1990). *Stiff-necked people, bottle-necked system: The evolution and roots of Israeli public protest, 1949–1986.* Bloomington: Indiana University Press.

Lewin-Epstein, N., & Semyonov, M. (2000). Migration, ethnicity, and inequality: Homeownership in Israel. *Social Problems, 47*, 425–444.

Maman, D., & Rosenhek, Z. (2011). *The Israeli central bank: Political economy, global logics and local actors.* London: Routledge.

Maman, D., & Rosenhek, Z. (2012). The institutional dynamics of a developmental state: Change and continuity in state-economy relations in Israel. *Studies in Comparative International Development, 47*, 342–363.

Mannheim, K. (1952). The problem of generations. In K. Mannheim (Ed.), *Essays on the sociology of knowledge* (pp. 276–322). London: Routledge and Kegan Paul.

Mason, P. (2012). *Why it's kicking off everywhere: The new global revolutions.* London: Verso.

Monterescu, D., & Shaindlinger, N. (2013). Situational radicalism: The Israeli 'Arab Spring' and the (un) making of the rebel city. *Constellations, 22*(2), 1–24.

Pabst, A. (2011). The resurgence of the civic. *Possible futures*. Retrieved from http://www.possible-futures. org/2011/11/29/the-resurgence-of-the-civic/

Pakulski, J., & Waters, M. (1996). *The death of class*. London: Sage.

Paz-Fuchs, A. (2009). Objectionable work in Israel. *Comparative Labor Law and Policy Journal, 31*, 471–486.

Peled, Y. (1998). Towards a redefinition of Jewish nationalism in Israel? The enigma of Shas. *Ethnic and Racial Studies, 21*, 703–727.

Piven, F., & Cloward, R. (1977). *Poor people's movements: Why they succeed, how they fail*. New York: Pantheon.

Rosenfeld, H., & Carmi, S. (1976). The privatization of public means, the state-made middle class, and the realization of family value in Israel. In J. Peristiany (Ed.), *Kinship and modernization in Meditarranean society* (pp. 131–159). Rome: Center for Mediterranean Studies.

Rosenhek, Z. (2007). Inclusionary and exclusionary dynamics in the Israeli welfare state: State building and political economy. In H. Herzog, T. Kochavi & S. Selniker (Eds.), *Generations, locations, identities: Contemporary perspectives on society and culture in Israel* (pp. 317–349). Jerusalem: The Van-Leer Jerusalem Institute and Hakibbutz Hameuchad Publishing House (in Hebrew).

Runciman, W. G. (1966). *Relative deprivation and social justice: A study of attitudes to social inequality in twentieth-century England*. Berkeley CA: University of California Press.

Shafir, G., & Peled, Y. (2002). *Being Israeli – The dynamics of multiple citizenship*. Cambridge: Cambridge University Press.

Shalev, M. (2007). The welfare state consensus in Israel: Placing class politics in context. In S. Mau & B. Veghte (Eds.), *Social justice, legitimacy and the welfare state* (pp. 193–213). Aldershot: Ashgate.

Shalev, M. (2012). The economic background of the social protest of summer 2011. In D. Ben-David (Ed.), *State of the nation report: Society, economy and policy in Israel 2011–2012* (pp. 161–220). Jerusalem: Taub Center for Social Policy Studies in Israel.

Shalev, M., & Levy, G. (2005). The winners and losers of 2003: Ideology, social structure and political change. In A. Arian & M. Shamir (Eds.), *The elections in Israel - 2003* (pp. 212–232). Brunswick, NJ: Transaction Books.

Standing, G. (2011). *The Precariat – The new dangerous class*. London: Bloomsbury Academic.

Steinmetz, G. (1994). Regulation theory, post-Marxism, and the new social movements. *Comparative Studies in Society and History, 36*, 176–212.

Swirski, S., & Konor-Attias, E. (2007). Workers, employers and the distribution of Israel's national income – Labor report: 2006. Tel-Aviv: Adva.

Swirski, S., Konor-Attias, E., & Abu-Khala, H. (2010). *Workers, Employers and the distribution of Israel's national income – Labor report: 2009*. Tel-Aviv: Adva Center (in Hebrew).

Tejerina, B., & Perugorria, I. (Eds.). (2012). *From social to political: New forms of mobilization and demo-cratization, conference proceedings*. Bilbao: Universidad del Pais Vasco.

Whittier, N. (1997). Political generations, micro-cohorts, and the transformation of social movements. *American Sociological Review, 62*, 760–778.

Wolbring, T., Keuschnigg, M., & Negele, E. (2013). Needs, comparisons, and adaptation: The importance of relative income for life satisfaction. *European Sociological Review, 29*, 86–104.

Yishai, Y. (2012). Escape from politics: The case of Israel. In T. Hermann (Ed.), *By the people, for the people, without the people? The emergence of (Anti)political sentiment in western democracies and in Israel* (pp. 288–313). Jerusalem: The Israel Democracy Institute.

Hashtags, ruling relations and the everyday: institutional ethnography insights on social movements

Bram Meuleman and Corra Boushel

School of Social and Political Science, University of Edinburgh, Edinburgh, UK

The role of social media (e.g. Facebook, YouTube, Twitter) in social movements has become the subject of academic and media discussion. This attention can be framed as debates over whether social media use encourages political participation, and whether the use of social media can be considered as a form of political activism. We suggest that analysis of social media in social movements can benefit from drawing on the work of Dorothy E. Smith. In this article we explain how paying attention to these media using an Institutional Ethnography perspective allows for insights on the activities of social movements and recognition of the use of social media without sliding into technological determinism. Following D. E. Smith, we argue that understanding contemporary social movements and their organisations in terms of the lived everyday/everynight experiences and interactions of historically situated people, texts and technologies provides a fruitful line of inquiry for further empirical research. We demonstrate the possibilities of such an approach by presenting examples from the Occupy Movement and the use of Twitter during political protests in Egypt (2011) and Iran (2009–2010). Taking this perspective allows us to identify and challenge the implicit boundaries drawn around what it means to be acting 'politically' in academic and media debates over social movements and social media.

New forms of social media have been incorporated into an increasing number of political actions over recent years, yet the role, influence and importance of these technologies are contested. On 17 September 2011, a group of protesters set up the Occupy Wall Street camp in the New York City financial district. Within four weeks, Occupy protests had spread to hundreds of cities in 82 countries, and within a year, the Occupy Wall Street website had over 130,000 Facebook 'likes' and had been the subject of over 35,000 tweets (www.occupywallst.org). But do social media statistics merit a mention in this description of political action? Are they statistics that describe and measure a social movement, or a (t)wittering distraction from the 'real' activity of politics?

Drawing on the work Dorothy E. Smith, we situate social media within the complex, intertwined social interactions and lived experiences of those involved in social movements. This article first defines the concepts of social movements and social media, and presents the principles behind Dorothy E. Smith's work. We then identify the three key features of current debates relating social movements and social media: whether the use of social media counts as political participation; the implicit hierarchy of offline and online political activism; and the relationships between privilege, social media use and political activity.

By adopting an Institutional Ethnography perspective, we are able to make explicit and critique some of the assumptions (in D. E. Smith's terms, the 'ruling relations') embedded in the framing of these discussions over what it means to be or do a social movement, or to act politically. Through our analysis, we demonstrate how debates about social media and social movements can perpetuate certain ideas of what it means to act politically, and how, in the process, they preclude some people from having the capacity to do so. It is not our aim to develop an alternative conceptualisation of political activity, but rather to highlight the relevance of everyday experiences to determining what does and what does not count as politics.

We demonstrate how an Institutional Ethnography approach can challenge the boundaries of existing academic debates by using illustrative examples drawn from the Occupy Movement and the use of Twitter during political protests in Egypt (2011) and Iran (2009–2010), and with data collected in the texts of other observers and participants. Furthermore, we draw from our experience as activists, observers and, simultaneously and perpetually, sociologists within social movements. Importantly, by examining how and where social media are present in the localised daily practice and formulation of contemporary social movements, we show how social media form a part of, rather than be a tool or a driver for, social movements.

Defining social movements and social media

Though definitions of social movements are almost as numerous as the number of people writing about them, one commonly accepted conceptualisation defines social movements as a broad network of (in)formal interactions, including both organisations and individuals/groups with no organisational affiliation that engage in collective action independently, but not separately from the realm of governmental institutions, and which is motivated by a shared concern about a particular set of political issues (cf. Rootes, 1999, 2007; Diani, 2000). Social movement organisations are very diverse, with organisational structures ranging from the highly organised, formalised and institutionalised to the radically informal, operating from the local to the global, and advancing causes that could be framed as single issues or more complex multifaceted problems like social justice or climate change.

In line with the Institutional Ethnography approach, social movements, and the debate over their definitions, fit into Dorothy E. Smith's observation of organisations more generally: 'We talk of these entities as objects or beings without finding their existence problematic, but as soon as we approach them, they dissolve into the air' (2001, p. 163). She contended this to be the case even when the organisations in question were highly formalised. Her research agenda focused on 'how what is thus named [as an organisation] comes into being out of the localed ephemeral of people's everyday doings' (2001, p. 160).

An Institutional Ethnography approach has been applied to social movements through ethnographies of political activists (e.g. G.W. Smith, 1990), which aimed to investigate social movements and their wider social contexts. However, to our knowledge, no work has yet used Smith's theoretical perspective in order to explain the role of social media in social movements.

In this article, while considering the broader role of the Internet in social movements, we focus on the specific subset of social media. Indeed, the use of social media in social movements is a recent phenomenon and has received less academic attention. Social media refers to 'online information generated by "users" (which could be companies or NGOs, but also includes individuals without a commercial aim) for the purposes of sharing, either publicly or with limitations on their audience, some self-presentation or disclosure' (Kaplan & Haenlein, 2010, pp. 60–62). Social media includes social network sites such as Facebook, 'content communities' such as YouTube or Flickr where the content is uploaded by users, as well as self-presentation texts such as blogs or Twitter.[1]

These social media activities fit with how Dorothy E. Smith defined texts in relation to understanding organisations. In her definition, texts include 'material in a form that enables replication (paper/print, film, electronic and so on) of what is written, drawn, or otherwise reproduced' (2005, p. 228). This broader meaning of text is adopted in this article, rather than social media specific meaning of 'text' as SMS message. Thus social media can be understood as similar to other reproducible texts that social movements, or more precisely, people, create and share.

An Institutional Ethnography perspective

Following G. W. Smith's (1990) approach, we conceptualise the texts of social media as a 'happening', namely a situated act incorporating on- and offline spaces, people, organisations and meanings. Two aspects of D. E. Smith's (1978, 1997, 2001, 2005) work are particularly relevant in the study of social movements and social media. First, Smith emphasises the particular, lived experiences that might be obfuscated in the process of nominalising certain verbs (2001). That is, when the activities of individuals communicating, organising and informing become abstracted into 'communication', 'organisation' and 'information', the intricate detail of exactly who is doing what, where, when, how and even why can more easily be overlooked. Smith considers these nominalisations as 'grammatical forms that repress the presence of people as agents' (1999, p. 39). Refocusing attention back onto human agency can lead to useful insights and understandings on the daily performance and practice of social movements, as seen in ethnographic work more broadly.

What is more specific to Smith's work is to prioritise looking at 'how abstractions are put together' (1992, p. 90) by drawing attention to the role of texts. She highlighted how texts 'enter into people's local practices' (2001, p. 160) as material objects and simultaneously can exist to codify, co-ordinate and order actions across times and spaces. Texts can prescribe roles that individuals then choose to act out, or offer interpretations of activities that observers, or participants, then select to make relevant or irrelevant to a particular situation.

Most significantly, D. E. Smith (2001) connects this effort of taking into account texts and people within their daily experience to an attempt at understanding what she terms the 'ruling relations'. She identifies the mapping of the local and particular actions of people into wider abstractions of social organisation as a method for understanding how the daily activities of others (and ourselves) fit together, are co-opted or excluded from the construction of capitalist modes of development, Weberian bureaucracy and relationships of power (1997, p. 38).

Her approach calls for attention to the everyday/night activities or statements that become deemed as useful, what gets transformed into objective 'facts' or abstracted concepts, and where and by whom this transformation takes place. The goal of such work is to make space for explicit reflection on how 'social organisation preserves conceptions and means of description which represent the world as it is for those who rule it, rather than as it is for those who are ruled' (1974, p. 267). We view this as a fruitful approach to analysing the use of social media in social movements, as well as how social media and social movements have been described in academic and media reports.

Debates over social media and social movements

Anduiza, Cantijoch, and Gallego (2009) identify three key academic debates related to the impact of Internet use on political participation that are present in discussions of social media use in social movements. The first concerns whether or not certain activities can or should be properly called 'politics' or political activity. The second involves a search for a causal relationship, to identify and measure the extent to which social media fosters levels of (other forms of) political participation. The third debate addresses whether social media broadens participation in formal politics. These questions are related and often conflated, but not necessarily mutually reinforcing. That is, modern technologies could be considered from inside or outside the frame of politics while still be seen to affect political participation.

Social media as politics

Though it is an intuitively appealing proposition that the emergence of a new medium would allow for novel forms and evolutions of political participation, there is no consensus on whether we can qualify the kinds of activity that social media enable as 'political', or relevant to social movements. Kahn and Kellner see the Internet as "creating the base and the basis for an unparalleled worldwide anti-war/pro-peace and social justice movement during a time of terrorism, war, and intense political struggle" (2004, p. 88). This argument identifies the activities of bloggers, tweeters, Facebook, etc. as political activities, and social media as relevant spaces of political action.

Social media supposedly facilitates community formation and lays the foundation for an online politics of alliance that can overcome the limitations of postmodern identity politics (Burbach, 2001; Dyer-Witherford, 1999). In their most 'cyber-utopian' form, these arguments tend to smudge the line between suggesting that the Internet (and social media in particular) can and does participate in political activities, and assuming that technology has the power to drive political action. This is easily identifiable in discourses of the various 'Twitter/Facebook/ 2.0 revolutions' of the Iranian 2009 protests and 2011 Arab Spring (Sullivan, 2009, June 13). Castells enthuses that the Internet is now 'a necessary though not sufficient component' of social movements all over the world (Castells, 2012, p. 229). This type of argument moves into territories of technological determinism, suggesting that modern social movements would/could not occur without these technologies.

However, not everyone sees the contribution of social media as important, or validly 'political'. Evgeny Morozov (2011a, 2011b) identifies social movements and their success as based on elite, expert coordination of activities, and sees their online counterparts as particularly shallow, ineffective forms of activism, which he refers to as 'slacktivism' (Morozov, 2009). His argument goes as far as to negate the political nature of activities such as joining Facebook groups or tweeting, when users are judged to be poorly informed or unwilling to participate in a campaign in other ways. In an exchange with Shirky, Gladwell argues: 'Just because innovations in communications technology happen does not mean that they matter' (Gladwell and Shirky, 2011, p. 153). Gladwell challenges the idea that use of social media counts as political statements because they do not require a 'real sacrifice' (2010, p. 47) on the part of the individuals concerned. In these 'cyber-cynic' discussions, it is worth pointing out the lack of scrutiny of the assumption that 'doing politics' should be defined as something difficult or dangerous, as well as the assumption that it is cost-free to undertake certain social media activities. Both of these assumptions will be considered further below.

Some of these cyber-cynic/utopian arguments are also more selectively applied when authors criticise the use of one medium, while embracing another. Lynch (2009, April 22), for example, distinguishes between different media forms, invalidating the relevance of some social media activities to politics, but endorsing others. For Lynch, blogging counts as a valid political activity and 'the torture of an unknown blogger should count as much as the harassment of Ayman Nour',[2] while arguing that joining online groups via Facebook is so easy as to be practically non-political:

> I have a hard time thinking of a communications technology more poorly suited for organizing high-risk political collective action than Facebook. Joining a [Facebook] group is perhaps the lowest-cost political activity imaginable, involving none of the commitment and dedication necessary to go out to a protest. (Lynch, 2009, April 22)

This differentiation is an interesting feature in discussions that are often framed in general, undefined terms and which refer to 'the Internet' or 'social media' in general. However, Lynch's argument indicates a conflation of what is considered as *effective* in political activity with what should be considered as *political*. A lack of capacity to influence or overturn formal political structures at the ease of a click (compared with what is assumed to be a time-consuming, potentially dangerous though plausibly effective physical confrontation) slides into a qualification of social media activities as non-political, and thus of minor or no importance in contemplating social movements.

Offline vs. online: political participation

A second strand of debate, conceptually separable but often intertwined with the arguments above, addresses whether social media use has an effect on other forms of 'traditional' political activity, most typically on physically manifested protests. To emphasise, these discussions do not require agreement on whether social media use should viewed as political per se. The debate appears most straightforwardly as an empirical question: did sending/receiving/viewing 'texts' through these media impact on the propensity of individuals to undertake other activities?

Determining the lines of causality for human behaviours is a complex business, but some have felt able to make generalisations. Castells states that in Tunisia, Iceland and Egypt 'the movement[s] went from cyberspace to urban space' (2012, p. 45) and 'the original spaces of resistance were formed on the Internet' (ibid., 56). Morozov strongly criticises the 'cyber-utopian' view that 'digital tools of social networking such as Facebook and Twitter can summon up social revolutions out of the ether' (2011a, March 7). Rather than comment directly on the (still sparse) statistical evidence (Wilson & Dunn, 2011; Occupy General Survey from Fuchs, 2012) we would like to point out features of the framing present in these discussions and their focus on social movements.

Though the contrast between the positions of Castells and Morozov could hardly be starker, their comments share an implicit hierarchy of forms of political participation. For both, social media communications are a poorer cousin to interactions in physical spaces, and thus social media are made interesting (or not) by their impact on those other forms. Such a narrowing of the discussion may sometimes be necessary for operationalising practicable research agendas, but the assumptions embedded in these views about what counts as activism, and what is more important – to the researchers, and passed on to their readership – about activism and social movements are debatable. If it is more interesting to know about whether tweeting leads to physical protesting than presence at protests leads to tweeting (or to use of other social media), this hierarchy should be scrutinised.

Not all of the research in this area assumes the existence of such a hierarchy between offline and online actions. Earl (2013) argues against the implicit notion of a 'ladder' of engagement, examining the impact of online activities independent from as well as embedded in wider offline campaigns or organisations (cf. Earl & Kimport, 2011). Such an approach suggests that social media use might not only increase participation in physical protests, but potentially shift 'the underlying processes driving and organising activism' (Earl, McKee Hurwitz, Mejia Mesinas, Tolan, & Arlotti, 2013, p. 472), for example by sharing information via Twitter on the activities of the police during protests, allowing strategies to be better countered and critiqued as part of a social movement, and in the future altering the ways in which police interact with protesters.

Social media as a political equaliser

The third strand of debate revolves around whether advances in technology are providing the structural elements necessary for the creation of more informed communities (Rheingold, 2002), who, in turn, should be more prone to engage in participation in social movements. This argument draws heavily from one of the most influential social movement theory traditions, resource mobilisation theory, which emphasises the availability of resources and the ability to face the costs of participation as the key determining factors in the decision of whether or not to take part in political activity (Edwards & McCarthy, 2007; Jenkins, 1983; Krueger, 2002; McCarthy & Zald, 1977; Verba, Schlozman, & Brady, 1995). As Ester and Vinken propose:

> The more important questions about the Internet are not about what it can do for real life or about how real life can best be mimicked with it, but about what it is as a constitutive force for the identity of people who engage in it, for the way people will experience the world and for the cultural forms that will arise from this. (Ester & Vinken, 2003, pp. 669–670)

First, we note how this discourse can belie the everyday use of social media. In contrast to the perception that 'everyone' is now online, in 2012, 15% of adults in the UK had never used the Internet (ONS, 2012). As noted by one individual involved in tweeting during the Egyptian Revolution, '[only] a certain class of activists are armed with smartphones' (quoted in Watkins, 2011). The relatively wealthy, Western and technologically savvy standpoint of many commentators both for and against the idea that social media enhance social movements is frequently obvious in statements about how 'easy' it is to join a Facebook group, or the possibility of Twitter starting a revolution, as others have noticed (e.g. Fuchs, 2012). In stating what we hope would be the obvious: gender, age, location, class, education and other 'usual' barriers to access can also apply to social media.

At the same time, we are wary of jumping to the conclusion that social media use (inside and outside social movements) is automatically a direct reflection of other social cleavages. As Qiu (2009) points out, there is not necessarily such a clear-cut binary of social media haves/have nots. He identified technological 'have-lesses' – people with limited or no access to electronic equipment – and complex, differentiated uses of social media in China. Within this argument, the discussion on who uses social media, and for what, is related to the debate above about what gets to be considered as a political activity.

Joining groups, commenting on online discussions, or signing petitions may or may not be considered as valid political participation depending on the standpoint of the theorist. Including or excluding these activities into a definition of politics, and social movements, can mean that we ignore or highlight the different daily experiences of social media users from the standpoint of an academic consideration of the relationship between social media and social movements. Taking a detailed, ethnographic approach to examining the spread, use and impact of social media within social movements may provide data to draw more reliable conclusions on the impact of social media use within social movements, as well as reflect upon the 'ruling relations' that are embedded in the definitions at play.

Texts as empirical vignettes

In the previous section we have briefly illustrated the three main debates surrounding social media use in social movements, drawing particular attention to the framing of debates and the definitions in use. In this section we present empirical data to illustrate how an Institutional Ethnography perspective could allow for a more thorough and nuanced understanding of the relations between social movements and social media use. Two cases will be explored: the Occupy Movement, in particular a photo submitted by a user on the Occupy related Tumblr blog 'We Are the 99%', and two quotes demonstrating the public perception of tweets generated during the Egyptian and Iranian Revolutions. These examples demonstrate how people's activities in local settings are organised across time and space into social relations by means of texts, although they have been left intentionally brief to allow for a more thorough theoretical discussion of the work of Smith and the current content of academic and media debates on social movements and social media.

Texts of the Occupy Movement

One important aspect of the social media output within social movements is the vast quantity of texts produced. While this can be overwhelming for analysis, we argue that this can be an example of Smith's conviction that texts are not (only) sources of information, but that they are coordinating devices, 'interpretable as expressions or instances of a higher order organisation, independent of particular people' (D. E. Smith, 2001, p. 180). The cacophony of texts, meanings, needs and desires that have formed the Occupy Movement are constitutive of its challenge to what is seen as hierarchical, minority control ('the 1%', financial markets, government). The texts of Occupy were written or recorded as activities that were interconnected (through common themes and debates, as well as technologies of tags, hashtags, links and pingbacks) as part of the lived experience of this social movement. It is the organisation as it is 'actually performed' and this social media output, we argue, has formed an important part of its performance.

In outputs from the Occupy Movement, effort is made to identify local happenings within and as part of trans-local relations, ordering and co-ordinating experiences to form a social movement. Consider the following example (Figure 1).

In this text, we see a person holding up a sign with details about her educational background, health status, age and education of her children, and some information regarding her financial situation. The social media forum on which this text was posted (wearethe99percent.tumblr.com) consists of a series of user-submitted photos adhering to the same implicit composition guidelines, in which the subject/participant/author holds up a usually hand-written sign[3] that tells some of their biographical detail and ends with the statement: 'I/We am/are the 99%'. Many choose to mention their debts, medical health and care, income, family situations, housing, education and employment history and aspirations. Some are not identifiable behind their pieces of paper or have been left outside of the framing of the photo, while others show their faces.

The decision to remain anonymous, as well as the depth of personal detail that some photos include, suggest that participation is far from 'slack' or emotionally easy for some. The majority of participants are American with their information written in English, but this is not inscribed in the rules of the blog. There is a link on the blog to a UK forum as well as a Spanish language version of the concept. Viewers are invited to submit their own photo. The archive of the blog displays the user-submitted photos displayed in a reverse chronological grid. Browsing through this archive invokes the concept of a photographic typology: the text composition implies that there exist other examples of what can be seen, and that comparing and juxtaposing these texts will reveal old and new meaning that are inherent in each individual text, and the collection of texts as a whole.

The administrator/editor/blogger(s) who run the blog do not identify themselves, but state their editorial control whilst refuting the idea that they are part of running any larger organisation: 'the only thing we are in charge of is this magic blog machine'. They directly (hyper)link the project to the Occupy Movement. The naming of the site is chosen to suggest that the individual stories presented in the user-generated photos have some unitary, meaningful connection: aggregating the uniqueness of each photo into a commonality of experience (of stress, hard work,

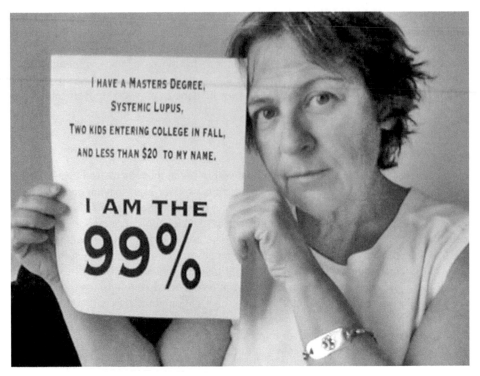

Figure 1. An example of a text in action as a coordinating device.

struggle, uncertainty, fear, bravery) that is shared amongst 'the 99%'. In this sense, the blog sim-ultaneously inscribes ways of mediating between people's experiences and the social movement of Occupy by encouraging the formulation and posting of user-produced texts, and at the same time it orders and coordinates user experiences as instances shaped by unfair social structures and relations of power. It shapes the 'personal' stories being displayed into a 'political' message.

Whether or not submitting content to the blog is tantamount to being part of the Occupy Movement – and acting 'politically' – is dependent on observers as well as the participant. The intertextual relations (D. E. Smith, 2001) between legal statute and the (re)production of social media have shifted in the last five years, with the US judicial system deeming social media as formative of social movements for the purposes of prosecution. Blog posts, comments and tweets are now called upon as evidence of organisational roles for social movement partici-pants: American courts have demanded data from the private Twitter accounts of some accused of illegal activities in the Occupy protests (Kravets, 2012). The meanings of reporting on, comment-ing or participating in the Occupy Movement can be mutually constitutive through such text–institution–person interactions.

Twitter and the production of texts

In the previous section, we have illustrated an example of how people's activities in local settings are organised across particular times and spaces into social relations by means of texts. Here we will briefly describe the ways in which texts inscribe roles by noting two contrasting descriptions of Twitter use in revolutions. Social media, and Twitter in particular, are increasingly becoming a forum on which some people edit, codify and categorise their everyday experiences, actions and thoughts (no matter how inane), including their participation in and formation of social movements. The entries in this real-time account, or tweets, are edited in the sense that the writer does not necessarily give a factual account of her doings, but rather produces a representation of these experiences and activities which is consequently codified and categorised through the use of 'hashtags' like *#Iranelection, #Egypt, #gr88, #jan25*, etc. These 'hashtags' function as markers that provide the reader with a digital context and a set of preliminary instructions for how to read a tweet. The politics of formulating, adopting and/or assigning particular roles for individuals and texts depends on what we can call a writer–text–reader interaction.

In their coverage of the Iranian elections, *The Economist* magazine derided the role of tweeters:

> Meanwhile the much-ballyhooed Twitter swiftly degraded into pointlessness. By deluging threads like #Iranelection with cries of support for the protesters, Americans and Britons rendered the site almost useless as a source of information—something that Iran's government had tried and failed to do. (*The Economist*, 2009, June 18)

Twitter users with a geographical location other than Iran that were tweeting about the Iranian Revolution are portrayed as being a hindrance to the efforts of those on the ground. Indeed, by using phrases like 'deluging' and 'cries of support' and suggesting that the tweets of Americans and Britons were actively aiding the regime, people tweeting from outside of Iran are not only described as not producing valid information, but even cast as obstructing the organisation of a more important (physically present) political activity. Furthermore, in this quote we can identify not only a hierarchy of Twitter users according to geography and perceived political relevance, but also to the aforementioned hierarchy of media in political participation. The phrase 'the much-ballyhooed Twitter' suggests a perceived inferiority of this social media forum to other, apparently less trivial and more valid forms of communication and political action.

In contrast, a second example ascribes a different set of roles to Twitter users and sheds a different light on the use of Twitter. Wilson and Dunn (2011) identify a network of users consisting of a small group of core nodes, or 'power users', located in Egypt during the revolution that were responsible for the creation of a large percentage of the tweets in their data set. They also describe a relatively small number of 'power users' in other countries, and a much larger group of relatively passive users, who contributed statements of support, shared related content, and retweeted content created by power users. In contrast to *The Economist*'s description of tweeting the Iranian Revolution, people tweeting about the Egyptian Revolution, regardless of geographical location, are described as forming a part of the expression and action of an international movement aimed at challenging the government in Egypt.

> [T]here is a clear indication that Twitter was used to actively and successfully engage an international audience in the Egyptian revolution. The dichotomous composition of the discourse is especially compelling, considering its geographic distribution and retweet frequencies. These characteristics suggest a model in which a small group of Twitter users in Egypt generated a significant amount of content that was consumed and mobilised by a small group of transnational actors, spawning discourse with very broad and largely passive participation (...), conveying the impression 'that the world was watching'. (Wilson & Dunn, 2011, pp. 1269–1270)

The creation and successful adoption of a particular role depends, as we have discussed, on some combination of the writer, text, technology and reader. The 'hashtags' used in a tweet are one set of 'authorisation rules [markers] which instruct the reader/hearer what criteria to use in determining the adequacy of the description and the credibility of the account' (D. E. Smith, 1978, p. 50). The extent to which the markers overlap with the intention of the message that the writer may want to send out, depends, in turn, on her knowledge and experience (i.e. an aware-ness of which hashtag is appropriate or insightful in a certain context) as well as her digital cunning, by which we mean her ability to make effective use of social media forums. A tweet containing relevant information, bearing the correct markers, and, at least in the eyes of some observers, originating from the correct geographical location is therefore more likely to be per-ceived as authoritative and relevant to a social movement.

Upon sending a tweet, however, it is the outcome of the text–reader interaction that determines how the text will be interpreted (D. E. Smith, 2005). Here we wish to highlight that it is not only the message itself, but also the roles of both the writer and the reader that are formed within the writer–text–reader interaction, due to the fact that each reader (e.g. fellow revolutionaries, Western media, academics, the US government) unpacks these edited, codified and categorised texts using their own knowledge, experience and digital cunning. The users, followers, hashtags and addressees that comprise the social media forum that is Twitter, create a social dynamic where tweets may be measured, taken as evidence, ignored or inspire as part of a social movement. As a result, the roles that tweets allow or oblige their author and reader to adopt are in constant flux.

Discussion

As these brief illustrations have shown, using an Institutional Ethnography approach allows for greater reflection on the 'doing' of social media use around social movements, and the ways in which everyday doings become interpreted, formulated and abstracted into and outside of defi-nitions of social movements. From this perspective, social movements are neither determined by, nor separate from, the use of social media. Where social media use forms part of the daily experience of people, we view it as a valid and interesting site of investigation in order to under-stand more about social movements and the 'ruling relations' which they may seek to overturn, or of which they may form a part.

In our example from the Occupy Movement, we argued that the text displayed is an instance of the social movement. The woman in the photograph has codified her everyday/night experience into text. By composing her text in accordance with the submission criteria of a particular social media forum – the texts show a picture of an ordinary person in an everyday setting holding up a sign with her personal story and the phrase 'I am the 99%' – she positions her activities within the context of a social movement. The social media forum orders and coordinates the everyday/night experiences of its users as happenings shaped by asymmetrical power relations and social struc-tures. Thus by formulating a text that adheres to and which becomes constitutive of the inscribed text composition guidelines of the 'We Are the 99%' blog, the woman in the text is allowed to adopt the role of the 99%. It is in this way that this individual text becomes *part of* the Occupy Movement.

What may be dismissed as easy, 'slack' activity by some may have been intensely fought, traumatic or risky decision within the daily activities of the persons involved. Retweeting or joining a Facebook group could be a straightforward act, or it could be a statement that a state authority could take and judge with significant (social, economic, political) repercussions for the person involved. In the midst of the protests surrounding the Iranian elections of 2009, in which president Ahmadinejad won a heavily contested victory, a senior member of the US State Department wrote an email to executives at Twitter urging them to postpone the scheduled daily maintenance of their website because the State Department believed the micro-blogging service was 'playing an important role at a crucial time in Iran' (Landler & Stelter, 2009, p. 12).

When the US government made a statement about the role of Twitter in the Iranian Revolu-tion, it not only described a situation, but also *enacted* it. Tweeting about the Green Revolution became an act that had received US approval, and one that was being defined as an anti-regime activity. Regardless of whether an academic consensus on the relative merits of social media use as a form of political participation has been reached, there is a contemporary reshaping of what is political by the tripartite of executive, legislative and judiciary powers. Ruling relations come to reinforce and delineate political access and participation by moving the boundaries of 'political' to exclude or include social media use.

The analysis of Twitter and text production brings to light the importance of the writer–text–reader interaction in creating and assigning roles. Our brief examination of two quotes on the use of social media in the Iranian and Egyptian Revolutions, respectively, exemplified how texts (or tweets) can be analysed as a site connecting people and organisations translocally and transtemporally. This writer–text–reader interaction allows texts to coordinate and inscribe roles, for example, a Briton whose tweets are interpreted as getting in the way of – or becoming part of – the Iranian/Egyptian Revolution. When this is put into the context of tweets and other social media output being used as evidence in court, it is clear that reader interpretations can have significant impacts for the writers of the texts.

Moreover, the way in which we discuss and analyse social media use in social movements reflects our framings of what it means to be political, and varies according to the more or less inclusive definitions of social movements and political activity adopted. Examining social media output as lived experiences of social movements allows us to identify the politics implicit in some of these debates. Hence, we refute an a priori analytical separation between (digital) utterances and (physical) presences. Defining, implying or simply ignoring digital activities as 'not really politics' is a powerful and political act in itself.

For instance, the Occupy Movement was criticised for its plethora of (often digital) output. The charge was that the movement could not be understood because of the sheer volume of this output combined with the lack of movement-wide acknowledged representatives and vision, and was therefore ineffective. This is in part based on a notion of politics that requires an organisation to produce unitary and consistent texts, directed towards influencing ruling institutions – in other words, that it is hierarchical and behaves like a modern, Western political party.

Some social movements are about engaging in direct action to affect change. But many are not, and even more are not *only* about that. Underpinning the hierarchy placed on social media activities, there are judgements about the purpose of social movements that may or may not chime with the purposes and hopes of participants themselves. Participating on a photo blog may or may not be effective in creating systemic change, but it may have been a successful *political* act in uniting individual circumstances into a frame that re-defines them as being affected by broader 'ruling relations'. An exclusive focus on macro-structural outcomes as a measure of efficacy for social movements can lead to overlooking beliefs and acts of self-emancipation or self-realisation as *political*.

Our point in this article, thus, is not to add our own definition of 'political' to the already sizeable list of definitions. Instead, following D. E. Smith (2001), we wish to draw attention to how lived everyday experiences are mediated by the textual output of social media, and highlight how writer–text–reader interactions map into wider social structures. The Institutional Ethnography approach seeks to highlight how and where the interpretation of the use of social media in social movements takes place within 'ruling relations', that is in ways that define power, that decide who has access to this power, and, subsequently, that determine what meanings are given to particular happenings.

Conclusion

In this article we suggest that adopting an Institutional Ethnography approach informed by the work of Smith can shed new light on the nuances of the use of social media in relation to social movements. The conceptualisation of the intertwining of social media and social move-ments proposed here fits comfortably with the view that social movements are a complex and sometimes 'messy' web of interactions (Diani, 2000). This description blurs the boundaries between social movement organisations and the everyday life of the individuals, technologies and texts whose doings become agglomerated under the banner of a 'social movement'.

Social media can be acknowledged within the activities of social movement activists, without necessarily insisting that these technologies are the drivers of action. Paying attention to social media and how we think about social media within social movements identifies the role of texts in mediating 'ruling relations', as they channel interpretations (in the example of the We are the 99% blog) and are open to multiple, contradictory interpretations (in the two cases of Twitter). We suggest that academic and popular discourse can approach the debates about whether or not social media played a significant role in the Iranian and Egyptian Revolution, or indeed, social movements more generally, by exploring the daily lives of the individuals and texts involved.

In this article we have identified a tendency in academic debates surrounding the relations between social media and social movements to conflate what is effective political activity with what can be considered as political activity. We have suggested that some imply the existence of hierarchy of forms of political participation that embed limiting assumptions about activism and social movements. Moreover, we have warned against assuming that social media use is a direct reflection of other social inequalities. Using an Institutional Ethnography approach allows us to identify and challenge the boundaries of the current debates, and avoid a conflation between what is being defined as 'political' with what might be viewed as politically effective in engaging with formalised, hierarchical political structures.

Dorothy E. Smith made clear that her approach was not to reduce 'organisations or institutions to the technologies of their architecture. Rather we are proposing that such "textual technologies" be recognised sociologically for how they co-ordinate people's work in particular settings' (2001, p. 173). We argue that the technology that enables the production of texts by historically situated people and the texts themselves are part of the enabling and sustaining of this network of everyday experiences we call a social movement. Exploring these daily activities moves us back from the *nouns* and into the *verbs* of being and doing social movements, and aids in associating everyday life with the situations of apparent power or powerlessness in which individuals may find themselves.

Notes

1. Kaplan and Haenlein's definition also includes virtual social worlds and games (e.g. Second Life, and World of Warcraft) although these have not, at least for now, played a role in large-scale social move-ment organisation and participation and will not be thus discussed here.
2. Ayman Nour was a candidate in the 2005 Egyptian Presidential election. He was the first person to stand against Husni Mubarak in elections, and was imprisoned soon afterwards on charges that were widely viewed to be politically motivated.
3. For the purposes of legibility, we have opted for a photo in which the subject is holding a computer printed sign.

References

Anduiza, E., Cantijoch, M., & Gallego, A. (2009). Political participation and the internet: A field essay. *Information, Communication & Society*, *12*(6), 860–878. doi:10.1080/13691180802282720

Burbach, R. (2001). *Globalisation and postmodern politics: From zapatistas to high-tech robber barons*. London: Pluto Press.

Castells, M. (2012). *Networks of outrage and hope: Social movements in the internet age*. Cambridge: Polity Press.

Diani, M. (2000). The concept of social movements. In K. Nash (Ed.), *Readings in contemporary political sociology* (pp. 155–176). Oxford: Blackwell.

Dyer-Witherford, N. (1999). *Cyber-Marx: Cycles and circuits of struggle in high-technology capitalism*. Chicago, IL: University of Illinois Press.

Earl, J. (2013). *The future of social movement organizations: The waning dominance of SMOs online*. Conference paper at COSM 2013, University of Arizona, April 2013.

Earl, J., & Kimport, K. (2011). *Digitally enabled social change*. Cambridge, MA: MIT Press.

Earl, J., McKee Hurwitz, H., Mejia Mesinas, A., Tolan, M., & Arlotti, A. (2013). This protest will be tweeted. *Information, Communication & Society*, *16*(4), 459–478. doi:10.1080/1369118X.2013.777756

Edwards, B., & McCarthy, J. D. (2007). Resources and social movement mobilisation. In D. Snow, S. Soule, & H. Kriesi (Eds.), *The Blackwell companion to social movements* (pp. 116–152). Oxford: Blackwell.

Ester, P., & Vinken, H. (2003). Debating civil society: On the fear for civic decline and hope for the internet alternative. *International Sociology*, *18*(4), 659–680. doi:10.1177/0268580903184002

Fuchs, C. (2012). Some reflections on Manuel Castells' book "networks of outrage and hope: Social movements in the internet age". *TripleC*, *10*(2), 775–797.

Gladwell, M. (2010). Small change: Why the revolution will not be tweeted. The New Yorker, 4 October 2010. Retrieved August 17, 2012, from http://www.newyorker.com/reporting/2010/10/04/101004fa_fact_gladwell

Gladwell, M., & Shirky, C. (2011). From innovation to revolution: Do social media make protests possible? *Foreign Affairs*, *90*(2), 153–154.

Jenkins, J. C. (1983). Resource mobilisation theory and the study of social movements. *Annual Review of Sociology*, *9*(1), 527–553. doi:10.1146/annurev.so.09.080183.002523

Kahn, R., & Kellner, D. (2004). New media and internet activism: From the 'battle of Seattle' to blogging. *New Media & Society*, *6*(1), 87–95. doi:10.1177/1461444804039908

Kaplan, A. M., & Haenlein, M. (2010). Users of the world, unite! The challenges and opportunities of social media. *Business Horizons*, *53*(1), 59–68. doi:10.1016/j.bushor.2009.09.003

Kravets, D. (2012, September 14). Twitter reluctantly coughs up Occupy protester's data. Wired.com. Retrieved October 3, 2012, from http://www.wired.com/threatlevel/2012/09/twitter-occupy-data/

Krueger, B. S. (2002). Assessing the potential of internet political participation in the United States: A resource approach. *American Politics Research*, *30*(5), 476–498. doi:10.1177/1532673X02030005002

Landler, M., & Stelter, B. (2009, June 17). Washington taps into a potent new force in diplomacy. *The New York Times*, p. A12. Retrieved September 9, 2012, from http://www.nytimes.com/2009/06/17/world/middleeast/17media.html

Lynch, M. (2009, April 22). Should we support internet activists in the Middle East? *Foreign Policy*. Retrieved August 17, 2012, from http://lynch.foreignpolicy.com/posts/2009/04/22/should_we_support_internet_activists_in_the_middle_east

McCarthy, J., & Zald, M. (1977). Resource mobilisation and social movements: A partial theory. *American Journal of Sociology*, *82*(6), 1212–1241.

Morozov, E. (2009, June 28). It feels like activism. *Newsweek Magazine*. Retrieved August 17, 2012, from http://www.thedailybeast.com/newsweek/2009/06/28/it-feels-like-activism.html

Morozov, E. (2011a, March 7). Facebook and Twitter are just places revolutionaries go. *The Guardian*. Retrieved August 17, 2012, from http://www.guardian.co.uk/commentisfree/2011/mar/07/facebook-twitter-revolutionaries-cyber-utopians

Morozov, E. (2011b). *The net delusion: The dark side of internet freedom*. New York: PublicAffairs.

ONS (2012). Statistical Bulletin: Internet Access Quarterly Update, 2012 Q2 (15 August 2012). Office for National Statistics. Retrieved February 6, 2013, from http://www.ons.gov.uk/ons/rel/rdit2/internet-access-quarterly-update/2012-q2/stb-internet-access-2012-q2.html

Qiu, J. L. (2009). *Working-class network society: Communication technology and the information have-less in urban China*. Cambridge, MA: MIT Press.

Rheingold, H. (2002). *Smart mobs: The next social revolution*. Cambridge, MA: Perseus Publishing.

Rootes, C. (1999). *Environmental movements: Local, national, and global*. London: Frank Cass.

Rootes, C. (2007). Environmental Movements. In D. Snow, S. Soule, & H. Kriesi (Eds.), *The Blackwell companion to social movements* (pp. 116–152). Oxford: Blackwell.

Smith, D. E. (1974). *The conceptual practices of power: A feminist sociology of knowledge*. Boston, MA: Northeastern University Press.

Smith, D. E. (1978). 'K is mentally ill.' The anatomy of a factual account. *Sociology, 12*(1), 23–53. doi:10.1177/003803857801200103

Smith, D. E. (1992). Sociology from Women's Perspective: A Reaffirmation. *Sociological Theory, 10*(1): 88–98.

Smith, D. E. (1997). Consciousness, meaning and ruling relations: From women's standpoint. In J. L. Abu-Lughod (Ed.), *Millennial milestone. The heritage and future of sociology in the North American region* (pp. 37–50). Toronto, Canada: International Sociological Association.

Smith, D. E. (1999). *Writing the social: Critique, theory, and investigations*. Toronto: University of Toronto Press.

Smith, D. E. (2001). Texts and the ontology of organisations and institutions. *Studies in Cultures. Organisations and Societies, 7*(2), 159–198.

Smith, D. E. (2005). *Institutional ethnography: A sociology for people*. Oxford: AltiMira Press.

Smith, G. W. (1990). Political activist as ethnographer. *Social Problems, 37*(4), 629–648. doi:10.2307/800586

Sullivan, A. (2009, June 13). The revolution will be twittered. *The Daily Dish*. Retrieved August 19, 2012, from http://andrewsullivan.theatlantic.com/the_daily_dish/2009/06/the-revolution-will-be-twittered-1.html

The Economist. (2009, June 18). Twitter 1, CNN 0: But the real winner was an unusual hybrid of old and new media. Retrieved August 14, 2012, from http://www.economist.com/node/13856224

Verba, S., Schlozman, K. L., & Brady, H. E. (1995). *Voice and equality: Civic voluntarism in American politics*. Cambridge, MA: Harvard University Press.

Watkins, S. C. (2011, February 18). Social movements in the age of social media: Participatory politics in Egypt. Theyoungandthedigital.com. Retrieved August 14, 2012, from http://theyoungandthedigital.com/2011/02/18/social-movements-in-the-age-of-social-media-participatory-politics-in-egypt/

Wilson, C., & Dunn, A. (2011). Digital media in the Egyptian revolution: Descriptive analysis from the Tahrir data sets. *International Journal of Communication, 5*, 1248–1272.

A matter of law and order: reporting the Salford riots in local news webpages

Sharon Coen[a] and Caroline Jones[b]

[a]Directorate of Psychology and Public Health, University of Salford, Allerton Building, Salford, UK;
[b]Directorate of Multiprofessional Practice Studies, University of Salford, Allerton Building, Salford, UK

On 9 August 2011, hundreds of citizens gathered in the streets of Salford, predominately in the precinct area. Violence escalated as commercial and domestic properties were set on fire and rioters engaged in widespread looting. Simultaneously, riots were taking place across the country in cities such as London, Birmingham, Bristol, Manchester and Liverpool and were covered extensively by national and local media. This paper focuses on local media coverage of the Salford riots in an attempt to shed light on the main interpretations which the local media offered to their readers. A (quantitative and qualitative) content analysis was conducted on news reported in four major local news websites during the period 9 August– 6 September 2011 ($N=100$) in order to identify the most common themes and frames presented by the media in reporting the Salford riots. Results show the overwhelming presence of a crime frame to the events: news outlets concentrated on policing and juridical aspects of the events with little room for political and larger social debates. The paper discusses differences between outlets and time frame, as well as the potential implications of imposing this type of framing on collective action.

Introduction

> You go and live in Syria, then or Iran or North Korea. How dare you compare oppressed people peacefully campaigning for democracy, with the criminal cowards infesting our streets. (Omni, Gtr. Manchester Comment Posted: 2011, August 10, at 22:08)

On 4 August 2011, Mark Duggan, a 29-year-old Tottenham resident, was shot dead by a police officer. Two days later, a peaceful protest arranged outside Tottenham police station to try and get information for Duggan's family turned violent; the violence spread and culminated in several days of rioting in London and across England. On 9 August, hundreds of citizens gathered in the streets of Salford, predominately in the precinct area around Salford Shopping City. Violence escalated as commercial and domestic properties were set on fire and people were engaged in widespread looting. Simultaneously, riots continued to take place in London and had begun in other cities such as Birmingham, Bristol, Manchester and Liverpool. These events were covered extensively by national and local media. In order to understand what sort of discourses and interpretative frames the media offer the public regarding these violent outbursts, an analysis of media coverage of such events is vital. Indeed, the extensive literature on media framing (Entman, 1993; Nelson, Clawson, & Oxley, 1997) suggests that the way that the media reports an issue can affect readers' perceptions, although the relationship between media framing and public's beliefs and attitudes need not be conceived as a simple unidirectional influence of the media, but as part of a complex set of relationships between members of the public, journalists, authorities and policy-makers (Schaufele, 1999).

While much academic work has focused on an analysis of national media coverage of the riots (as outlined in the following section), little is known about how local media outlets have presented the events to their public. This study aims to fill that gap by presenting the results of an analysis of Online Local Media Outlets' coverage of the riots in Salford.

National media coverage of the 2011 riots

Two main characteristics emerge in the literature on media coverage of the riots: first, the prevalence of a crime frame and second, the use of social categories to discriminate rioters.

Riots as crime

Although the media placed the initial Tottenham riots in the context of previous riots in the area – particularly those in 1980/1981 and 1985 (Murij & Neal, 2011), Cavanagh and Dennis (2012) note that there have been shifts in the media portrayal of riots since those in 1981. Where the media framed those riots in terms of deprivation 'exploited by "infiltrators"' (p. 375), the 2011 riots were couched in terms of criminality and mob rule. In line with this analysis, Reicher and Stott (2011), in a summative discourse analysis of media coverage of the Tottenham and Croydon riots, note how the headlines dedicated to the riots mainly used negative words such as '"mayhem" (The Guardian), "anarchy" (The Sun, Daily Star and Daily Mail) and "mob" or "mob rule" (The Daily Telegraph, The Times and Independent)' (p. 183). The prevalent discourse of media was therefore accentuating the contrasts between local communities and authorities and denying the social psychological underpinnings of the riots, while discounting the events as the evil actions of criminal groups. As Reicher and Stott (2011) state, 'within a week of the riots there was a consensus that riots were all about criminality and that they happened because our society and our police had become too soft on indiscipline, on disrespect and on crime' (p. 30). The authors further suggest that this might have played an important role in framing the public's understanding of the events.

A lost generation in a degraded society

Cavanagh and Dennis (2012) also highlight that the 2011 riots were framed in the National press as a *youth* phenomenon, a mindless action of lost kids with no values or ethics – a 'lost generation' (pp. 378–379). Indeed, Yates and Shukla (2011) notice:

> The England riots of 2011 and much of their post-riot reportage propelled apocalyptic versions of our society and the disenfranchisement of its youth around the world. Claims were made of a feral underclass, with no hope, opportunities or civility: a whole demographic pushed into the fringes with no future and no stake in society. (p. 4)

These themes are echoed in several analyses of media coverage of the riots (Ball & Drury, 2012; Cammearts, 2012; Cavanagh & Dennis, 2012; Reicher & Stott, 2011).

Local media and communities

According to Cammearts (2012), although media in general tend to present riots and social movements under a negative light, this is not always the case: community radio stations in particular are 'important actors in countering the mainstream framing of movement messages and protest actions' (p. 125). This suggests that local and community media may offer a different viewpoint to mainstream media by providing a richer and more varied interpretation of the events. Nonetheless, Fenton, Metykova, Schlosberg, and Freedman (2010) stress that due to market pressures, local media might be falling short of this important function.

Local media, market pressures and online news

In 1997, the local press was the second biggest advertising medium in the country (after television) with a yearly investment of £1.9 billion (Advertising Association, 1997 as cited in Beamish, 1998). Beamish (1998) notes how 'detailed examination of many local newspapers reveals how carefully they are geared to the needs of their local communities – both in content and in style' and that 'Many local and regional newspapers now have their own Internet World Wide Websites, carrying a variety of news content and advertising. They are attractive, regularly updated and well used. They complement the printed product for advertisers and readers alike' (p. 144). Like in the case of National press, local newspapers have seen a progressive diminishment of their readership and their advertisement revenues, which is forecasted to fall below £1 billion in 2013 (Sweeney, 2012). News outlets tried to cope with this crisis in several ways (for a summary, see Gulyas, 2012) which include a strengthened investment in multimedia platforms. For example, in 2009, the *Manchester Evening News* launched a mobile app. which proved to be extremely successful, attracting on average 1000 downloads a week in the period between October 2009 and February 2010 (Deans, 2010). This shift towards online technology for news delivery makes the analysis of online content particularly interesting.

The context: city of Salford

Although geographically in very close proximity, Salford and Manchester are actually separate entities. Each a city in its own right, the two have different identities despite Salford being too often identified as being in Manchester (posters for national tours frequently cite Salford's Lowry theatre as being 'the Lowry Theatre, Manchester'). Boundary change proposals put forward in 2011 to incorporate parts of Salford into a 'Manchester Central' constituency were met with disgust by many Salford residents (Salford Disappears in Boundary Changes, 2011), as well as a successful campaign to oppose the idea (Salford Constituency Saved from Oblivion, 2012). Therefore, it is unsurprising that the nature of the events of 9 August differed between the two. The Manchester riot appears to have been predominantly a matter of looting (Reicher & Stott, 2011). People came into the large city centre from outside in order to steal from mainly higher end shops and businesses, but there does not seem to have been a great deal of animosity exhibited towards authority in the form of the police or civic buildings. In Salford, where around the area in which the riot took place there are child poverty rates of almost 75% (Morrell, Scott, McNeish, & Webster, 2011), there are no high end shops and while cheaper alternatives such as Lidl, Bargain Booze and Cash Converter were looted, a lot of the violence, anger and hatred was directed towards the police, who were pelted with bricks at various points in the evening, a clear demonstration of the city's deep rooted animosity towards authority.

Evans, Fraser, and Walklate claim that relations between the people of Salford and the police 'have always been somewhat fragile and tentative' (1996, p. 365), citing a historical tradition of mutual distrust stemming from the harsh social and economic conditions found in Salford. From the late 1800s, the city was a poverty ridden dockland area until the closure of the Terminal Docks in the 1970s and continues to be an area of deprivation. Salford has also has a history of 'riots', from 1931s Battle of Bexley Square (a demonstration against means testing which turned violent when protesters were attacked by the police) to a fortnight of violence in 1992 between the police and young people in the Ordsall area – the last major outbreak of rioting in the area before the riots of August 2011. As Evans et al. point out, there is a feeling of safety for those established within the community coupled with an ingrained culture of anti-police feeling and a strict 'no grassing' policy.

With this in mind, it is therefore not surprising that *The Guardian*'s 'Reading the Riots' study found that 85% of participants interviewed saw policing as an important or very important factor in the riots. The tensions between police and population in Salford are reflected in the police's routine practices. For example, while the Equality and Human Rights Commission found last year that someone is 21 times more likely to be stopped and searched by Greater Manchester Police (GMP) if they are black, in Salford this is not primarily a race issue but one of class, with young working-class men in particular claiming to be the victims of disproportionate numbers of stop and searches. The Scarman report into the 1981 Brixton riots identified stop and search as a contributing factor and the stop and search rate overall in Greater Manchester is higher than average at 22 per 1000 population, putting the area sixth in the country. Between 1 April 2006 and 31 March 2007, for white people in Salford it was 20.3. However, this number may be perceived locally to be much higher, since, as retired Deputy Assistant Commissioner and HM Assistant Inspector of Constabulary David Gilbertson points out in his 2012 Bernie Grant Memorial Lecture (Gilbertson, 2012), 'There are therefore many instances of such interactions which the police do not recognise or even record, but the public regard as "Stop and Search". So we have a difference of perception' going on to relate: 'Many years ago, whilst I was researching the subject, an officer based at Salford in Greater Manchester told me that he regarded "stop and search" as, "a contact sport to keep the crimes on their toes"'. In Salford then, there is a history of tension and struggle between police and the white, working-class section of the society, something less prominent in the rest of the Greater Manchester area.

A wide range of people have picked up on this difference: the Bishop of Manchester stating that while 'looting was at the heart of it, in Salford, there was a bit more anger behind it all' (BBC News, 2011), a statement echoed by Home Secretary Theresa May in front of the Home Affairs committee (in House of Commons Home Affairs Committee, 2012, p. 30), Guardian journalists Helen Clifton and Eric Allison (2011) and GMP Chief Constable Peter Fahy (in Clifton & Allison, 2011).

To summarise, while there are some similarities between the two riots, the differences are greater, requiring a separate analysis for each event, and, for this reason, we narrowed our field of study to Salford. Salford was chosen over Manchester due to the body of evidence suggesting that the events here went beyond simple looting for personal gain.

Method

We conducted a mixed-method content analysis of five local media sources available online: the *Manchester Evening News*, a daily newspaper covering Greater Manchester; the *Salford Advertiser*, a weekly paper covering Salford; *This is Lancashire*, a web portal combining articles from nine Lancashire and Greater Manchester newspapers, though none specifically from Salford; *Salford Online*, an independent community interest website; and the *Salford Star*, an independent Salford-based magazine. These are the main sources of local news for the Salford area as well as being the only outlets to generally cover Salford.

Table 1.   Sampled articles across time and outlet.

Frequency	Manchester Evening News Daily	Salford Advertiser Weekly	Salford Online Daily	Salford Star N/A	This is Lancashire Portal based	Total
Week 1	9	2	30	5	4	49
Week 2	11	2	13	0	5	31
Week 3	3	2	7	0	1	13
Week 4	0	3	2	0	1	6
Total	23	9	52	5	11	100

The methods utilised in the content analysis were: a thematic analysis of news headlines, an analysis of news sources featured in the articles and a quantitative analysis of prominent words. In order to offer a more in-depth insight on the results of the quantitative analyses, the researchers supplemented it with a more in-depth – qualitative – interpretation by analysing features and nuances of the use of particular themes, source categories or words. The procedure adopted for each component of the analysis is further illustrated in the following paragraphs.

Selection of articles

The articles analysed were published within a four-week period from the start of the riots in Salford on 9 August 2011, a time frame used to allow analysis of changes in the articles over time. Articles were retrieved via the individual sites' search engines, using the terms 'Salford' + 'Riots'.[1] The search initially returned 146 articles. Of these, 100 specifically addressed the events in Salford and constituted our final sample (see Table 1 for a breakdown of the sampled articles across the four weeks of coverage and the sampled websites).

Analysis of headlines

Daniel Dor (2003) claims in his empirical study of a Tel-Aviv news-desk: 'the importance of the role of headlines in the communicative act performed by newspapers can hardly be exaggerated' (p. 695), going on to describe headlines as 'relevance optimisers' and 'textual negotiators' (p. 696) between readers and the stories which sometimes summarise, sometimes highlight and sometimes quote from the article (p. 297). During the period following the riots, there were numerous articles on the subject, so the job of encouraging the reader to read each article further would be an important function of each headline, making it 'a communicative device whose function is to produce the optimal level of affinity between the content of the story and the reader's context of interpretation, in order to render the story optimally relevant for the reader' (Dor, 2003, p. 720). Indeed, Giles and Shaw (2009) suggest that headlines can give important indication on the characters/situations the reader is invited to identify with.

Titles – or headlines – of the articles were analysed via a computer-aided thematic analysis using NVivo (versions 8 and 9). Data were analysed following the step-by-step procedure proposed by Braun and Clarke (2006). The researchers read the whole sample of titles repeatedly and identified themes which appeared to address the topics recurring in the titles. The two coders then identified all the titles which fitted in the set of themes proposed by the head researcher and proposed the addition/modification of such themes. The head researcher then identified broader themes in which the set of sub-themes could fit. The researchers then re-coded the data on the basis of the agreed coding scheme. Ambiguous titles or titles on which coders had doubts were discussed among coders, as were further suggestions for refining the coding scheme. A final coding scheme was then agreed and coders re-coded the data on that

Table 2. Summary of themes identified in news headlines.

Theme	Description	Examples
Arts sports celebrities	Characters from arts sports and celebrities commenting on the events, poetry competition	Nigel Pivaro on Salford Riots Salford Riots: a poem from Daniel Clarke
Business	Effects on business and attempts of business to cope	Businesses left to count the cost Business reaction to Salford riots
Comments and explanations	Comments on and attempts to explain or contextualise – the events	Paul Taylor: do riots mark the death of liberalism? Deanna Delamotta: feckless parents are where the blame lies for Manchester and Salford riots
Descriptive	Description of events	Young thugs turn streets into war zone More eyewitness reports on Salford riots
Police work, authorities and justice	Information about the police, information from the police, calls for – and reports of – punishment	Police chief: we will catch looters Police get new powers to move troublemakers Probation pledge on riot yobs Prison for Salford rioters
Politics	National and local politicians' reaction and comments	Barbara Keeley MP pays tribute to police in Salford and calls on government to rethink police cuts Council promises tough action on riots
Positive campaigns and cleanup	Calls for participation and reports on positive campaigns and cleanup initiatives	Advertiser campaign: show your love for Salford Salford people back applause campaign

basis. This led to the identification of seven macro-categories into which each title was then coded (see Table 2 for summary, description and examples of the themes identified). The inter-rater reliability (IRR) was assessed by the coders re-coding 50% ($n = 50$, the minimum number necessary for a reliable IRR) of the headlines and resulted in a Cohen's κ of .95.

Analysis of sources

Giles and Shaw (2009) eloquently argue for the inclusion in any media framing study of an analysis of the 'dramatis personae', the key characters which appear recurrently in the story. Such characters serve, they argue, multiple purposes: they serve as interpretative frameworks and they aid deeper processing of the story by giving the opportunity to develop – or build on pre-existing – parasocial relationships.

We were interested in going a step further by not simply looking at the characters appearing in the stories but at those who were actually given a voice. We therefore decided to analyse the sources quoted in the news. Our rationale was that identification and the establishment of a parasocial relationship with a character would be facilitated by being exposed to their words and thoughts. Moreover, the recent advances in technology have meant that journalists can now rely on a much wider range of sources of information beyond the 'Official' sources: indeed, in the case of protests, we have seen a rise of 'citizens' journalism' whereby citizens actively seek and diffuse information concerning the events. It is not by chance that the role of Social Networking sites in protests has been at the centre of both academic (Gerbaudo, 2012) and political debates, which culminated in a meeting between Theresa May and Social Networking executives (*Salford Online*, 2011a). We were therefore interested in exploring the extent to which local editors and journalists relied on different sources of news.

The analysis of sources followed the same multi-step procedure used for the identification of themes. Thus, after identifying all sources cited, these were categorised in larger categories by the head researcher and then categorised by both researchers, who amended the coding scheme where necessary. Once the final categorisation scheme was agreed, the entire data-set was re-coded accordingly. The resulting categorisation consisted of six macro-categories: authorities and public services, business, informed citizens, political, public/Vox Populi and anonymous/celebs/arts/sports/others. The IRR was assessed by the coders re-coding 30% (to guarantee to reach the minimum number of $N = 50$) of the articles and resulted in a Cohen's κ of .94.

Word frequency

It is possible though that looking only at headlines and sources might misrepresent the content of the articles sampled. We therefore turned to a more systematic analysis of the prevalent words appearing in the articles. This procedure, while quite crude in its nature since it does not give indi-cation of the wider context in which the words appear, provides an idea of how the media rep-resented the riots during this period and of where they placed the most emphasis in their framing of events. To this end, we performed a word count of the 10 most frequent words featured in the news. The analysis was conducted using NVivo 9. The search criteria were required to identify the 10 most frequent (minimum four letter) words (including stemmed words, such as police, policing; riot, rioting, riots; and shop, shopping, shops). A list of stop words (words that were frequent, but did not carry any specific meaning or relevance) was compiled.

Results and discussion

Headlines

As Table 3 shows, headlines in the reports focused mainly on the work carried out by the police during the riots (the – sometimes ineffective – attempts to contain the damage, the hunt for the indi-viduals responsible for the riots, as well as the arrests which took place in the aftermath of the events reported). Titles covering this theme were often very factual such as 'More CCTV images released following disorder' (*Salford Online*, 2011b). Only three headlines focused on the anti-police nature of the riots. One quoted police officers denouncing the extent of the violence ('"Outnumbered" police officers tell home secretary "We could have been killed"', Linton & Keeling, 2011) and the remaining two quoted the Chief of Police Peter Fahy, who claimed that the riots were organised by criminals in the area to get back to the police who had worked hard to reduce crime rates in the area (Peter Fahy: Criminals Organised Salford Violence as 'Payback' for Police Action, 2011 and 'Hate shown to Police in Salford was astonishing' Keeling, 2011).

A theme often appearing in the headlines concerned the impact that the events had on business. Coverage focused mainly on business associations and spokespersons' estimates of the damage and initiatives that businessmen and business associations alone or in collaboration with the council and the political authorities put in place in an attempt to bring the public back to the shopping centre.

Headlines often reported a simple and descriptive account of the events (for instance, 13% of titles were merely descriptive). The frequent use of numbers to illustrate the impact of the events as well as the damage to businesses (36% of titles describing events or concerning business fea-tured this characteristic, e.g. '1000 police incidents, 150 fires, 12 hurt, 113 people arrested in night of violence in Manchester and Salford', Wheatstone, 2011) is interesting. In this case, numbers are used to frame the protest as dominated by a *logic of damage* (Cammearts, 2012): presenting the public with numerical data indicating the extensive damage caused by the riots often de-legit-imises the protest while emphasising 'the violent mob frame the media is looking for and eager to overexpose (Donson et al., 2004)' (Cammearts, 2012, p. 125).

Table 3. Themes appearing in news headlines across outlets.

Theme	Manchester Evening News		Salford Advertiser		Salford Online		Salford Star		This is Lancashire		Total
	N	%	N	%	N	%	N	%	N	%	N
Arts sports celebrities	1	4	–	–	2	4	1	20	–	–	4
Business	5	22	3	33	3	6	–	–	–	–	11
Comments, explanations	4	17	–	–	–	–	1	20	1	9	6
Descriptive	1	4	1	11	6	12	3	60	2	18	13
Police work, authorities and justice	8	35	3	33	29	56	–	–	8	73	48
Politics	1	4	–	–	6	12	–	–	–	–	7
Positive campaigns and cleanup	3	13	2	22	6	12	–	–	–	–	11
Total	23	100	9	100	52	100	5	100	11	100	100

National and local politicians' reaction to the events and comments on the way in which police and magistrates should deal – or dealt – with the event and the people involved featured frequently in the headlines.

A significant proportion of the coverage focused on the 'cleanup initiatives' initiated by authorities (the 'shop-a-looter-and-make-them-pay' initiative by the GMP and the 'I love Salford' campaign promoted by the City Council), as well as initiatives taken by media outlets (see the *Manchester Evening News* appeal to join the 'fight back' by posting comments on the reasons why readers love Salford or the *Salford Advertiser*s' analogous campaign, 'I love Salford').

From a more discursive point of view, it is interesting to notice how these pro-social initiatives are often framed in negative terms, as a 'fight back' (e.g. 'Join the fightback, tell us why you love Manchester', Williams, 2011), as a war against the rioters which the community will 'win' (Manchester Businesses Will Beat the Rioters, 2011), often appealing to the 'spirit' of the 'Salford community' ('Salford spirit will save the city', Rogers & Burton, 2011), thus implying that those involved in the riots are not part of the community. Campaigns such as the 'Shop a Looter and Make Them Pay' (*Salford Online*, 2011c) are illustrative of this point. Indeed, some members of the public responded promptly to these appeals, as well as to calls to sign e-petitions to rip the people condemned during the hearings from their housing benefits ('Thousands sign e-petition to axe rioters' benefits', *Salford Online*, 2011d).

The 'rioters/looters' rarely appear in the headlines, and when they do, the terms used refer to them as 'criminal', 'thugs', 'looting yobs', 'troublemakers', 'riot yobs' or in terms of their age 'young' or 'teenager', once again an element which creates distance between most readers and the individuals involved.

Significantly, very little space was overall given in the headlines to potential explanations of the events.

The relative proportion of themes appearing in the headlines does not vary substantially across news outlet (Table 4): with the exception of the *Salford Star* (for which we have also a very small number of articles) the theme appearing most frequently was that of police work, authorities and justice. Little differences can also be observed across time, with the only exception of 'descriptive' titles, which, as it could be expected, appear only in the first two weeks of coverage ($n = 12$ in week 1 and $n = 1$ in week two) and of titles concerning the political debates/reaction that appear mostly in the first week of coverage.

Sources

We defined news sources as those who are quoted (directly or indirectly or paraphrased) in the story. Results showed significant differences in the extent to which different types of sources were quoted in the media (χ^2 (5) = 138.44, $p < .001$, see Figure 1).

The largest proportion of individuals quoted in the news was composed of representatives of the authorities: police officers and representatives (84 overall to this type of source appeared in the sampled articles), ambulance, fire and rescue services (20 references) as well as representatives of the justice system (e.g. judges, magistrates and lawyers, 24 references).

National and local political figures are frequently quoted in the articles (69 quotes came from politicians, of which 36 were references to local politicians and 33 to national politicians) as well as representatives of the business world, from shop owners to representatives of business consortia (53 references in text).

A significant minority of news sources consisted of members of the public (35 references overall). Of these, some provided an eyewitness testimony of the events (5 references) and others commented on the events (23 references). People actually involved in the riots rarely

Table 4. Changes in headlines, sources and text across time.

		Week 1	Week 2	Week 3	Week 4
Headlines					
Arts sports celebrities	N	1	2	1	0
	%	2	6	8	0
Business	N	7	3	1	1
	%	14	10	8	17
Comments, explanations	N	3	2	0	1
	%	6	6	0	17
Descriptive	N	12	1	0	0
	%	24	3	0	0
Police work, authorities and emergency services	N	20	17	8	2
	%	40	55	62	33
Politics	N	4	2	0	1
	%	8	6	0	17
Positive campaigns and cleanup	N	3	4	3	1
	%	6	13	23	17
Total	N	50	31	13	6
	%	100	100	100	100
Sources					
Authorities and public services	N	48	46	28	1
	%	35	37	60	8
Business	N	29	21	0	3
	%	21	17	0	23
Informed citizens	N	15	7	6	0
	%	11	6	13	0
Political	N	24	28	11	4
	%	17	23	23	31
Public, Vox populi	N	18	15	1	1
	%	13	12	2	8
Anonymous, celebs, arts and sports and others	N	5	7	1	4
	%	4	6	2	31
Total	N	139	124	47	13
	%	100	100	100	100

figured. Of the seven quotes from people allegedly involved in the riots, five were quotes of a man wrongly accused to have partaken in the riots and only two were quotes from people who actively participated. No space was offered to parents or relatives of the individuals who were arrested or under trial. It is yet to be established whether this is because parents or relatives refused to comment on the events of because they were not offered this opportunity.

There were some differences in the extent to which different outlets gave voice to the various sources: first, newspapers relied differently on sources in general (Kruskall–Wallis test, χ^2 (4) = 11.75, $p < .05$). Looking at the average scores, the *Manchester Evening News* quoted more sources than the other news outlets. Second, there were significant differences within each outlet in the extent to which different sources were represented: as Figure 1 shows, *Manchester Evening News* and *Salford Advertiser* relied heavily on all 'official' sources (authorities, political and business), at the expenses especially of informed citizens and the general public, whereas *Salford Online* and TIL were heavily skewed towards authorities and – for *Salford Online* – political sources and less on business (all $\chi^2 > 15.6$, all $p < .05$).[2]

Overall, the analysis of sources closely reflects the analysis of the themes appearing in the headlines, with a clear prevalence of criminal/justice systems related information offered to the audience. Similarly to the headlines, minor changes can be noticed across times in the relative

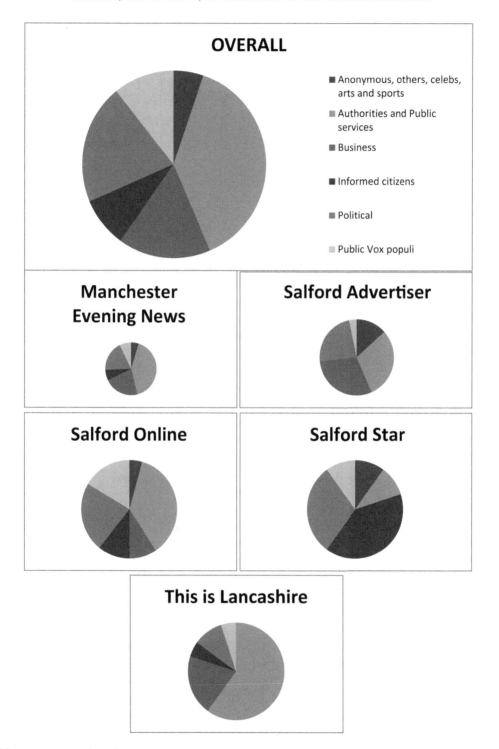

Figure 1. Proportion of sources cited across news outlets.

Table 5. Most frequent words appearing in news items across outlets (top 10 rank).

Rank	Overall Word	Count	Manchester Evening News Word	Count	Salford Advertiser Word	Count	Salford Online Word	Count	Salford Star Word	Count	This is Lancashire Word	Count
1	Police	277	Police	100	People	19	Police	115	People	24	Police	36
2	People	253	People	83	Police	19	People	111	Riots	16	Riots	20
3	Riots	186	Riots	57	Riots	18	Riots	75	Council	13	People	16
4	Officers	105	Officers	53	Shopping	17	Disorder	36	Services	12	Disorder	14
5	Disorder	76	Rioters	32	Campaign	12	Officers	33	Riot	10	Charged	13
6	Council	71	Fire	25	Support	12	Community	31	Young	10	Looters	11
7	Fire	66	Prince	25	Chief	10	Fire	30	Youth	10	Court	9
8	Riot	61	Home	24	Close	10	Violence	30	Cuts	9	Damage	9
9	Violence	61	Sentences	22	Love	10	Council	28	Members	8	Looting	9
10	Chief	59	Chief	21	Officers	9	Local	28	Police	7	Public	9

Table 6. Word frequency across time.

Word frequency Rank #	Week 1 Word	Count	Week 2 Word	Count	Week 3 Word	Count	Week 4 Word	Count
1	Police	171	Riots	73	People	38	Riots	13
2	People	145	Police	70	Prison	27	Police	11
3	Riots	77	People	60	Police	25	People	10
4	Officers	70	Rioters	35	Riots	23	Shopping	8
5	Disorder	48	Shop	27	Love	16	Campaign	7
6	Violence	42	Prince	25	Officers	16	Market	7
7	Fire	37	Council	24	Public	14	Home	6
8	Chief	35	Fire	23	Council	11	Support	6
9	Businesses	34	Sentences	21	Sentences	11	anti-social	5
10	Council	33	Business	19	Support	11	Disorder	5

weight of the various sources across the four weeks of coverage: authorities remain the most prominent source throughout three of the four weeks, followed by political and business sources. By week four, though, the authorities' presence is significantly reduced (χ^2 (3) = 15.09, $p < .01$), while business and political sources remain prominent (see bottom part of Table 4).

Word frequency

As Table 5 shows, news featured words concerning policing and justice, with police being among the top four most frequent words in all but one outlet. Indeed, other words relating to this theme occurred frequently, such as officers, sentences and chief. Almost as a contrast, the third most frequent word overall was 'people'. Also recurring frequently are words related to the events and their consequences (riots, fire, disorder and damage) and business (business and shops).

It is indeed interesting to notice how the word 'people' is often used as a category separate from that of the rioters, creating a contrast between the 'real' people and those involved in the riots.

The following are examples of such occurrences:

This is nothing more than senseless violence with no absolutely no regard for people, their property or livelihoods. (ACC Gary Shewan in *Salford Online*, 2011, August 10)

The majority of the people living in Salford are, quite rightly, disgusted by what they saw happening in their city last night. (Councillor John Merry in *Salford Online*, 2011, August 10)

Decent Salford people, she said, are going to be really, really angry. (Hazel Blears MP in *Salford Online*, 2011, August 10)

Looking at the individual outlets, this rough analysis shows how the emphasis shifts from three outlets focusing mainly on the 'crime' frame (the top three words in the *Manchester Evening News*, *Salford Online* and *This is Lancashire* were police, riots and people or police, riots and charged for *This is Lancashire*) to the more 'commercially' oriented *Salford Advertiser* (shops, riots and people) to the more 'socially' concerned *Salford Star* (riots, people and reasons). The analysis of word frequencies across the four weeks of coding highlights how little change can be observed in the most recurring words across time (Table 6). Although 'police' and 'people' recur very often in the four weeks, in weeks two and three words related to the work of the courts ('prison' 'sentence/s') gain prominence. In weeks three and four, the articles also frequently feature words related to the campaigns (campaign and love – in reference to the 'I love Salford' campaigns).[3]

Conclusion

The riots which took place in August 2011 generated an abundance of media coverage in both national and local news. While National news coverage has been extensively explored in research (Ball & Drury, 2012; Cavanagh & Dennis, 2012; Murji & Neal, 2011; Winlow & Hall, 2012), little attention has been given to local realities. Indeed, Reicher and Stott (2011) suggest that riots should be analysed and interpreted in the specific context in which they occur. The authors further highlight how the 2011 riots had different characteristics and followed different dynamics in different locations. For this reason, the present study looked at local media coverage of the riots in Salford, Greater Manchester, in order to understand whether, due to their awareness of community-specific issues and dynamics, local media's coverage differed from the prevalent discourses presented at National level.

We readily acknowledge some limitations in the methods adopted in the study: first, the sample size is limited by our choice to only include articles which allowed for user-generated comments. This choice was driven by our intention to look at the public's reaction to the reports (Coen & Jones, 2013). This analysis will allow us to have an indication of the immediate effects of framing on the readers (see Giles and Shaw for a similar methodology). Second, as mentioned in previous sections, the analysis of word counts is a rather rough measure. However, we believe that it does reflect accurately of prevalence of themes in the news, as shown by the substantial consistency of its results with our analysis of sources and headlines, thus providing support for its convergent validity. Third, the quantitative analysis of sources provides only indicative guidelines of the main voices featured in the news. A qualitative analysis of the themes emerging in such quotes would provide a much more complete and in-depth account. We nonetheless believe that our study provided some interesting indications of trends in the local media coverage of the Salford riots.

Results show that patterns of coverage at a local level did not differ significantly from those identified at national level: indeed, the riots were framed as mindless criminality perpetrated by 'young' 'thugs' and focused mainly on the criminal prosecution of the rioters, the activity of police and courts (Cavanagh & Dennis, 2012). This supports Reicher and Stott's assertion that, according to the media at least, the riots were very quickly 'all about criminality' (2011, p. 30). Moreover, a large proportion of news items simply consisted of announcements or images offered by the authorities, with little or no contextualisation. Therefore, it appears that there is an emerging media template (Kitzinger, 2000) for the coverage of riots in which the emphasis seems to be on law and order-related themes. Online local news outlets by adhering to this template missed the opportunity to provide an alternative, community-specific account and contextualisation of the events, thus confirming Fenton et al.'s claim that while local and community media may offer a different viewpoint to mainstream media, they generally fail to do so (2010).

Online local news outlets relied heavily on official sources such as police, judges and lawyers, and national and local politicians. Local business and its representatives find a significant proportion of space and voice in the local media. Sources involved in or connected to people involved in the riots were extremely rare or absent. A second missed opportunity for local media is therefore failing to provide a more comprehensive coverage of the different voices and to provide the community's support for families and relations to those who were accused – rightly or wrongly – to have taken part in the events and who were framed in extremely negative terms in the media, as shown in our analysis of headlines.

Finally, members of the local civic society and informed citizens offering a reading of the events in the context of the specific issues faced by the 'young' generation in the local community rarely featured, although frequent were references to the 'decent Salford people' and the appeals to support 'fight back' initiatives by identifying looters or posting comments. Readers are, therefore, strongly encouraged to identify with these characters: 'decent' people, property owners, business people and representatives of the law (Giles & Shaw, 2009). In line with their national analogues, online local news outlets tended to identify, isolate and derogate a section of the society (mindless, young and 'thugs') against which the rest of the community should 'fight'. Appeals to the public were therefore mainly directed to a retrospective *collective reaction*, rather than a forward looking *collective action*.

While reliance on authoritative sources is an integral part of journalism, a larger representation of members of civic society and informed citizens would provide a more balanced and community-based coverage of the events. The 'mob rule' media frame fails to acknowledge or promote a deeper understanding of the social and political issues underlying the events, which, if properly reported, could then potentially be addressed by the communities that the local media aim to represent.

Notes

1. In view of future developments of the project, we only selected articles which allowed users to post comments.
2. The analysis did not yield to significant differences for Salford Star, but this might be due to the extremely low number of articles ($n = 5$ and of sources $n = 10$).
3. It is to be noted that the word 'social' appearing in the list might be misleading: a closer analysis shows how in the nine instances in which the social appears, it is either a component of 'anti-social' ($n = 5$) or of 'social networking' ($n = 4$).

References

Ball, R., & Drury, J. (2012). Representing the riots: The (mis)use of statistics to sustain ideological explanation. *Radiation Statistics, 106*, 4–21. Retrieved from http://www.radstats.org.uk/no106/BallDrury106. pdf

Beamish, R. (1998). The local newspapers in the age of multimedia. In B. Franklin & D. Murphy (Eds.), *Making the local news local journalism in context* (pp. 135–148). London: Routledge.

BBC News. (2011). *Bishop says Manchester and Salford riots 'different'*. Retrieved December 20, 2012, from http://www.bbc.co.uk/news/uk-england-manchester-16325950

Braun, V., & Clarke, V. (2006). Using thematic analysis in psychology. *Qualitative Research Methods in Psychology, 3*, 77–101.

Cammearts, B. (2012). Protest logics and the mediation opportunity structure. *European Journal of Communication, 27*(2), 117–134.

Cavanagh, A., & Dennis, A. (2012). Framing the riots. *Capital & Class, 36*(3), 375–381.

Clifton, H., & Allison, E. (2011, December 6). Manchester and Salford: A tale of two riots. *The Guardian*. Retrieved from http://www.guardian.co.uk/

Coen, S., & Jones, C. (2013). *An analysis of the public's reaction to local news reports of the Salford riots in local newspapers*. Manuscript in preparation.

Deans, J. (2010, February 5). MEN scores success with palm pre-app. *The Guardian*. Retrieved from http://www.guardian.co.uk/

Dor, D. (2003). On newspaper headlines as relevance optimizers. *Journal of Pragmatics, 35*, 695–721.

Entman, R. M. (1993). Framing: Towards clarification of a fractured paradigm. *Journal of Communication, 43*(4), 53–58.

Evans, K., Fraser, P., & Walklate, S. (1996). Whom can you trust? The politics of 'grassing' on an inner city housing estate. *The Sociological Review, 44*(3), 361–380.

Fenton, N., Metykova, M., Schlosberg, J., & Freedman, D. (2010). *Meeting the news needs of local communities. Executive report for mediatrust*. Retrieved from http://www.mediatrust.org/uploads/128255497549240/original.pdf

Gerbaudo, P. (2012). *Tweets and the streets. Social media and contemporary activism*. London: Pluto Press.

Gilbertson, D. (2012). Policing matters: The road to recovery after the riots. *Bernie Grant Memorial Lecture*. Retrieved from http://www.berniegrantcentre.co.uk/

Giles, D. C., & Shaw, R. L. (2009). The psychology of news influence and development of media framing analysis. *Social and Personality Psychology Compass*, 3(4), 375–393.

Gulyas, A. (2012). Changing business models and adaptation strategies of local newspapers. In J. Mair, N. Fowler, & I. Reeves (Eds.), *What do we mean by local?* (pp. 27–33). Suffolk: Arima Publishing.

House of Commons Home Affairs Committee. (2012). *Policing large scale disorder: Lessons from the disturbances of August 2011, Volume II*. London: Stationary Office.

Keeling, N. (2011, August 12). Hate shown to police in Salford was astonishing, says GMP Chief Peter Fahy. *Manchester Evening News*. Retrieved from http://www.manchestereveningnews.co.uk/

Kitzinger, J. (2000). Media templates: Patterns of association and the (re) construction of meaning over time. *Media, Culture & Society*, 22(1), 61–84.

Linton, D., & Keeling, N. (2011, August 11). 'Outnumbered' police officers tell Home Secretary: 'We could have been killed'. *Manchester Evening News*. Retrieved from http://www.manchestereveningnews.co.uk/

Manchester Businesses Will Beat the Rioters. (2011). *Manchester Evening News*. Retrieved March 9, 2013, from http://manchestereveningnews.co.uk/

Morrell, G., Scott, S., McNeish, D., & Webster, S. (2011). *The August riots in England: Understanding the involvement of young people*. London: NatCen.

Murji, K., & Neal, S. (2011). Riot: Race and politics in the 2011 disorders. *Sociological Research Online*, 16 (4), 24.

Nelson, T. E., Clawson, R. A., & Oxley, Z. A. (1997). Media faming of a civil liberties conflict and its effect on tolerance. *American Political Science Review*, 91(3), 567–583.

Peter Fahy: Criminals Organised Salford Violence as 'Payback' for Police Action. (2011, August 12). *Manchester Evening News*. Retrieved March 9, 2013, from http://manchestereveningnews.co.uk/

Reicher, S., & Stott, C. (2011). *Mad mobs and Englishmen? Myths and realities of the 2011 riots*. Constable Robinson. Kindle ed. Retrieved from http://www.madmobsandenglishmen.com/

Rogers, T., & Burton, A. (2011, August 11). Salford people spirit will save the city. *Salford Online*. Retrieved from http://www.salfordonline.com/

Salford Constituency Saved from Oblivion. (2012, October 16). *Salford Star*. Retrieved March 9, 2013, from http://www.salfordstar.com/article.asp?id=1542

Salford Disappears in Boundary Changes. (2011, September 13). *Salford Star*. Retrieved March 9, 2013, from http://www.salfordstar.com/article.asp?id=1095

Salford Online. (2011a, August 29). May hosts social network meeting over riots. *Salford Online*. Retrieved from http://www.salfordonline.com/

Salford Online. (2011b, August 10). More CCTV images released following disorder. *Salford Online*. Retrieved from http://www.salfordonline.com/

Salford Online. (2011c, September 3). Shop a looter and make them pay. *Salford Online*. Retrieved from http://www.salfordonline.com/

Salford Online. (2011d, August 14). Thousands sign e-petition to axe rioters' benefits. *Salford Online*. Retrieved from http://www.salfordonline.com/

Schaufele, D. A. (1999). Framing as a theory of media effects. *Journal of Communication*, 49(1), 103–122. doi:10.1111/j.1460-2466.1999.tb02784.x

Sweeney, M. (2012, December 11). UK newspaper advertising facing bleak forecast for 2013. *The Guardian*. Retrieved from http://www.guardian.co.uk/media/2012/dec/11/uk-newspaper-advertising-bleak-forecast-2013

Wheatstone, R. (2011, August 10). 1,000 police incidents, 150 fires, 12 hurt, 113 people arrested in night of violence in Manchester and Salford. *Manchester Evening News*. Retrieved from http://www.manchestereveningnews.co.uk/

Williams, J. (2011, August 23). Join the fightback, tell us why you love Manchester. *Manchester Evening News*. Retrieved from http://www.manchestereveningnews.co.uk/

Winlow, S., & Hall, S. (2012). A predictably obedient riot: Postpolitics, consumer culture, and the English riots of 2011. *Cultural Politics*, 8(3), 465–488.

Yates, K., & Shukla, N. (2011, October 27). *Summer of unrest: Generation vexed: What the English riots don't tell us about our nation's youth* (Kindle locations 37–39). Kindle ed. Retrieved from http://www.amazon.co.uk/Summer-Unrest-Generation-English-ebook/dp/B005ZVE5WI

The moral economy of the UK student protest movement 2010–2011

Joseph Ibrahim

Department of Psychology, Sociology and Politics, Sheffield Hallam University, Sheffield, UK

The winter of 2010 through to the spring of 2011 saw a number of high profile, nationally and locally organised student protests and occupations of university campuses all around the UK. These were a direct response to the UK government policy to lift the cap on higher education (HE) tuition fees and the reduction in government funding for HE institutions in England. To explain this revolt, I draw on the work of Thompson [1971. The moral economy of the English crowd in the 18th century. *Past & Present, 50,* 76–136; 1993. *Customs in common: Studies in traditional popular culture.* New York, NY: New Press] to argue that they were a 'moral economy' of protests. This paper draws on a two-and-a-half-year ethnographic study of the student political community. I argue that the student community have mobilised in defence of an embedded tradition – affordable HE – and that they are politically motivated by what they consider to be an entitlement violation.

The old customs which still linger on in the obscure nooks and corners of our native land, or which have survived the march of progress in our busy city's life. (Ditchfield, 1896, as cited by Thompson, 1993, p. 2)

Some of us used to joke that if corporations could bottle and sell the air that we breathe they would do it. Well, now nobody is laughing anymore. (Hubbard & Miller, 2005, p. 1)

Free education has now become an old custom from a bygone era; for a time it did survive the march of the free market, but not anymore. The neoliberal victory over the higher education (HE) system in the UK, arguably because of the research excellence framework, the emphasis on grant capture and the new increase in HE tuition fees, is almost complete. These are all examples of how the UK university sector is becoming increasingly commodified and marketised. It was the increase in UK tuition fees and cuts to the HE budget that provoked the student revolt 2010–2011. During this period, the UK saw a number of high-profile student protests on 10, 24 and 30 November; 9 December; 29 January and 26 March and occupations at 40 universities. These protests and occupations were in direct response to the Independent Review of Higher Education and Student Finance undertaken by Lord Browne (also known as the Browne review).

The review started in November 2009 and ended in October 2010. The main aim of the review was to consider the balance of contributions between students, the taxpayers, employers and graduates to university funding in England. The review put forward three main recommendations. First, the government should remove the cap on HE fees (then £3200 per annum) to enable universities to set their own fees. Second, loans should be provided by the government to pay for students' fees and living costs. The loans would not have to be repaid until student's pre-tax earnings were above £21,000. Any remaining monies owed would be written off after 30 years. Third, part-time students – who had to pay fees upfront – should be treated equal to full-time students in terms of access to loans to pay for their fees (Browne, 2010).

In May 2010, the newly elected Conservative–Liberal Democratic coalition government decided to accept the core of Browne's recommendations. On 3 November 2010, the following government proposals (based on the Browne review) were put forward by David Willets, the Minister of State for Universities and Science: both part-time and full-time students would be entitled to loans. These are to be repaid at a rate of 9% on earnings over £21,000, per annum, any remaining debt to be written off after 30 years. One of the main differences between Browne's recommendations and the government proposals was the ability of the university to set its own fees. The government decided instead to raise the cap to £9000 per annum. In addition, government policy stipulated that universities wishing to charge over £6000 per annum must demonstrate a commitment to widening participation. On 9 December 2010, the government bill was passed by the House of Commons by 323 votes to 302. In 2012, 94 out of 122 universities have announced that they will charge students the full £9000 across all courses (Morgan, 2012). It was because of the government proposals and Parliament subsequently voting in favour of these proposals that students took to national and local protests in London and around the UK, including occupying a number of university buildings.

In this paper, I argue that these protests and occupations throughout the UK are a moral economy, in E. P. Thompson's sense of the term. A tradition of entitlement – affordable HE – has been violated (in this case HE tuition fees are set too high) and as such students have taken to direct action to contest the UK Parliament's decision to raise the cap on tuition fees and implement cuts to HE. Thompson's work is under utilised in social movement studies and sociology in general. I argue it has much to offer when it comes to explaining the political motivations and political actions of a community when they decide to mobilise. Thompson's approach enables us to consider how the protests and occupations by the students concerned are a political negotiation between cultural expectations of a community and economic pricing. And how, if a community entitlement is violated, this can lead to political action. To this end, this paper offers a new application of Thompson's moral economy to explain the student revolts 2010–2011.

The moral economy approach

In an earlier article (Ibrahim, 2011), I provided a rapid response and preliminary analysis to these waves of protests and occupations by claiming that they were politically motivated by a sense of injustice felt by the students since the new fee structure represents a new toll on HE and a very real barrier for some trying to access it (Ibrahim, 2011). My initial response drew tentatively on Thompson's (1971, 1993) notion of moral economy, in particular, on how the fees were an assault on traditional entitlements and moral sensibilities. In this paper, I expand and develop the theoretical application of Thompson's moral economy to the said protests and occupations.

The theoretical application used in this paper is drawn mainly from two of Thompson's writings: 'The moral economy of the English crowd' (1971) and *Customs in common* (1993). His arguments centre on the emergence and political motivations of crowds in the eighteenth century who rioted against the increases of the price of food. The increases are a result of free market forces, but the riots should not be read merely as an instrumental reaction to the affordability of food or hunger. Although these are important, it is the crowds moral outrage and political motivations that provide the explanation for their mobilisations against certain parties in that community such as millers, bakers, etc. The moral economy refers to the difference in what something ought to cost, according to the expectations of a community, and the reality of the price rise. This gap is where the tensions emerge because it is seen as unfair, unjust and an attack on the communities' moral sentiments.

There are certain key ideas within the moral economy framework that provide an explanation as to why free market reforms result in collective action (collective action in this context refers to protests, riots and political mobilisations). The central idea is that of legitimation. This refers to whether the rise in the price of food is perceived as legitimate by the community (i.e. the relevant stakeholders). If the price rise is perceived to be illegitimate within a community then this might result in collective action being taken.

Collective action, sanctioned by the community, generally draws upon a stock repertoire of political methods to defend against a price rise. The defence could include rioting or threat of riot, if a good (in the case of the eighteenth century this was food) is not returned to what is con-sidered to be a reasonable price. The riot, in the eighteenth century, was considered to be a reason-able form of political action taken to defend an entitlement. Therefore, political action in this context arises because entitlement to food through rising prices has become unaffordable and is considered to be an entitlement violation. Each party within that community has a role and func-tion based on traditional norms and values that are understood by the members of that community. As such, if a violation occurs, even the authorities and elites within the community understand that certain members have a right to defend a tradition against a threat imposed by market forces.

Although used to analyse riots in the eighteenth century, it is evident that Thompson's ideas have currency in the twenty-first century. For example, Patel (2009) and Patel and McMichael (2010) have used the moral economy framework for analysing the wave of food riots that took place around the world including those in Italy and Haiti in 2007. However, I would argue that the framework has explanatory power beyond analysing food riots. It offers a powerful frame-work for understanding the underlying moral antagonism towards free market reforms in terms of how communities express their collective and political grievances when faced with a threat from the imposition of free market policies more generally. In fact, Thompson (1993, p. 340) himself has stated that the Great British miners strike of 1984–1985 was a moral economy since it was political resistance against 'free market' reforms including pit closures, which threa-tened to take away the miners' entitlement to a livelihood, a tradition that they had had for gen-erations. Moreover, another more recent application comes from Bagguley (1996) who has used the moral economy argument to explain the very popular and UK wide anti-poll tax campaign of the 1990s, which brought about a change in UK government policy. Following in this tradition of appropriation and adaptation, I argue that the concept of moral economy can be applied to explain why students campaigned against the increase of tuition fees and the cuts to the UK HE budget implemented by the UK coalition government.

Although tuition fees for HE in parts of the UK have been in operation since 1997, payment for tuition has always been a source of contention for students. This is to be expected, because students know that their parents did not have to pay for their HE, they also know that students who enrolled before the rise in fees pay around one-third of what they pay for the same education. The parents of today's students pass on folk memories and stories of free education and, in some cases, entitlements to maintenance grants. It is arguable that HE in the UK before 1997 was a tra-ditional entitlement for students. So even though free at the point of use HE has not been an enti-tlement for sometime, it is reasonable to assume that students are aware of the erosion of such an entitlement. It is the case that most students have come to expect that fees need to be charged; however, the threefold increase may have resulted in political action by the student community since the fee may now be considered to be too high.

Applying Thompson's framework to today's situation, the coalition government's decision to increase HE tuition fees and introduce budget cuts are examples of reforms that are a move towards further marketisation of the UK university sector. This could be seen as an assault on an embedded custom – affordable HE – and an 'entitlement violation' (Sen, 1981). The Browne review and the coalition government's policy of lifting the cap on tuition fees and the implementation of £2.9 billion cuts in the HE budget are the reality which is out of line with what is classified as fair and reasonable amongst the student community. This gap in expectation and reality has opened up as a result of the further commodification of the university sector and the implementation of free market forces – this has led to moral outrage by the student community and this is why they have taken to protest and occupations.

Why the moral economy?

Thompson's notion of moral economy is relatively under utilised in sociology, much less in social movement studies. This, therefore, begs the question, why use the moral economy argument in this case? The main reason is that the established social movement theories are deficient when it comes to explaining collective action that is driven by moral concerns. Two schools of thought, resource mobilisation theory (RMT) (McCarthy & Zald, 1977) and the political process approach (PPA) (McAdam, Tarrow, & Tilly, 2001) do not really consider political motivations beyond resources, economic incentives and structural opportunities. Although these theories are very useful when it comes to identifying under what conditions protests and mobilisations can occur and what the incentives for political action might be, in the specific case of affordable HE neither theory can explain why political action was undertaken by the students. This may largely be due to the fact that RMT is rooted in rational actor theory (RAT), which makes recourse to methodological individualism.

Whilst RAT dispels myths about protest being irrational, it tends towards the other extreme of being too rational. The theory suggests that political activists only engage in action when there is an individual benefit to be had. This proposition is difficult to apply to the thousands of students who protested on the days mentioned, since many were already enrolled on courses that would not be affected by the increase. Although it is sometimes argued that selective incentives are possible for politicos, particularly those already in a position to further their political career (perhaps within formal student politics at the branch or national level of the students union and I am not convinced of this argument), many of the student activists on demonstrations do not seek incentives. Rather, they expressed outrage at an injustice and argued from a moral standpoint, displaying outrage that an entitlement had been violated. Furthermore, the student protests were based on normative arguments against increased tuition fees, which were collective in nature, they were not individualistic.

The PPA school of thought developed out of RMT and whilst it has been adapted it also falls foul of the resource-based argument outlined above. However, one of the main ideas in PPA is that political organisations seek to influence government policy through the political opportunity structure. To some extent, this is can be used to explain why students have little success in influencing government policy – especially in this case – since they are not close to the polity and as such they have little political leverage. However, it does not explain their values, ideas and normative political motivations, which led to the mobilisations. The moral economy approach in this case does.

The study

The research carried out for this paper was part of larger project funded by the Leverhulme Trust, which investigated the politicising effect of the university campus on students (Crossley, 2008). The research was primarily carried out at the University of Manchester, UK. This project lasted two years in total from January 2009 to December 2010. The project took an ethnographic approach, which included conducting 53 semi-structured interviews with student politicos, observations of demonstrations and meetings of student political societies and groups (on and off campus) and analysis of 100 documents produced by political groups and societies based at the University of Manchester. During the project an 'upswing' of a 'cycle of contention' by student protestors occurred in light of the Browne review and the anticipated increase in tuition fees (Tarrow, 2011; Tilly, 1995; Traugot, 1995). Therefore, after the official ending of the project, for the next 12 months I continued to collect data derived from university blogs (especially those involved in protest occupations), the national press and documents produced by the student community. In addition, I revisited earlier interview data and analysed further themes that were central to student politics. In particular, their feelings towards the commodification and marketisation of HE and the new fee structure which was to be implemented. The next section of the paper details the methodology used.

Methodology

The aim of this ethnography was to understand the campus political world, as such I attempted to capture the everyday political life including the culture and social practices of the students under study in their natural settings (Brewer, 2000). To achieve this, the University of Manchester became a case study. A case study was appropriate in this context, since it was not possible to conduct meaningful research at more than one politically active university campus because of time and funding constraints of the project. The justification for the use of case studies in these circumstances are widely written about, both at a general methodological level and in the field of social movement studies more specifically (Klandermans & Staggenborg, 2002; Yin, 2009). In short, a single case can be used as an 'analytical generalisation' (Yin, 2009). However, to offset any potential local bias, I used student blogs which were reporting on the occupations and protests from different parts of the country. The statements made by the occupiers clearly stated their moral outrage against fees, which was consistent with the local, University of Manchester, student view.

The main methodology employed within this ethnography consisted of 53 semi-structured interviews with student political activists. Students were asked a series of open-ended questions on their political and moral values, activist biography including their political activities and experiences with social movements and campaigns (McAdam, 1989), their social and political networks and how and why certain methods of recruitment were used to gain support for particular campaigns. Two sampling techniques were used to identify potential respondents. First, purposive, this refers to choosing respondents 'who are nested in particular contexts' (Gray, 2004, p. 324). In this case, I contacted politicos via university student websites, posters and leaflets who were involved in the students union and those who were chairs of the political societies on campus. These respondents were excellent knowledge sources who were involved in the everyday life of political activities, organising and taking part in campaigns and meetings as well as the day-to-day minutiae of campus political life. Having made these contacts, I then employed a second sampling technique, that of snowball sampling, by asking the chairs of political societies and the students' union branch officers to put me in touch with other politicos that they knew on campus. All interviews were recorded and subsequently transcribed and analysed. Although there are biases with these types of sampling, there is little choice when one wants to understand a campus political world. There are no ready-made sampling frames of activists that one can randomly select from. Furthermore, purposely choosing politically active students for this study ensures that every respondent is suitable for interview according to the aims of the project.

Alongside arranging and carrying out interviews, I immersed myself, in so far as is practical, in the everyday life of student politics. I would regularly go to the students' union building to see what events were occurring that day or week and regularly meet with student union branch officers and chairs and members of political societies to find out what, if anything, was happening on or off campus that was politically motivated. Some meetings were simply routine and party political matters, which helped with the aims of the wider project on how and why students become politically active. However, discussions at certain meetings did reveal a moral critique of neoliberalism. I kept field notes during certain events, for example, I observed several occupations and demonstrations that were connected with a wider anti-neoliberal critique of not just the university but with society more generally. These included the occupation of the roof top of the student university union branch of the Royal Bank of Scotland by the group People and Planet, who were arguing that the student population should evict them from the union premises because of perceived unethical investments (February 2009); the student contingent who went along to the G20 Protests in London (March 2009), the Roscoe building occupation as a response to the increase in tuition fees and HE budget cuts (March 2011) and the demonstrations by the University of Manchester branches of University College Union (UCU) and the National Union of Students (NUS) as part of the national protest on 26 March 2011, because of the expected increase in HE tuition fees in light of the Browne review.

The documents collected included posters, flyers, the student union newspaper, the national press and online blogs of universities involved in occupations. The paper documents were mainly used to supplement the other main methods mentioned and to keep me in touch with current political issues on campus. They were a vital resource in informing me when and where meetings or events were to be held. The online blogs, taken together (of which I drew upon 10), provided up-to-date knowledge of the ongoing occupations taking place all around the country. Within these blogs there was a definite sense of political solidarity. Students writing on these blogs were voicing their support for the wider student political community.

The following results are presented through three sections. The first is a national overview of the occupations and protests, which are largely drawn from the national press and online blogs. This section provides information on the wide geographical spread and the numbers involved in the political actions. The second section draws upon my interview data and upon activists' writings on the online blogs. Here, I discuss the social and political dissatisfaction felt by students at what they perceive to be the marketisation and commodification of the university sector, which I argue is a precursor to the moral economy. The third section draws on field notes and online blogs, which discuses students' perspectives on the rise in tuition fees and how the protests constitute a moral economy.

Protests and occupations: a national overview

The NUS organised national protests against the proposals of the Browne review between November 2010 and March 2011. The first was on 10 November and was jointly organised with the UCU (the lecturers union) an estimated 50,000 students turned out to express their opposition. It was the most controversial protest because 200 students broke away from the main demonstration and stormed Conservative Party headquarters at 30 Milbank, London. The demonstrators smashed windows and property and occupied the rooftop. It was estimated that another 1000 students supported this occupation from outside the building. These actions received criticisms from both the president of the NUS (Aaron Porter) and the UCU (Sally Hunt). This infuriated many students and subsequently caused a division between some of the more radical elements of the student protestors and the leadership of NUS (Solomon, 2011, p. 15). In addition to the said unions, the National Campaign Against Fees and Cuts became involved in organising protests on the 24 and 30 November, which included staged walkouts of schools and colleges across the country. On 9 December, the day parliament voted on the proposals, 'an estimated 40,000 students protested in London' (The Guardian, 2010).

As well as local and national marches, around 40 university occupations with a very wide geographical spread took place. In the south of England, occupations were held at the Universities of Plymouth, Bristol, West of England, Kent, East London, London School of Economics, London Metropolitan University, Goldsmiths and Cambridge. In the midlands and North: Universities of Nottingham, Bradford, Leeds, Manchester and Newcastle. For the purposes of this paper, it is interesting to note that major Scottish universities and Scottish students, who are not affected by the increase in fees and cuts in the same way as English Universities, also held occupations in solidarity with their English counterparts at the universities of Edinburgh, Glasgow, Strathclyde and St Andrews (Hensby, 2012, 2013).

Marketisation and commodification as a precursor to the revolts

Revolts as part of the moral economy do not emerge overnight. Marketisation and commodification of a good or service are usually a precursor to such political actions. A revolt is likely to emerge when a price increase is perceived to be a financial barrier to what was once free or considered affordable, and or, the conditions of a good or service are considered inferior to expectations based on a normative understanding of what is value for money. Market reforms of the HE system in parts of the UK have been impacting on the student experience for sometime, arguably, since 1997 when fees were first introduced.

Protests associated with the moral economy are not a matter of a simple price rise of a good, but a systematic implementation of market forces which causes social and political dissatisfaction. It is arguable that the marketisation and commodification of the university sector has been at the root of student dissatisfaction for sometime. This might be inferred from the fact that the government proposals announced on 6 November was followed by a series of protests very quickly (10, 24, 30 and 9 December and so on). For students to mobilise so quickly, it must mean that they were already primed and ready for political action in anticipation for the next round of marketisation in the university sector. To make this claim, the University of Manchester provides a good empirical case study as some of the grievances outlined by the student activists are generalisable to the university sector.

Before I started the research project outlined above, there had been a student political campaign at the University of Manchester called 'Reclaim the University'. This campaign had arisen because students were dissatisfied with the condition of the education they were receiving. This included dissatisfaction with what was considered to be a low amount of contact time (formal and informal teaching), lack of access to lecturers and tutors, lack of feedback from essay assignments and exams and lectures conducted via video link because numbers on courses were too large to fit into one lecture theatre. These issues were interpreted by some students as the university trying to save time, and by implication money, and as such the education as a service good was seen as overpriced. This provoked a political response by some student union candidates who stood on a platform claiming: 'if elected, I will demand a lecturer in front of every student' (i.e. not via video link) or 'vote for me, I am hungry for exam feedback' (evidence derived from election posters during student election campaigns).

In addition to these issues, whenever there was a complaint or sense of dissatisfaction amongst the social science students at the University of Manchester, it often became known amongst staff and students as the 'Arthur Lewis effect'. This referred to The Arthur Lewis building, which houses the social science subjects. It is an open plan building, as such a swipe card entry procedure (for staff and PhD students only) is in place. Undergraduate students must make an appointment in advance to see a lecturer and must phone them from the reception area before being met and allowed in. This building became an object of student grievance at the University of Manchester because it was seen as an embodiment of commodification and marketisation. As one interviewee put it: 'It is the building where lecturers are not accessible,' 'working behind closed doors writing for the Research Assessment exercise' (now Research Excellence Framework) (Interviewee 1). And unable to give students the academic attention they expected. One activist explained that he and others set up the 'reclaim the university' campaign to address 'the commodification of the university'. Part of the campaign included organising 'a large occupation of the Arthur Lewis building' (Interviewee 5). The reclaim the university campaign is particularly interesting since it signified the depth and breadth of discontent amongst the student population. This campaign attracted student politicos from a variety of political societies including Conservative Future, Labour students, Liberal Youth and the Socialist Worker student Society – groups not known for working together politically. Yet, when I interviewed them they all felt that they had been ill treated as students.

To gain further understanding of this from the students' perspective, I asked them their thoughts on the way the HE system was becoming more commodified and subject to market forces. What was striking is that the students I interviewed articulated their particular situation with the wider issues of commodification and marketisation of the university sector more generally. Two interviewees explained their thoughts on this:

> Looking at the commodification and marketization of higher education … I'm paying three thousand pounds a year and I'm getting four hours contact time a week and a glorified library subscription … or you can look at it from a sort of – a much broader national level as well, the introduction of fees has changed the very nature of how we interact with higher education. So you know, before it was – could see it as a pursuit of knowledge and now it's a commodity that you want to get which is a sort of financial investment. (Interviewee 1, January 2009)

> You pay your fees and expect to have a higher paying job at the end of it, and so university suddenly becomes a – a financial investment rather than the pursuit of knowledge as an end in itself. (Interviewee 2, February 2009)

Their comments are applicable to the university sector as a whole, particularly their concerns as regards to lack of contact time, the cost and employment after university.

During the revolts of 2010–2011, students from the occupation at the University of Sussex also framed their critique in terms of being against the marketization of HE and echoed some of the same concerns:

> not only are these cuts damaging our current education, but are changing the face of the education system as we know it. The hole in finances left by government cuts will inevitably be filled by private interest. This marketization of education will destroy the prospect of free and critical academic enquiry, on which universities should be based. ('Statement from the occupation', 2010, p. 1)

In addition to the University of Sussex, the Universities of Manchester, Leeds and East London all held teach-ins, which were attempts to create a community where people could exchange ideas in the spirit of education rather than as consumers.

It is clear from the above critiques that students think the nature of HE has changed from an institution in which the pursuit of knowledge was the end goal to one that now simply functions as an instrumental mechanism for gaining employment. As such, the experience of being a student has become functional and utilitarian. In this respect, the capitalist market (such as charging higher fees) 'has offended against community norms and called into being a "moral" antagonist'

(Thompson, 1993, p. 340 citing Charlesworth & Randall, 1987, p. 213). This is particularly apt in the example of student fees and budget cuts to HE. The encroachment of the free market has clearly created discontent amongst the student population and I would argue that this gives rise to the moral economy of protest.

The moral economy of student protests 2010–2011

It is important to explore Thompson's (1993) arguments outlined in the chapter on the 'moral economy of the crowd' (pp. 185–258). As I have argued above, the student protests cannot simply be understood in terms of the rising price of education. Rather, the protests are under-pinned by a moral economy. Thus, Thompson's arguments are useful for understanding collective action beyond immediate economistic prices rises and to that end help explain why the crowd saw the new price rises of HE as illegitimate:

> By the notion of legitimation I mean that the men and women in the crowd were informed by the belief that they were defending traditional rights or customs; and, in general, that they were supported by the consensus of the community. It is of course true that the riots were triggered off by soaring price rises, by malpractices among dealers, or by hunger. But these grievances operated within a popular dis-course as to what were legitimate and what were illegitimate practices in marketing, milling etc. (Thompson, 1993, p. 188)

The moral economy is a political negotiation between economic rationalisation and cultural norms. Although fees for tuition had been in operation for sometime this recent trebling of fees was considered unfair, unjust and morally wrong. In 2010, student's protestors were of the view that they were defending the traditional right to HE and that the implementation of the new fee structure would hinder some students from less affluent backgrounds from accessing it. Some examples from my field notes express students' moral sentiments about the unjust nature of the increase in fees:

> How are students from working class backgrounds going to afford the new rises? They are not, simple as that! (Interviewee 3, field notes, 26 March 2011)

> Education will be for elites now. Many students won't want to be saddled with that type of debt. (Inter-viewee 4, field notes, 26 March 2011)

The University of Sussex blog reinforces this point:

> The trebling of tuition fees will further exclude another swathe of society and make university acces-sible only to the rich. ('Statement from the occupation', 2010, p. 8)

The very fact that these students who were protesting and occupying would not be affected by the price rises suggests that the political actions are moral and not simply a utilitarian and individual reaction. This mirrors Thompson's argument that the rioters in the eighteenth century were part of wider social and political community who shared similar values and all had a normative under-standing of traditions and entitlements. Thus, protests against price rises are part of an expected response when traditions and entitlements are violated as the following quote suggests:

> [practices were] … grounded upon a consistent traditional view of social norms and obligations, of proper economic functions of several parties within the community, which taken together, can be said to constitute the moral economy of the poor. (Thompson, 1993, p. 188)

In the case of the tuition fees, some of the university authorities explicitly supported the student action, even including occupations. 'The Moral economy includes reference to shared understandings, memories and agreements' (Crossley, 2002, p. 129). This means that even those in authority often share the same values and are sometimes in agreement with the actions of protestors. An example was at Leeds Trinity University from 2010 to 2011. The then Vice Chancellor, Professor Freda Bridge, commented on the protests and occupations taking place at the University:

> We are supportive of their campaign against government cuts in higher education and have worked positively with them to ensure they can carry out their protest. The students initiated a sit-in in December which they have continued to date. (Garner, 2011, p. 2)

The students were even given an office space from which to conduct their campaign:

> By providing them with an office base we placed our trust in them to continue their activities in a peaceful manner and they have respected this by maintaining a well-organized protest that is not disruptive to our business and they have been professional at all times. (Garner, 2011, p. 2)

As well as outright support, there is also evidence of attempting to apply an emollient of sorts. According to the blog pertaining to represent the University of Manchester student occupation, the President (Vice Chancellor) of the University of Manchester made a statement to students during the occupation of university buildings in 2010:

> Let me be absolutely clear; for those of you already enrolled on courses here, there is absolutely no question of your tuition fees suddenly going up. ('Manunioccupation', 2010, p. 1)

> The University will clearly need to adapt to future financial challenges – but we will do so in a way that fulfills our key commitment to delivering an outstanding student experience. ('Manunioccupation', 2010, p. 1)

When there has been a violation of entitlement, Thompson is clear that the authorities and elites realise that part of the moral economy is that a community has a right to defend their tradition when under threat. We see from the above statements that there is an acknowledgement that students have a right to protest against rising tuition fees and cuts to the HE budget. This suggests that the introduction of cuts to the HE budget was seen as illegitimate (normatively speaking) not just by the student population but by some university authorities. This is broadly congruent with Thompson's account of how in some instances Justices of the Peace (JPs) were called to arbitrate between the crowd on the one hand and the marketer on the other hand. The JP would often side with the crowd (Thompson, 1971).

Repertoires of contention

Thompson has argued that collective and direct action was not only a rational response to rising food costs, but also required a consensus of support from the community (1993, p. 238). In actuality, 'the popular ethic sanctioned direct action by the crowd' (1993, p. 212). Such political practices develop over time. Thompson explains that they are 'an inherited pattern of action' (1993, p. 238). These political practices are diffused down from previous generations. Therefore, the riot and other forms of direct action – e.g. seizing food through force and making threats against marketers, bakers, millers, etc. – are all part of the eighteenth-century repertoire of contention. They are learned, rational and bounded by the historical period in which they exist. As Tilly (1995, p. 26) has argued 'repertoires are learned cultural creations … they emerge from struggle. People learn to break windows in protest, attack pilloried prisoners, tear down dishonoured houses, stage public marches, and petition, hold formal meetings, and organize special interest associations'.

As Crossley (2002, p. 18) has argued, protesters' repertoires are selected from a stock available in a particular historical period. In a similar way, occupations, demonstrations, petitions and now blogging are established repertoires of contention for today's students just like the food riot was for the eighteenth-century crowd.

Although we are now in the twenty-first century, and so the political actions of students may seem very different to the peasants in the eighteenth century, there are some important similarities that should be pointed out. The wider student community has shown enough support for fellow students involved in the protests and occupations to constitute the term community. No community is ever totally homogenous, not even an eighteenth-century one. However, my argument is that these student protesters are, by and large, supported by the wider student community and they do share enough common ground to constitute a community. They have certainly demonstrated solidarity with students across a wide geographical spread, in this sense they could be seen as a political crowd. Or why else would there have been 40 occupations in universities from the north to the south of the UK? And by Scottish students who are not even affected by the fee rises? Indeed, a plausible answer can be that students shared a strength of feeling and moral outrage to the rise in fees and cuts in the HE budget. Further evidence can be seen in the statement below which shows support from Universities of London and Sussex after the protestors at Milbank were criticised by the NUS and the UCU:

> We reject any attempt to characterize the Milbank protest as small, 'extremist' or unrepresentative of our movement. We celebrate the fact that thousands of students were willing to send a message to the Tories that we will fight to win. Occupations are a long established tradition in the student movement that should be defended. ('Defend the right to protest', 2010, p. 2)

It is evident too that students chose tangible objects to occupy and/or smash, not to dissimilar to the rational outrage [sic] experienced by pre-industrial communities when the price of bread increased. Farmers' houses were sometimes placed under threat, for example. As Thompson (1993) makes clear it is important to understand the underlying symbolism of the action not just the action itself. This is why students on national demonstrations occupied Milbank and, at the University of Manchester, the Arthur Lewis building, these sites were seen as tangible and symbolic objects responsible for their grievance.

Conclusion

Using new empirical evidence, I have argued that the student protests and occupations of 2010–2011 should be seen as a moral economy (Thompson, 1971, 1993). Analogous to the crowds and mobs of the eighteenth century and the citizens who protested against the poll tax in the twentieth century (Bagguley, 1996; Thompson, 1971, 1993), the students of the twenty-first century are fighting as much against the immorality of the increase in price and unfair practices of those concerned than that of the actual financial increase. There are a number of important analogies in order to make this claim.

The first is marketisation and resultant entitlement violation. The student mobilisations did not happen overnight or even over a year or two. Indeed, for around 16 years we have seen the increasing marketisation and commodification of the university sector which has provoked a number of student protests in different parts of the UK. This latest issue – fees and cuts – provoked a massive response and we saw an upswing in contention because the price set for fees was considered to be too high. This is analogous to the political and rational crowd in the eighteenth century fighting over the rising cost of bread.

It might be questioned how 'bread' in a subsistence economy may be considered the same as 'education' in an advanced capitalist society. This question would miss my point, however. My claim is not that bread in the eighteenth century is the same as education in the twenty-first century, especially because having the former could mean the difference between life and death. Rather, attention should be directed to notions of entitlement and tradition and how violation of these invokes a moral economy. In this case, students believed they were entitled to affordable HE and it is this that has been taken away because of the imposition of market forces.

Second, in a similar way to pre-industrial protesters, the students have no effective mediating institution that they can turn to in order that fees be reversed. The only way open for students to politically negotiate their position is through protest; there is no other way to challenge the market or the politicians who made the decision. Indeed, the NUS does not have any power in Parliament, or elsewhere, to challenge government policy.

This lack of institutionalised power meant that students, just like the pre-industrial protesters, occupied and attacked objects of their grievance they perceived to be symbolic and legitimate targets. This is analogous to the mills and machines which were smashed by crowds in the eighteenth century and toll gates in the nineteenth century when the price of bread increased, livelihoods were threatened, or when rights of way became privatised (Hobsbawm & Rude, 1969). Of course the methods of protests are different, but this is because action repertoires change over time. Nevertheless, demonstrations and occupations were used to attempt a political negotiation against what was perceived to be an illegitimate price increase.

Finally, the idea of community is apparent in both periods. Although students cannot bring sanctions against those who did not participate, it does not alter the fact that the reasons for the grievance are there and as I have argued elsewhere universities produce a critical mass for students to mount campaigns (Crossley & Ibrahim, 2012). Indeed, political communities are formed on university campuses. Students have the resources akin to a political community on campus including media and communication networks to put themselves in touch with other politicos across the campus and the country's multiple universities and it is through these twenty-first century ways of political networking that a community is formed (Crossley & Ibrahim, 2012). Ideas of legitimacy, campaign tactics and general information are shared and are grounded upon similar political values.

Acknowledgements

The initial ideas and some material in this paper were originally written in a rapid response article. I thank Taylor and Francis for granting permissions to reproduce some of the material here. A full acknowledgement is at http://www.tandfonline.com/doi/full/10.1080/14742837.2011.614110.

Funding

Some of the material presented here is based on a research project funded by the Leverhulme trust. I am grateful to the trust for their support.

References

Bagguley, P. (1996). The moral economy of anti-poll tax protest. In C. Barker & P. Kennedy (Eds.), *To make another world: Studies in protest and collective action* (pp. 7–24). Aldershot: Avebury.

Brewer, J. (2000). *Ethnography*. Buckingham: Open University Press.

Browne. (2010). *Securing a sustainable future for higher education*. Retrieved from http://www.bis.gov.uk/assets/biscore/corporate/docs/s/10–1208es-securing-sustainable-higher-education-browne-report-summary.pdf

Crossley, N. (2002). *Making sense of social movements*. Buckingham: Open University Press.

Crossley, N. (2008). Social networks and student activism. *Sociological Review, 56*(1), 18–38.

Crossley, N., & Ibrahim, J. (2012). Critical mass, social networks and collective action: Exploring political worlds. *Sociology, 46*(4), 596–612.

Defend the right to protest. (2010). Retrieved March 26, 2011, from http://teneleventen.wordpress.com

Garner, R. (2011). *Student protest against Leeds Trinity's fee rises is longest sit-in in the country*. Retrieved October 1, 2012, from http://www.independent.co.uk/news/education/higher/student-protest-against-leeds-trinitys-fee-rises-is-longest-sitin-in-the-country-2308061.html

Gray, D. E. (2004). *Doing research in the real world*. London: Sage.

Hensby, A. (2012, September). *'Going to a party where you don't know anybody' – paths and barriers to mobilization in the 2010/11 student protests against fees and cuts*. Paper presented at the Politics, consumption or nihilism: Disorder and protest, the UK and beyond conference, Sheffield Hallam University, Sheffield, UK.

Hensby, A. (2013). Networks, counter-networks and political socialisation – paths and barriers to high-cost/risk activism in the 2010/11 student protests against fees and cuts. *Contemporary Social Science*. http://dx.doi.org/10.1080/21582041.2013.851408

Hobsbawm, E. J., & Rude, G. (1969). *Captain swing*. London: Phoenix Press.

Hubbard, G., & Miller, D. (2005). *Arguments against the G8*. London: Pluto.

Ibrahim, J. (2011). The new toll on higher education. *Social Movement Studies, 10*(4), 415–421.

Klandermans, B., & Staggenborg, S. (2002). *Methods of social movement research*. Minneapolis, MN: University of Minnesota Press.

Manunioccupation. (2010). Retrieved March 26, 2011, from http://manunioccupation.blogspot.co.uk

McAdam, D. (1989). The biographical consequences of activism. *American Sociological Review, 54*(5), 744–760.

McAdam, D., Tarrow, S., & Tilly, C. (2001). *Dynamics of contention*. Cambridge: Cambridge University Press.

McCarthy, J. D., & Zald, M. N. (1977). Resource mobilization and social movements: A partial theory. *The American Journal of Sociology, 82*(6), 1212–1241.

Morgan, J. (2012). 'Exception' becomes the rule as three in four charge £9 K fees. *The Times Higher*. Retrieved March 4, 2013, from http://www.timeshighereducation.co.uk/420686.article

Patel, R. (2009). Food riots. In I. Ness (Ed.), *The international encyclopedia of revolution and protest*. Blackwell Reference Online, Blackwell Publishing. Retrieved from http://www.revolutionprotesten cyclopedia.com/subscriber/tocnode?id=g9781405184649_chunk_g9781405184649571

Patel, R., & McMichael, P. (2010). A political economy of the food riot. *Review, A Journal of the Fernand Braudel Center, 12*(1), 9–35.

Sen, A. K. (1981). *Poverty and famines: An essay on entitlement and deprivation*. New York, NY: Oxford University Press.

Solomon, C. (2011). We felt liberated. In C. Solomon & T. Palmieri (Eds.), *Springtime: The new student rebellions* (pp. 11–16). London: Verso.

Statement from the occupation. (2010). Retrieved August 2, 2011, from http://defendsussex.wordpress.com/2010/11/

Tarrow, S. (2011). *Power in movement*. New York, NY: Cambridge University press.

The Guardian. (2010). Student protests as they happened. Retrieved December 11, 2010, from http://www.guardian.co.uk/education/blog/2010/dec/09/student-protests-live-coverage

Thompson, E. P. (1971). The moral economy of the English crowd in the 18th century. *Past & Present, 50*, 76–136.

Thompson, E. P. (1993). *Customs in common: Studies in traditional popular culture*. New York, NY: New Press.

Tilly, C. (1995). Contentious repertoires in Great Britain, 1758–1834. In M. Traugot (Ed.), *Repertoires and cycles of collective action* (pp. 15–42). Durham, NC: Duke Press.

Traugot, M. (Ed.). (1995). *Repertoires and cycles of collective action*. Durham, NC: Duke Press.

Yin, R. K. (2009). *Case study research: Design and methods* (4th ed.). London: Sage.

Networks, counter-networks and political socialisation – paths and barriers to high-cost/risk activism in the 2010/11 student protests against fees and cuts

Alexander Hensby

School of Social and Political Science, University of Edinburgh, Edinburgh, UK

Why might people sympathetic to the goals of a protest campaign choose not to participate? What distinguishes them sociologically from those who do participate? This paper uses the 2010/11 UK student protests as a case study for understanding how contemporary social movements mobilise individuals for high-cost/risk forms of activism participation. The protests saw large-scale regional and national demonstrations take place, along with the formation of a network of simultaneous campus occupations across the UK, presenting a greater scale and diversity of protest participation opportunities than had been seen for a generation. Nevertheless, students' political background and network access remained significant not only for shaping attitudes towards the efficacy and meaningfulness of protest, but also making protest participation appear an 'available' option. This paper uses interviews with participating and non-participating students from four UK universities to explore the range of pathways to mobilisation for national demonstrations and campus occupations.

Introduction

The final three months of 2010 saw the UK's student population engage in perhaps its most sustained, coordinated and widespread acts of protest for a generation. This followed the publication of the Browne Review into higher education funding in October 2010 and the Conservative–Liberal coalition government's subsequent proposal to increase tuition fees for English students from £3290 to £9000 per year from the 2012/13 academic year, as well as cut 40% from the higher education teaching budget by 2014/15. Much of the public anger was initially directed at Nick Clegg's Liberal Democrats, as the party had campaigned extensively on the issue of higher education in the run-up to the 2010 UK general election, pledging to vote against any parliamentary proposals to increase fees whilst promising to abolish fees altogether if voted into government. When the election result produced no majority victory, however, the Liberal Democrats took the position of junior coalition partners in government with David Cameron's Conservatives. Clegg's decision to reverse his party's position and support plans to increase fees represented a double blow for many young people: not only did it represent defeat on one of the few exclusively youth-based election issues, it arguably reflected an instant betrayal to the thousands of first-time voters targeted by the party's election campaign.

---

†This research was completed with the assistance of an ESRC PhD studentship (ES/I018425/1).

Given the broader context of the 2008/09 financial crisis and successive governments' plans to enact widespread public sector cuts, there had already been tremors of student activism prior to the 2010 election. The Browne Review had been commissioned in 2009 by the preceding Labour government, prompting a number of pre-emptive departmental cuts at universities (Swain, 2011). Amidst growing discontent from independent student campaign groups, the National Union of Students (NUS) announced a national demonstration to take place in London on 10 November 2010.

The NUS demonstration was a remarkable event, unanticipated both in scale and its radicalism. Having attracted the participation of around 52,000 students, with over 100 universities represented (*Guardian*, 10 November 2010a), events soon escalated when a small group of students broke off from the main march to attack the Conservative Party's campaign headquarters at 30 Millbank. With some of the crowd diverging from the main march route to watch events unfold, the building's front windows were smashed and approximately 200 protesters entered inside. This was followed by clashes between protesters and police, culminating in injuries to 14 people – including police and activists – and the arrest of around 50 protesters (*Guardian*, 10 November 2010a).

Although 'Millbank' (as the event came to be known) divided students and was condemned by the NUS, it gave the fees issue a public visibility that inspired more students to take action. With the NUS having distanced itself from the demonstration's more radical elements, students were left to plan a second remarkable event: on 24 November, the National Campaign Against Fees and Cuts facilitated a 'National Walkout and Day of Action', in which a reported 130,000 college and university students took part in protests across the UK (Solomon, 2011, p. 15). This served as a springboard for students staging occupations of campus buildings, with as many as 50 individual occupations taking place between November and December (Solomon & Palmieri, 2011, p. 60). Occupations became spaces for planning protests, negotiating demands with university management, communicating with the media, hosting events, as well as informally discussing and debating political ideas. The protests climaxed with parliament's vote on the government's bill to treble tuition fees on 9 December. A demonstration in London attracted a reported 30,000 participants and featured further violent confrontations between protesters and police, especially once news spread that the bill had been passed, albeit narrowly, by parliament (*Guardian*, 10 December 2010b). With academic term drawing to a close, most campus occupations ended soon after.

As a case study of paths and barriers to mobilisation, the narrative of the student protests gives us much to unpack. Between October and December 2010, the combination of the NUS, student unions and independent activism groups created multiple local, regional and UK-wide opportunities for students to take part in numerous protest activities. Utilising McAdam's (1986) distinction, these ranged from 'low-cost/risk' forms including signing petitions or joining Facebook groups to 'high-cost/risk' activities such as national demonstrations and occupations. This article focuses on paths and barriers to participation in the latter. The unique nature of the university campus gives us an interesting opportunity to study protest participation and non-participation side by side. Previous studies of high-cost/risk participation have tended to focus on explaining those who *do* participate, with non-participants usually considered too diffuse and amorphous to study as a critical mass in their own right. In this article, interviews with students from four UK universities will be used to critically compare the paths and barriers students encounter when broadly sympathetic to a movement's goals. In focusing on specific protest opportunities where participatory costs and risks were relatively similar for all students, one can gain a deeper understanding of the essential motivations and contexts which frame individual action.

Understanding protest participation and non-participation: theoretical approaches

Over the years, theories of social and political movement participation and non-participation have variously focused on the rationality of individual decision-making (Olson, 1965), individuals' emotional and moral engagement with certain issues and grievances (Jasper, 1997) and the collective identities that sustain involvement (Melucci, 1996). Given the unique spatial nature of the university campus, however, it is useful to draw on the work of Crossley (2002) who, following Bourdieu, argues that becoming an activist requires the acquiring of an 'activist habitus' through sustained engagement with activism fields. This places important emphasis on the *process* of gaining such an identity: one does not become an activist simply by choosing to be one – he or she is expected to acquire distinct forms of political knowledge, the social and cultural capital that generate opportunities to participate, and the practical skills and experience gained through participating. This view challenges rational choice assumptions that decision-making processes are highly individualistic by emphasising the *embeddedness* of social agents, where choices, priorities and opportunities are framed by the fields and networks an individual interacts with.

For some activists, the construction of an activism habitus has its roots in family and upbringing. Coles (1986) observes how children learn about the political world through the experiences and attitudes of their family. Political socialisation might involve the specific and comprehensive absorption of values, ideologies and practices or a more basic appreciation for political engagement and self-expression. In their life-course study of youth activist leaders from the 1960s, Braungart and Braungart (1990) found that most had followed the political direction of their parents' politics, albeit in different ways. Some reflected on the influence of their early exposure to activism through parents taking them picketing, whereas for others a more general inspiration came from the significance of activism in their family history. In either case, it is clear that political socialisation equips activists with a political disposition that gives them a head start for taking on activism opportunities later in life.

Of course, not all student activists come to university with an activist background, indicating a need to explain mobilisation beyond simple cultural reproduction. In his study of the conditions that facilitated participation in the 1964 Freedom Summer project, McAdam (1986) argues that applicants were more likely to participate if they already held memberships in other political organisations, had prior activism experience, and knew of friends also applying. The latter especially reflects the *social* costs of decision-making, where fulfilling social obligations and expectations might initially seem as important as the political cause itself. Moreover, applicants with a background in politics and activism might be better equipped to anticipate the costs and risks of participation and prepare accordingly. In contrast, those without such attributes may be more inclined to lose their nerve and withdraw their application, which given their lack of social connections, carries less social burden of 'letting the side down'.

Adapting McAdam's perspective for the university field, Crossley and Ibrahim (2012) depict the modern campus as featuring activist networks which coalesce around certain identifiable foci such as the student union and political societies. Although foci might operate as mobilising agencies for student campaigns, Crossley and Ibrahim argue that the overall *network* is ultimately responsible for developing and sustaining activist identities on campus. This is because it operates as a tightly integrated political world around which 'information, rumours, resources and directives are likely to pass very quickly' (Crossley & Ibrahim, 2012, p. 603). Collective action opportunities are also enhanced by the denser these networks become as this enables activists to keep one another 'in the frame' (Crossley & Ibrahim, 2012, p. 607). In practical terms, this might be facilitated through student activists living together, forming relationships or co-running political groups. Moreover, these networks may draw in other students who are connected to activists in other ways, such as housemates, course-mates, friends, partners or siblings.

Network approaches can also explain aspects of non-participation. Individuals with political interests but no network context through which to participate might find it difficult to seek out protest opportunities. Illustrating this point, Oegema and Klandermans (1994) draw a distinction between 'non-conversion' and 'erosion' in their research on prospective petition-signers in the Netherlands. The first can be explained by individuals' lack of opportunities to convert their support into action, which might come from not being targeted during campaign drives or not belonging to networks which discussed the issue and what they might do about it. As a result, the *lack* of social pressure to think or act causes non-conversion. Erosion, on the other hand, is caused by facing the 'reality' of participation. This might be the result of network 'cross pressures' where cynics or opponents of the issue discourage individuals from acting upon their original willingness. In other words, participating might cause *too much* social pressure and antagonism, thus making non-participation the easier option.

Certainly, protesting involves putting oneself politically 'out there', and this commitment has consequences for how individuals choose to present themselves to their peers. An example of this can be found in Norgaard's (2006) study of attitudes towards climate change activism in Norway. She found that non-participation was often *collectively* managed by individuals through certain shared narratives. An example of this in practice was citizens' use of 'selective attention strategies' to negotiate anxieties over climate change. For some, this involved engaging in certain environmentally friendly activities in order to appear to be doing at least *something*. Others adopted a 'perspectival selectivity' to deflect personal responsibility in favour of narratives that express either an individual's powerlessness to effect meaningful change (i.e. 'my participation does not make a difference so why bother') or the supposed neglect and culpability of others (i.e. 'we might not be perfect, but *they* are far worse').

The desire to maintain favourable images of the self in front of others recalls the social psychology of impression management (Goffman, 1969). In the case of politics this can work both ways: in some contexts, acting upon one's moral code might draw admiration from peers whereas in others participation may incur the risk of 'making a fool of oneself' (Eliasoph, 1998, p. 135). It is therefore important to examine the social context of mobilisation – and how this influences individual decision-making – as much as the mobilisation opportunities themselves.

The study

This paper uses interviews with 41 students from four UK universities – the University of Warwick, the University of Edinburgh, the University of Cambridge and University College London – who as participants or non-participants engaged in some way with the 2010/11 student protests.[1] Interviews took place between March and October 2012 and focused on students' general level of political engagement and their attitudes towards, and interactions with, the student protests. The four universities were chosen on the basis that each featured a certain level of high-cost/risk activism during this time, including campus occupations and union-arranged travel to the NUS demonstration in London. Although this selection should not be viewed as representative of UK universities overall – all are large, wealthy Russell Group institutions – they do provide opportunities to compare the experiences of participants and non-participants who broadly shared the same opportunities to convert their sympathies into action.

The majority of interviewees were recruited through an online survey distributed to students across a range of different departments at each university. In addition, interview recruitment was supplemented by snowball sampling, with interviewees invited to suggest the names of other willing candidates. For accessing students who took a role in planning campus occupations and transport to the NUS demonstration, purposive sampling was used through posting messages on a protest group's blog or Twitter accounts. Interviews typically took place on campus and lasted between one and two hours. Interviewees ranged from students who played an active part in national demonstrations and campus occupations to students who only expressed a passing interest in politics. A degree of representativeness was sought in capturing the story of how each occupation was organised by ensuring that interviews featured a minimum of four students from each university who took an active role in planning and facilitating their occupations.

Results

What follows is an attempt to explore the narrative of the student protests using the various access points through which students mobilised into participating in national demonstrations and occupations. As a counterpoint, these access points are contrasted with the experiences of those who, whilst similarly predisposed politically, did not take part.

Pre-university activist socialisation

All students who played a part in organising occupations in 2010 on their campuses spoke of having had some sort of political background prior to coming to university. Most recalled 'discussing politics around the dinner table' as well as having access to political knowledge and media. Andrew recalled the significance of finding a copy of Bertrand Russell's *History of Western Philosophy* in the family bookcase, whereas Lindsey became interested in environmental politics through having copies of *New Scientist* 'by the loo at home'. For most students in the 2010/11 cohort, their school years coincided with the 2003 anti-Iraq War protests, which provided opportunities to become more politically engaged through reading contemporary writers such as Noam Chomsky and George Monbiot ('the slightly clichéd anti-establishment thinkers' as one recalled). A minority had been taken on demonstrations by their parents – including the 'million march' against Iraq – which helped to give them a familiarity and comfortableness towards protest. For some student, activists, politics and protest played a stronger part in their family history and they were able to speak knowledgably about relatives' experiences and involvements:

> I've been left-wing all my life really – my family is political. My grandfather was very involved in the miners and stuff like that. My aunt was actually a full-time student organiser for a number of years. (Peter, Edinburgh)

> I grew up being aware that when [my parents] were students they went on protests and that kind of thing. Protest has always been something that is kind of like, 'that's what we did'. I know that my mum was at Greenham Common for a while. (Angie, Cambridge)

Although many spoke admiringly of their family's political heritage, most saw only limited overlap between their 'political upbringing' and current activist identity. This generally reflected how much students felt their personal politics had developed during this time. In other words, family background provided activists with the *platform* to embark on their own political journey, which was then driven by a desire to find the most appropriate means of expressing their ever-developing political views. Most described themselves as socialists or anarchists, though many had arrived at this point via membership of political parties or single-issue campaign groups. In contrast, politically *inactive* students had experienced no such comparable journey and consequently found that their political outlook still had much in common with their parents and family. This suggests that family background can produce political *apathy* as well as participation:

> The main reason people vote the way they do is because that's what their parents voted, and I make no pretence that I'm not active because I'm just copying them [...] We're political in that we complain a

lot, but there's never been any kind of 'let's go and make a difference, let's go and protest'. We wouldn't write a letter to our MP or anything like that. (Sharon, Warwick)

For a small number of students, opportunities to become more politically engaged and active came through school. Not only did they have the chance to study politics at AS-Level, they were also influenced by other pupils who already *had* a politically active background, which helped generate opportunities to participate in protests. For these students in particular, their formative experiences of protest had a profound effect on their development and self-identification as 'activists'. For Ronnie and Andrew, both spoke of experiences of witnessing injustice (such as a friend being a victim of racism) and then seeing a related protest action succeed in achieving its goals and empowering its participants. For Andrew and Damon, school provided opportunities to gain experience of mobilising people for protest actions:

> I'd say that I've always been aware of [political] problems, but it wasn't until about 5 or 6 years ago that I ever thought it would be possible to act in a way where you could effect change ... I think the fact that the first demonstration I went on was so effective – that was in Derbyshire, you know the BNP conference? That was considered by the people engaged in it to be a very successful action – it pretty much shut down their conference. (Ronnie, Warwick)

> The first real form of activism I took was when I was in the sixth form the English Defence League had one of their first marches was in Manchester, so I mobilised a group of students from my sixth form to go down to the Unite Against Fascism demo ... It was quite a terrifying experience because it was the first time I'd ever actually done something with my politics apart from read about it. (Andrew, Cambridge)

> I think the Iraq War had a big influence on me. As a school kid I was 14 and spent two weeks organising and taking part in walkouts. That was radical, and it felt invigorating [...] My school was very left-wing, certainly liberal. The head teacher gathered the whole school for an assembly and said 'I know that some of you may be thinking about walking out – I don't really mind'. (Damon, UCL)

Not all activists who participated in the student protests spoke of a politically active background, however. Many recounted having few opportunities to participate in protests due to the lack of an interested peer group, or because they grew in areas where 'nothing really happens' (Jeremy, Edinburgh), suggesting a 'non-conversion' of sorts. A very small number of student activists claimed to have had little interest in politics prior to arriving on campus. Nevertheless, of those who helped to *organise* high-cost/risk protest events in 2010, all spoke at least of political engagement at a formative stage and most had participated in some form of activism prior to coming to university.

The university as a critical mass

For students already-equipped with protest experience, it is perhaps unsurprising that they saw university as an opportunity to build on these experiences by immediately getting involved in political societies, campaign organisation branches and the student union. Many knew what sorts of groups and societies they wanted to join, with some even being able to draw on network links with existing members via activism elsewhere. Similarly, freshers hitherto lacking in opportunities to convert their political interests into political participation saw the campus as providing an important corrective:

> I researched it and found out exactly what I wanted to do before I even came here. I found this little group, so I made contact with them, probably in the first week of being here, or so, and then joined in at that point. (Raphael, Warwick)

> Something that I found really nice about coming to university is that I could get involved a bit more. Part of the reason why I chose King's as my college was because I knew it had a reputation for left-wing politics. (Angie, Cambridge)

Of course, the visibility and accessibility of activism networks depended in many ways on the sorts of network foci available to students. Although research did not extend to a formal social network analysis of campus political worlds, interviewees did touch on the often diverse range of interconnected groups hosted at each university, similar to the network identified by Crossley and Ibrahim (2012) at the University of Manchester. As with Manchester, Cambridge, Edinburgh, UCL and Warwick, all have a student population in excess of 18,000 students – a population size which contributes to the maintenance of a large and well-funded student union.

Nevertheless, it is worth noting that 2006–2009 represented a relative fallow period for student activism at UK universities. As Ibrahim (2010) points out, protest cycles do little to deter already engaged students from getting involved in activism groups on campus, but the lack of mass mobilisation opportunities arguably has a greater effect on those who do not yet self-define as activists. Much therefore seemed to depend on students' halls of residence: some freshers with little prior interest in politics were provided with unexpected opportunities to become more active via their neighbours, whereas others who *had* intended to get involved in politics found that they lacked the appropriate network context. Given the sometimes fragile confidence that might come from entering a new and unfamiliar social setting, Bekka's experience suggests a demobilising effect from encountering network 'cross pressures':

> I remember in first year getting a bit involved in Socialist Worker, and a lot of my friends that I made in halls – who aren't my friends anymore – were kind of like condemning me for that, and didn't really understand the reasons for wanting to get involved more in politics […] I think as well when you're first starting to engage in politics and going on demos, especially if you don't know people, your friends aren't doing it, it can be kind of alien[ating]. (Bekka, Edinburgh)

In some ways, these cross-pressures add a further dimension to Crossley and Ibrahim's (2012) findings, namely that belonging to the *wrong* networks can delay or preclude participation. Bekka's experience also recalls Oegema and Klandermans's (1994) concept of 'erosion': in cases where participating threatens to cause *too much* social pressure and antagonism – especially among friends – non-participation becomes the easier option, with the student trapped in what effectively becomes a political *counter-network*.

The NUS demonstration

At the beginning of the 2010/11 academic year, it was clear to many student activists that tuition fees and university funding cuts were likely to be major mobilising issues. Of the campuses studied, the planning of protest actions in anticipation of the Browne Review's publication coalesced around the larger activism networks typically comprising of the leftist wing of the student union, Trotskyist factions and free education groups. In the initial meetings of the new term, established student activists noted an upsurge in attendance compared to before:

> Some people were involved in setting up something called the Cambridge Left Group ... By the second meeting there were suddenly 80 people there. That was the day after the Browne Report, and we realised that we were entering a different period now. So the Cambridge Left Group became a kind of anti-Browne Review meeting, and it happened every Wednesday and eventually we had to book bigger rooms. (Eric, Cambridge)

Under pressure from activists, student unions provided significant resources for mobilising for the upcoming NUS demonstration on 10 November. Tasked with mobilising students for an 800 mile round trip, Edinburgh's union was especially keen to ensure a strong turnout, to the extent that – according to sabbatical officers John and Peter – it spent around £8000 on hiring five coaches to travel to London with 250 students paying only a £5 deposit (including a free lunch). This arguably helped tip the balance for many predisposed students:

> I was going to go on the demo because a friend – a new friend at uni – said 'let's go on this, it looks like fun'. And so I thought 'yeah, this is what you do at uni: yeah, what a great opportunity – £5 bus to London and back'. (Jeremy, Edinburgh)

> I was aware of it, but it wasn't until I actually received a letter through that mailing list which said why you should go, this is how you sign up, it's only a £5 deposit, you'll get the money back. And then I found out that my flatmate, one of my friends, was going … I decided I would go, but a big concern with going on this trip was not knowing anyone on it – that was a terrifying concern, so it helped that I knew she was going. (Danny, Edinburgh)

Although the union succeeded in making the trip to London appear as easy as possible, the above quotes also highlight the fact that for most people attending a demonstration is a fundamentally *social* activity. For those who had not been on demonstrations before, this social context helped them to share and make sense of the experience. In contrast, the lack of this social context not only removes a key motivation to participate, it might also function as an active motivation for non-participation. Consider the following two quotations:

> I was interested in [politics], but I wasn't an activist. It was just something I didn't encounter in my life until … yeah. I had a boyfriend at Oxford who was incredibly political and as soon as the Browne Review came out, all my friends at different universities were talking about it, and he got involved immediately in organising something. So I was hearing about that a lot, and I was talking about it with my friends, and some of my friends were quite political – not activists – they were keen Labour supporters. But I wasn't. So we were all talking about it, and we decided to go on the first demo which was on 10th November. My whole friendship group went on that march. (Donna, UCL)

> I had my opinions about [the fees increase]. I thought – and still think – that it's absolutely disgusting and it's elitist. But I wasn't really as engaged as I should have been – I didn't go to any of the things in London, and I don't feel guilty about that but I kind of feel that I should have stopped being so lazy and done it. Me and my flatmate were just like, 'oh yeah, we should really go to that, yeah, we should really go, oh whoops, we haven't gone'. (Bekka, Edinburgh)

Having initially struggled to find social opportunities to take part in activism, Bekka did not start regularly participating in protest groups and actions until the following academic year – her last as an undergraduate. In contrast, Donna came to university with comparatively little desire to get involved, yet found herself in a social environment where politics and activism were accepted as relatively normal activities. In this sense, converting her political views into action carried a 'social pressure' similar to those identified by McAdam (1986). For Bekka, however, the lack of these pressures made the thought of going to a demonstration akin to - in her words - 'going to a party where you do not know anybody'.

Interviewees who *did* make it to the NUS demonstration spoke of the overwhelming scale and the atmosphere of the day which many found empowering. Because of this atmosphere, many recalled the storming of Millbank as a seemingly inevitable outcome, as it provided the march with a more suitable climax than the NUS's planned rally and speeches. Nevertheless, Millbank proved a controversial and divisive issue. In the week following, campus activism networks and affinity groups spent time in discussing and analysing what had happened. Whereas some were steadfast advocates, others were uncertain about how Millbank could be *defended* on a political or tactical level. As a result, the debates that took place that week among activist networks were crucial to building a shared consensus on how Millbank should be framed:

> I'd been politically active for a long time but it was the first time I'd been on a huge demo, the first time I'd had to contemplate issues of violence against property as a political statement, so it took me quite a while to let it sink in and analyse it. I spent a lot of time thinking about it myself, and then I started talking to other people about it, bouncing ideas off people – political friends whose opinions I trusted ... and I realised that I'd been thinking about it in a kind of reactionary way. (Andrew, Cambridge)

At this point, many student activists had also become aware that media coverage of Millbank – though often critical – was helping to amplify their grievances surrounding the Browne Review to a wider audience. This not only helped revive a student as activist identity, but also provided students with a sense of agency that defeating the parliamentary bill (still four weeks away) was indeed possible.

University occupations

The week following the NUS demonstration saw public meetings take place on each of the four campuses to formulate ideas on how to take the protests forward. It was in these meetings that activists were able to float the idea of occupations as a means of bringing the 'spirit of Millbank' to individual campuses. Whilst Millbank clearly inspired some activists, however, attending the NUS demonstration was not necessarily converted into participating in the occupations:

> I wasn't involved in the occupation – I remember thinking it was a bit ridiculous. I walked through there a couple of times, saw people, didn't know any of them, and didn't want to approach them! Didn't really understand why they were occupying the university when it had nothing to do with fees, especially in Scotland. (Danny, Edinburgh)

> When I came here I considered myself a left-winger, and then I actually met left-wingers at my college ... they were mental, so I jacked that in quite quickly! (laughs) It's full of the annoying side of the left – vegans and self-proclaimed Trotskyites, people who were living in squats and stuff like it was a political statement or something. (Mick, Cambridge)

> I think it's awful that tuition fees have changed, but I'm not sure than an occupation is the right way to do anything ... It became a place for people partying ... I just saw people becoming 'martyrs to the cause'. Its supporters were in the minority across the university [...] Clubs and societies – zero support. (Louise, UCL)

This withdrawal partly reflected students' lack of network links to make occupying seem a desirable *social* as well as political option. Mick's attitude also indicates that some students might have dis-identified with the *individuals* in occupation, suggesting a symbiotic relationship between networks and identity: although supportive of Millbank, his lack of social connections and identification with participating students meant that he shunned the occupation. This does not necessarily correlate to 'erosion' in the same way as Oegema and Klandermans describe, since opposing the fees increase and participating in high-cost/risk activism are of course two very different things. However, one can argue that certain networks helped *reinforce* narratives of cynicism and dis-identification towards the occupation through processes similar to those described by Norgaard (2006). Louise, for example, was anti-fees but claimed to have had little in the way of a political background. As an English student and member of UCL's boat club, she belonged to two contrasting networks – the former had a critical mass of supportive and participating students and the latter, she claimed, had neither. Her membership of the latter network – combined with the lack of a politically active background – was mutually reinforcing and ultimately overrode the activism opportunities she had as an English student.

Nevertheless, occupations *did* attract the participation of many students with little or no experience of protest. Due to the need to organise semi-covertly (so as to avoid alerting university management of their intentions) participation in their organising relied strongly on existing networks of experienced activists. Crucial to an occupation's establishment was achieving a critical mass of participants that could outnumber security staff and 'hold the room'. Activists at Edinburgh and Warwick consequently adopted a strategy that in many ways replicated the Millbank occupation the previous fortnight: with student unions having agreed to organise a local march on 24 November, activists disseminated ideas for occupation through the crowd, so that a sizeable number then followed them to their intended destination. Although numbers dropped off once the march adopted this tactical switch, both occupations were successful in attracting upwards of 200 students to their intended locations.

UCL took an even more daring approach. Activists advertised and then staged a mock rally, promising to lead its students to the main demonstration in central London. Instead, they left UCL only to march back onto campus and occupy the Jeremy Bentham Room. This had the advantage of effectively tricking many of the students on the march into occupying and whilst some quickly left for their originally intended destination, the occupation was boosted by a sizeable number of anti-fees students who had not expected to find themselves engaged in direct action but decided to stay on.

Cambridge had initially planned their occupation in much the same way as Edinburgh and Warwick, but had found their intended location – the Old Schools Combination Room – had been locked up by facilities staff. Consequently, a group of students planned to stage an occupation a few days later. This was akin to a military operation in which a group of 20 students occupied the Combination Room at 10 am, followed by another 20 students who locked the doors. Occupiers then called, texted and emailed their friends inviting them to come and join, as well as putting word out through Facebook and the student press. Although the occupation did not spontaneously attract participants in the same way as the others did, it nevertheless attracted over 100 students by the first evening.

Despite the relative openness in how they mobilised students, one can generally observe that occupations drew heavily on pre-existing networks and affinities. Significantly, all occupants interviewed were able to identify at least two pre-existing friendships to other attendees, though the more experienced activists were likely to be better connected than first-year undergraduates. As a result, some who had been drawn in via affinity networks found themselves initially unsure of their role as occupants:

> I know so many people that were like me that came in on the first day of the occupation and kind of got involved because there was this massive spirit of 'we're doing something amazing here'. Within a couple of hours they realised that they didn't really have a place to fit in. Lots of people had friends already there that were vaguely politically active, and were just like 'I believe in this cause but I have no idea of what you're talking about; texts you've read from a hundred years ago' ... it was so alienating. Luckily I had this tiny little thing with Twitter which meant that I had a *role*, [otherwise] I would have felt really, really obsolete. (Justine, UCL)

> I think I was just intellectually a bit out of my depth, but I stayed because I wanted to learn and hear all the stuff and decide what I thought about it ... It was me and a close friend who both came from the same position where we hardly knew anyone. We liked the people who were there; we just didn't know them very well. (Rhiannon, Edinburgh)

To get students more involved, activists with previous experience in occupations were keen to establish working groups – process, media, kitchen, etc. – to engage students who whilst lacking in activism experience might have other valuable skills to offer. Over time,[2] however, the process of socialising and sleeping at the space, organising in working groups and attending daily meetings built strong ties between participants. Moreover, the fees issue arguably helped publicise the occupations as much as the occupations helped publicise the fees issue, which helped bring likeminded students on campus together and make connections. This helped spread the experience of high-cost/risk activism outwards to less active students:

> It was almost like a beacon. So for instance, my girlfriend had never done anything political ever, and her friend got involved in it and a guy that she knew – a PhD student who was working at the coffee shop she went to – gave her a leaflet, and she looked at it and saw that her mate was going along and decided to go with him. And now that's opened her up to a whole new group of people and a whole new set of ideas. (Eric, Cambridge)

> People invited their friends to come – like, my brother came to visit; people from other universities when their occupations ended, they came down, like, all the Oxford lot came and stayed for a bit. (Donna, UCL)

> It was mostly King's people there – partly because it was next door to King's. And people from other colleges who came in were like, 'oh, it's always all King's people'. So I guess you're drawing from a slightly different pool of people, people who weren't necessarily even that interested in politics, who were vaguely onside, but they were coming up because that's where people were hanging out on an evening. (Angie, Cambridge)

As the above quotes suggest, students' routes to joining occupations operated mostly via existing social ties. To attract the more distantly connected, occupations employed multiple outreach strategies, including holding talks and debates as well as social events such film screenings and ceilidhs. There was also an information desk during the day for students to visit and discuss issues. Although occupants recalled mostly positive responses from visitors, accounts from both sides suggest invisible barriers in terms of converting engagement into action:

> In the lobby we had tables out where people would be sat all day, talking to students. So we would be engaging with people that way, we had people out flyering. On campus people were unsure of what to make of it, because this is very much something new. So people weren't saying 'oh no, we disagree with this' or anything, there were just lots of people saying, 'yeah, it's quite right that you're doing this' – not committing themselves, but saying 'yeah, I agree'. (Jeremy, Edinburgh)

> Most of the people who I actually hang out with face-to-face are sort of in the same boat as me – they think these things are terrible but will not necessarily actually go out and join in a protest […] I think Appleton Tower was occupied for a while and I had classes in there, so I would walk past and they would have a banner and stuff and a little table saying 'ask us about occupy' kind of thing. And I was just, like, looking at this and thinking 'this is good', and just continued on! (laughs) It was like, 'I support this' but I'm not going to sleep in Appleton Tower, or whatever they were actually doing. (Rick, Edinburgh)

In general, sympathetic students who paid brief visits to occupations tended to cite a lack of available time to devote to getting more involved. Again, a key differential is their apparent network position. For participants such as Justine, Donna and Angie, their mobilisation was influenced by (friendly) social pressure from their peers, whereas non-participants such as Rick, Danny and Mick lacked the equivalent network context through which comparable social expectations might have arisen. As such, none recalled feeling particularly 'guilty' or self-conscious about their non-participation. Louise, however, belonged to both 'pro' and 'anti' social networks. Having sided with the latter, she recalled the student protests soon becoming an awkward conversational 'no-go area' when in the company of her politically active course-mates.

Of course, the prospect of sleeping in a lecture theatre and participating in daily meetings and working groups whilst maintaining their academic study is what makes occupying a high-cost/risk activity, especially considering that many non-participants admitted to not understanding the connection between opposing government legislation and occupying a room on campus. Whilst this raises broader questions about the perceived efficacy of certain protest repertoires, it is also worth considering that these views did not differ significantly from the initial thoughts of many who *did* occupy. Most occupants had little expectation of occupations lasting as long as they did, let alone sleeping over for most of its duration. For those with little prior activism experience, their initial *social* motivations laid the foundations to their deeper involvement and commitment over time. Indeed, the experiences gained from participation by the end were often more profound than they ever could have expected – experiences that understandably proved difficult to translate to those on the other side of the 'welcome' tables:

> I had expectation of being part of an occupation, although I was, like, I really need to work on my PhD – I'll go there for two days at the very most, try and sneak a bit of work in as well ... [but] I found it a really intensive, fast-track learning experience, just coming into contact with all these people from different political traditions, people coming to talk to us: unionists, academics, activists, journalists; taking part in negotiations with management...So yeah, it was a big learning experience for me, definitely. (Brett, UCL)

> I said this to my tutor the other day 'I love everything I've done in this degree and I've had such a good time, but the three weeks I spent in the first UCL occupation I learned more than I have in my entire three years at UCL ... ' There aren't even words to say the amount that I changed in that three weeks, it's ridiculous. (Justine, UCL)

> Looking back it was kind of the golden days of the anti-cuts group ... Lots of friendships. Almost all of my friends are from that group. And my girlfriend as well. (John, Edinburgh)

Conclusion

By its very nature, high-cost/risk activism demands more from its participants than other forms of protest. At a fundamental level, the time and resources required of demonstrations and occupations make it easier for certain people to participate than others. On campus, however, the differentiation of biographical availabilities is arguably narrower than in other fields. Whilst this can vary more with international students and postgraduates, students nevertheless have much in common. A key differential found in interviews is the expectations students have of getting involved in politics and activism when they first arrive at university: certainly, those already with knowledge and experience are better resourced to quickly get involved in activism. In contrast, individuals without such a background have to work hard over time to catch up with their more experienced peers.

Among those wishing to catch up, students relatively well-connected to activist networks were placed at a clear advantage. Such connections sometimes had little initial basis in politics, reflecting friendships established in halls of residence, but in any case it meant that they were well-placed to convert their political interests into participation. One can also argue that these social networks are more likely to be converted into political networks during times of 'political opportunity' for activism. This was certainly true of the student protests against fees and cuts – the issue was simple for students to take a position on and resonated particularly with those who voted in the 2010 election. Furthermore, the parliamentary vote gave the protests a clear goal which many felt was achievable.

To explain the *non*-participation of sympathetic students, we can broaden Oegema and Klandermans (1994) notion of 'erosion' to consider the possibility of counter-networks which (at least temporarily) neuter students' desires to convert their political interests into action. This could occur through explicit arguments made against participation or by more implicit means, i.e. where participation had no precedent in the group or was collectively a low priority. For students without a background in politics and activism, overcoming these barriers to participation might have seemed socially costly, especially when the costs of participation were high with few perceivable rewards.

Of course, one should be resistant to framing mobilisation as a socially deterministic process: clearly, it remains possible for individuals to participate in activism *without* possessing strong network ties or a political background. One may question whether individuals with certain personalities or identities might be more predisposed to overcome a lack of network opportunities or withstand erosion and ultimately 'go to a party where they do not know anybody'. Certainly, the social and political science literature from McAdam (1986) to Jordan and Maloney (2007) has identified those who are habitual 'joiners' as more likely to convert their interests into collective action. This may have its roots in socialisation processes – where individuals have both the opportunity and the encouragement to try their hand at new things – as well as psychology. In this sense, the interaction between network opportunities and self-identity requires closer examination for studies in political mobilisation.

Notes

1. All names of interviewees have been changed in this article.
2. Warwick's occupation lasted one night and so is not included in the following discussion.

References

Braungart, M. M., & Braungart, R. G. (1990). The life-course development of left- and right-wing youth activist leaders from the 1960s. *Political Psychology, 11,* 243–282. Retrieved from http://www.jstor.org/stable/3791689

Coles, R. (1986). *The political life of children*, Boston, MA: Atlantic Monthly Press.

Crossley, N. (2002). *Making sense of social movements*. Buckingham: Open University Press.

Crossley, N., & Ibrahim, J. (2012). Critical mass, social networks and collective action: Exploring student political worlds. *Sociology, 46,* 596–612. doi:10.1177/0038038511425560

Eliasoph, N. (1998). *Avoiding politics*. Cambridge: Cambridge University Press.

Goffman, E. (1969). *The presentation of self in everyday life*. London: Allen Lane.

Guardian. (2010a, 10 November). *Demo 2010 student protests – live coverage*. Retrieved from http://www.guardian.co.uk/uk/blog/2010/nov/10/demo-2010-student-protests-live

Guardian. (2010b, 10 December). *Prince Charles and Camilla caught up in London violence after student fees vote.* Retrieved from http://www.guardian.co.uk/education/2010/dec/09/charles-camilla-car-attacked-fees-protest

Ibrahim, Y. (2010). Between revolution and defeat: Student protest cycles and networks. *Sociology Compass, 4,* 495–504. doi:10.1111/j.1751-9020.2010.00289.x

Jasper, J. (1997). *The art of moral protest*. Chicago: University of Chicago Press.

Jordan, G., & Maloney, W. (2007). *Democracy and interest groups*. Basingstoke: Palgrave Macmillan.

Melucci, A. (1996). *Challenging codes: Collective action in the information age*. Cambridge: Cambridge University Press.

McAdam, D. (1986). Recruitment to high-risk activism: The case of freedom summer. *American Journal of Sociology, 92,* 64–90. Retrieved from http://www.jstor.org/stable/2779717

Norgaard, K. M. (2006). 'People want to protect themselves a little bit' emotions, denial and social movement non-participation the case of global climate change. *Sociological Inquiry, 76,* 372–396. doi:10.1111/j.1475-682X.2006.00160.x

Oegema, D., & Klandermans, B. (1994). Why social movement sympathizers don't participate: Erosion and nonconversion of support. *American Sociological Review, 59,* 703–722. Retrieved from http://www.jstor.org/stable/2096444

Olson, M. (1965). *The logic of collective action.* Cambridge, MA: Harvard University Press.

Solomon, C. (2011). We felt liberated. In C. Solomon & T. Palmieri (Eds.), *Springtime: The new student rebellions* (pp. 11–16). London: Verso.

Solomon, C., & Palmieri, T. (Eds.). (2011). *Springtime: The new student rebellions.* London: Verso.

Swain, D. (2011). The student movement today. *International Socialism, 130,* 95–112. Retrieved from http://www.isj.org.uk/index.php4?id=723&issue=130

Something's wrong here: transnational dissent and the unimagined community

Brian Callan

Social Sciences, Loughborough University, Loughborough, UK

Based on ethnographic research in 2011–2012 this paper explores the production of a transnational community through various dissenting practices in Israel–Palestine. In a critique of instrumental and structural approaches to transnational dissent, from micro-level framing processes to the macro-level concepts like Global Civil Society (GCS) and networks, it builds understandings of the affective dimensions of protest and proposes that a transnational community is being produced through a shared feeling of *wrongness*. Drawing upon recent reassessments of community conceptualisations [Amit, V., & Rapport, N. (2002). *The trouble with community: Anthropological reflections on movement, identity and collectivity.* London: Pluto; Djelic, M.-L., & Quack, S. (Eds.). (2010a). *Transnational communities: Shaping global governance.* Cambridge: Cambridge University Press; Rapport, N., & Amit, V. (2012a). *Community, cosmopolitanism and the problem of human commonality (anthropology, culture and society)* (Kindle.). London: Pluto Press], this paper asks why the moral actors from GCS limit their imagined community in spatial terms. In a world of movement, where the everyday practice of community is as likely to be defined through shared worldviews as it is though shared place, the challenge is to ask how we may engage in recognising and re-imagining transnational activism as not merely an episodic and instrumental *gesellschaft* but as a praxis of fluid, interconnected and self-reproducing *gemeinschaften*.

Introduction: imagining the community

> Positive change does not come quickly and demands ongoing effort. If we become discouraged we may not attain even the simplest goals. With constant, determined application, we can accomplish even the most difficult objectives. (Dalai Lama, n.d.)

For millennia Jerusalem has been a crossroads and a destination, a site of transnational social emplacement where armies triumphed and retreated, merchants paid their toll and kept their piece and migrants and pilgrims came and went and stayed. The city is a repository of the unending cultural accretion of thoughts, tongues, texts, deaths and lives that touch upon its hills. Today 'pro-Palestinian' activism is a significant contributor to these ongoing processes and the practices of Palestinians, Israelis and Internationals coming together are clearly producing a community of sorts. In addition to the instrumental practices like demonstrations, documentation and dissemination, there are also avenues for occupational specialisation, economic channels and spaces and occasions for casual socialisation.

The notion of community is used by this highly heterogeneous collective of dissenters. However, it is often imagined to be small weak and fractured. Its boundaries are thought to terminate at municipal or state borders and it is fractured along ideological spectra, prognoses and tactics. The categories used by members to describe the community reflect traditional and idealised understandings of community, as a geographically bounded population which possesses a relatively harmonised outlook on the world.

Contemporary research of transnational social processes in fields such as economics, international relations, migration studies, knowledge production and global elites are decoupling the notion of community from 'place' and finding communities of 'purpose', 'practice', 'episteme' or 'interest'. Building on this body of work, this paper asks why the field of transnational activism studies has 'on the whole not used or appropriated the term "community", preferring terms such as "networks" or "social movements"' (Djelic & Quack, 2010b, p. 40). This absence also highlights certain problematics that the practice of transnational activism poses for established paradigms and concepts in social movement theory, at both the micro-level specificities of framing process theory and the macro-level abstraction of Global Civil Society, and the metrics used to describe and analyse the concept.

In the first instance, framing process theory or collective action frames are found to be more divisive than cohesive and often unsuitable for addressing the elusive and fluid nature of contemporary transnational power and resistance. Emphasising both social and psychological dimensions, framing process theory has developed richly since Goffman's early work, providing in-depth analyses of a crucial component of social movement practice. Originally conceived as schemata of interpretation 'rendering meaning, organizing experiences, and guiding actions' (Goffman, 1974, p. 21), frames are now understood as complex, contested and cascading processes which must resonate on both cognitive and affective dimensions (Borah, 2011; Gould, 2004; Schrock, Holden, & Reid, 2004). Yet, between the local and the global, the transnational dimension of contemporary dissent challenges the effective development of collective action frames which can resonate across cultures and social-groups (Bennett & Segerberg, 2011; Olausson, 2009).

Moreover, terms such as Global Civil Society (GCS) and Transnational Networks are structural abstractions which though descriptively and analytically powerful can obscure the affective and potentially productive dimension of 'belonging' that community affords. By the turn of the millennium, GCS was an idea of 'unusual promiscuousness' (Keane, 2003, p. xi) employed both by academics as a major sociological potential (Beck, 2005) and by proponents as 'an expression of the love of life, freedom, community and democracy that resides deep in the soul of every human being' (Korten, Perlas, & Shiva, 2002). Like grand ideas such as nation or society, GCS has always been a fuzzy concept, at once manifest yet difficult to empirically define.

Network analysis proved a sophisticated and empirically grounded methodology from which to approach the various emergent instances of GCS. Its tool kit allows us to compare how signature characteristics facilitate goal achievement, communication flows and mobilisation processes, the extensity, intensity and velocity of its macro-structure and the constitution of global public spheres through hyper-network structures of inclusion and exclusion (Anheier & Katz, 2004).

Though well suited to describing and analysing transactional exchanges, many affective dimensions of dissent have also been addressed through network concepts. Juris (2008) in particular highlights how the shared experiences of intense emotions at mass events like Seattle, Prague or Athens generate affective solidarity, which is 'particularly important with fluid, network based movements that rely on non-traditional modes of identification' (p. 63). Nonetheless, in the tension between descriptive and normative capacities of social sciences there is always the problem of reifying our object of analysis through our methodology and our abstractions can become essences in the minds of academics and its practitioners alike. Pro-Palestinian[1] dissenters are keenly aware that they are part of a transnational network and they do imagine themselves as belonging to such a structure.

However, in this paper I wish to suggest that another significant affective process is occurring but is overlooked both by academics and practitioners, the practice of community. I believe that this affective consequence of dissent may be significant for just as the sense of community belonging is leveraged by major polities to promote cohesion and durability (Anderson, 1991; Berezin, 1999, 2001; Billig, 1995), it is possible that by imagining themselves as part of a wider transnational community dissenters may also overcome fragmentation and fatigue.

Community is also a fuzzy subject having both concrete and constructed connotations (Olwig, 2002). Certainly there are concrete relationships involved and as with any community these may come to be defined through both friendship and enmity, but I suggest that the practice of dissent by a diverse and distributed population is also akin to what is normally seen as an imagined community. This is partially a consequence of the ongoing nature of the conflict for, in contrast to the intense affect of mass mobilisation described by Juris, dissent sociality in Israeli and Palestine is shaped by long duration, scheduled protest and the interim and uneventful daily routine of being a dissenter. Though there are often intense confrontations, these happen mostly on Fridays and Saturdays in locations far removed from each other. Many members of the professionalised dissenters, those in local or international NGOs may not even attend or are contractually prohibited from participation in such events. In the weekly interval between protests there may be special actions organisations or the ongoing efforts of NGOs. But there are also the unspectacular and banal everyday practices of daily life such as the meeting of friends, family and colleagues, going shopping, writing emails, dropping the kids off to school or going or taking the bus. However, over time it is precisely through such familiar and concrete routines and faces that we come to feel we belong (Rapport & Amit, 2012a).

The established choreography of weekly protest in Israel and Palestine, the specific places in time where protests are organised, lead to 'emplaced sociality' (Pink, 2008) in which diverse backgrounds converge and share experiences and feelings which in turn enable the future sharing of those stories with others and the recognition of those experiences amongst peoples whom have never actually met. This is as much an imagined community as Anderson (1991) could have conceived of, though not one controlled by a constructed collective memory but by a shared sense that *something is wrong*. This feeling of wrong need not amount to or be sustained at the level of 'moral outrage' (Nepstad, 2004; Nepstad & Smith, 2001; Risley, 2012; Warren, 2010) but it has been felt wrong enough for long enough to bring people to particular places in Israel and Palestine. The emplaced sociality continues in the days between demos where quiet streets, shops, schools and offices are also shared sites of dissent sociality and in which participants become as loosely, intimately or indirectly familiar as the people meet each Friday. Though the concrete community is certainly experienced, there is a wider and fluid population of unmet dissenters whose emplacement happened at different times and places but whom nonetheless share the sense of wrongness. It is the imaginable yet unimagined community which this paper addresses.

The present paper is based on 12 months ethnographic research which began in October 2011. The field was approached through the Israeli contingency by regularly attending two weekly protests in Jerusalem. Methodologically I did not join any particular movement or place of protest and was not closely involved with the strategic workings of an organisation or ideological goals of a protest. Following Jean-Klein's (2003) lateral ethnography, I limited my own inclinations and followed the movements and suggestions of participants. This approach resulted in an emphasis on the social aspects of dissent over the strategic or instrumental. I begin by describing a typical weekend protest routine which brings together a highly heterogeneous group of activists on a regular basis.

Even within this small gathering, which constitutes only a fraction of the concurrent protests in the region, there is an impressive diversity of critiques and imagined solutions. Examining this diversity highlights the utilitarian limits of framing processes when transnational activism opposes diffuse power systems. Nonetheless, a high degree of unity is achieved by the consensus that something is wrong. Following on from Prinz' (2007) equation of morality with non-cognitive affective appraisal, the elusiveness of transnational framing is overcome and the uncodified moral impetus of GCS is found to function well enough (Beck, 2005; Keane, 2003). Taking this embodied judgement to be the shared motivator, I suggest that despite the 'moral multiverse' by which the diversity of actors come to practice dissent the shared feeling of wrongness in turn produces a sociality that is equivalent to what we can call 'community-like' practice. In focusing on the strategic outcomes and reifying network abstractions, academics may be overlooking the sense of community which may be crucial in dissent's ability to reproduce and endure over time (Jasper, 2011). In doing so, we also fail to legitimise such practices as being community in the imagination of dissenters. With this paper, I hope to contribute to the large body of work on emotion, morality and social movements and to be 'movement relevant' by arguing that dissenters may access the positive potential and greater extent of community, if they can legitimately imagine it so (Berezin, 2001; Bevington & Dixon, 2005; Goodwin & Jasper, 2004; Goodwin, Jasper, & Polletta, 2001; Gould, 2004).

Who are we? Protest demographics and discourses in Jerusalem

There are places across Israeli and Palestine where the sociality of dissent occurs. Some, like the regular weekend protests, are scheduled in time and space. Others, like the cafes, bars, info-centres and offices, are available during trading times and yet more like the city streets, the private homes and the social media sites afford random access. Below I provide a description of a one Friday's fieldwork in which out of the dozen or more weekly protests occurring across the region I visited two in Jerusalem. Fridays and Saturdays are routine for these are the days on which protest is regularly scheduled. Perhaps routine is the key notion in the case of Israel and Palestine. Of the two events, *Sheikh Jarrah* has been held every week since 2009 and the *Women in Black* have been holding their vigil for over 25 years. The main tactical consideration is to persist and so the same Palestinians and Israelis come to practice dissent together week after week and year after year. Additionally, these protest performances are, like tourist honey-pots and Broadway musicals, well known and accessible to International dissenters throughout the year. Though they may come and go, Internationals from all over the world also have the ability to exchange common experiences of place, protest, emotions and critique even though the sharing occurred at different moments in time. I consider the diversity of critique found at these protests and the use of complexity as a barrier to social change, before considering the potential of community as an unintended and unimagined product of taking action when something feels wrong.

I leave the kids off to nursery on Friday morning before getting a message that the protest at *Walaja* is called off so I go to West Jerusalem to join the weekly silent vigil held by *Women in Black*. Dina who keeps the black hand-shaped placards usually arrives first with Tanya. They are joined by half a dozen, other Israeli women dressed in black. About three to five Internationals with the Ecumenical Accompaniment Programme in Palestine and Israel (EAPPI)[2] also arrive. They are volunteers on three-month rotations in the region and their movement between protest sites or security checkpoints is dictated by their coordinator. I met Mia and Marco here on my first day in the field, she from Finland and he from Switzerland had also just begun their three-month placements with the Jerusalem team.

The vigil is laid out along three sides of *Kikar Paris*, a small square that sits between four of the Western city's major thoroughfares. Given the small size of the group, which is usually no more than 20 people, the protest body is dispersed in clusters rather than grouped together. I usually chat with a few different people catching up on the weekly news both personal and political and keeping an eye on fellow protesters being angrily berated or insulted by passers-by. The silent vigil has gathered here in West Jerusalem every Friday for the last 26 years calling *Di LaKibush*.[3] Having abjectly failed to achieve this end I asked Tanya why they continue? 'We keep this space open, so that people know they can come here on any Friday'. At the stroke of two the women greet the end of the vigil with smiles and light-hearted relief. There is small bustle of chit-chat as everyone comes back together to return the placards to Dina's bag and with a criss-cross of *Shabbat Shaloms* everybody heads on their way.

This leaves me an hour or so to cross the city centre to the weekly protest in *Sheikh Jarrah*. The distance is walk-able and takes you from predominantly Jewish West Jerusalem, up to the Old City walls and down past the commercial heart of predominantly Palestinian East Jerusalem at *Bab al-Amud*.[4] On the way, there is enough time to drop into the Educational Bookstore on *Salah Ad-Din* Street. Mia and Marco had told me about this place, full of books in English relating to the conflict and cappuccino and cakes. The EAPPI teams are brought here as part of their induction training. This is also where I met Avner properly for the first time, a young Israeli man whom I would have seen several times before at *Sheikh Jarrah* chanting out slogans in Arabic over the mega phone. In the quiet proximity of the bookshops, our glances of recognition turned to handshakes and first names exchanged and we walked on down the road together to join the *Sheikh Jarrah* protest at four.

Dina and Tanya are usually parking by the time I get there. I see Mia and Marco with some others from the EAPPI and am drawn by their smiles. A handful of local men who have been evicted or face eviction from their homes constitute the core of the group. One brings a fine frilled Palestinian flag on a long pole. Occasionally other locals join, children play with crayons and Palestinian activists from the Hebrew University turn up. A regular group of Israelis bring a mega phone and a bag of placards. Sometimes the *Yasamba* drummers add volume to the protest. There are activists with *Ta'ayush, B'Tselem, Breaking the Silence* and any number of Israeli left-wing organisations, visitors from the *International Solidarity Movement* and fact-finding Christian missions. Some people take signs from the bag and stand by the road side or around the samba band and join in the chants, but the majority hang back in small intimate groups, surprised and smiling when they meet someone they have not seen for a while. Its normally quiet, there are no police here now and only occasionally tensions rise with some of the Jewish settlers who now live in the evictees' homes. At the end of the protest the activists disperse, heading home perhaps or to meet friends or prepare for Friday dinner. I head to *Uganda*, one of a few places in West Jerusalem that stays open on *Shabbat*.[5] It is usually quiet at this time and I write up my field notes, but often others I know drop-in at this time. Like Nur who I recognised from a march in Tel Aviv. She is here to meet Rachel, a Jewish activist arriving from England and we talk over beer and humus. Rachel kindly offers me a place to stay in London for my upcoming conference.

Though initiated and led by local Palestinians, the *Sheikh Jarrah* protest is not particularly constituted either by the local community or a particular movement. This is generally true of most of the weekend protests which are impressively transnational in their make-up but number less than 100 people at best. Not present at the protest are teams of lawyers engaged in the ongoing court cases deliberating the evictions. The Norwegian Refugee Council, which along with several other local and major international NGOs are based in the area, also coordinate some of the legal assistance. Journalists, researchers and various other agencies monitor, assist, publicise and interject in *Sheikh Jarrah* in various ways. This is a snapshot of a moment in the dissenting community in Israel and Palestine. The protest is temporal social 'performance' in Turner's (1988) terms which for an hour or two brings together people from various neighbour-hoods, cities, countries and predilections. Aside from a few organisers and shapers of the protest practice, the majority are not fully engaged with a given script for this performance. It is not a Durkheimian cohesion ritual focused on a collective totem (Durkheim, 1912) nor a carnival affair or intensely affective direct action event (Juris, 2008). Some chant, some do not, some do not like certain slogans, the volume of the drums annoys one while others do a little shimmy. Mostly people are sitting or standing in small groups chatting casually and on the whole participation is fluid, informal and elective. I began to explore the various understandings of the situation by appropriating the classic protest chant and asking participants 'What are we fighting for?'

The moral multiverse

Nilli: 'What are we fighting for – oh that's a hard one – we're fighting for different things you see – I don't know, can I get back to you on that'

Vered: 'I'm fighting so I can go camping, hiking at the weekend. I want a normal life'

Moshe: 'I could give you the political answer, justice, equality, bla-bla-bla, but I just want to live in a normal city. Like Montreal'

Khalid: 'This is not political this is social'

Kate: 'I'm here in solidarity with the Palestinians'

As the above responses demonstrate, ideological discourse is also fluid and relatively un-ascribed. While Palestinian national flags are present and the chants call out 'Free Free Palestine', such overtly nationalist symbols and notions are often rhetorical devices. This is true even for the Palestinian organisers, as Khalid's statement shows. Though in many imaginations the Two State Solution is the obvious answer, Farouk from *Al-Tariz* tells me he does not care what flag flies 'so long as I'm left alone to build a house and raise my family, find work – that's what peace is'. Amongst Internationals, Palestinian national liberation and justice are strong tropes, as is anti-Semitism according to one Israeli activist. Others talk of respect for Human Rights or liberal democratic values, while some defer judgement saying they are on 'fact-finding' tours. Israeli critiques and visions of the future are also fragmented. While the *Women in Black* call for an end to occupation, Yigal from *B'Tselem* thinks this 'a rather outdated notion'. The One State Solution is openly posited while another sees hope in the future primacy of urban polities and focuses his efforts on Jerusalem. Subjective critiques are unfolding and coming to *Sheikh Jarrah* has also changed peoples' perceptions. Moshe, an Israeli citizen raised in the USA 'came to *Sheikh Jarrah* a classic left-Zionist Two State activist ... after that year I was an anti-Occupation activist'. Tomer, who had never protested, came here because he 'did not think it was right that the police were arresting people' and is now with *Anarchists Against the Wall*.

Sheikh Jarrah is fairly typical of much of the 'Popular Committee' form of protest activity which has been prevalent for the past decade or more. Its focus is a particular localised instance of dispossession, it insists on being peaceful and avoids overt alliance to the major Palestinian political parties. It invites Israelis and Internationals to join and persists in the face of physical coercion and incarceration by state and private security agencies. These protests are all monitored by numerous Palestinian, Israeli and international NGOs, journalists, filmmakers and researchers. Reportage is published in local and international media outlets and is also included in publications by and for major global governance organisations such as UNICEF, UNDP, The European Union and the Quartet. Efforts at direct contact and coordination between the various protests are now being attempted through personal networks, conferences and strategy meetings. However, with the exception of one or two isolated cases there have been few instrumental gains. In the absence of any political opportunity structure over the last number of years, these protests are critiqued by some as symbolic acts (Al Saafin, 2012). Debates on indices of success or failure and the importance of symbolic acts aside, we can concretely say that these protests have managed to persist for years and have played a significant role in the growth of international dissent to Israeli policies (Landy, 2011). Though instrumentally we can rightly call this diverse set of peoples and practices a network, what sustains these protests week after withering week is the affective component of the sociality of prolonged dissent, which is producing what maybe properly understood as a transnational community.

Division through complexity

There are though significant obstacles to a sense of unity amongst such a collection of peoples, both real and imagined. This is an impressively heterogeneous group containing a liberal mix of cultures, experiences, genders and generations. It holds a multitude of different understandings of the problem and its resolution and such diversity of opinions is inevitable for three main reasons. First, there is the obvious relativity of acculturated understandings, experiences and expectations of Palestinians, Israelis and Internationals. This is further compounded by the historical depth and unfolding nature of the situation and its complexity of narratives and counter-narratives. These narratives have been central characters in a major geo-political performance for over a century now with each character vying for the attention, sympathies and assistance of audiences and powers near and far. Third, in this period of 'relative quite' expropriation of Palestinian land and property is not simply a state-controlled exercise. It is a transnational project where private capital, diaspora resources, urban planning, archaeological preservation, environmental quality, messianic beliefs and other stakeholders devolve the state from culpability.

Much of the differentiation between dissenters' understandings is to be found in the modes of dispossession employed by 'pro-Israeli' agencies. In East Jerusalem alone a property developer and a religious tomb are driving evictions in *Sheikh Jarrah*; in *Silwan*, illegal homes are demolished and a bronze-age archaeological dig undermines foundations; a national park is established on the land of *Issawiya and* a by-pass road is set to cut *Beit Safafa* in two. In *Area C* of the West Bank, where the Israeli military has jurisdiction over the Palestinian civilian population,[6] dispossession occurs by various means. The construction of the West Bank 'barrier' around *Walaja*, the settlement security fences near *Beit Ummar* and the military Firing Zone 918 all confiscate land on the grounds of security needs. Construction companies expanding settlements and their road systems are all part of infrastructure development and 'natural growth'. Absence of infrastructure is also effective, as when raw sewage from the *Betar Iilit* settlement pollutes Palestinian agricultural land below. Bureaucracy and the rule of law are also significant. Palestinian villages like *Susiya* remain 'unrecognised' and so they are not connected to transport, water and power infrastructures and have their homes, schools, sheep pens and porta-loos demolished on the grounds that they are illegal constructions.

Attributing blame and proposing a resolution on which there can be consensus is difficult. For collective action framing there is simply no unifying diagnostic to describe the problem, no definitive protagonist to highlight and no certain prognosis for resolution. Framing process theory sees movement actors as 'signifying agents actively engaged in the production and maintenance of meaning for constituents, antagonists, bystanders or observers' (Benford & Snow, 2000, p. 613). Collective action frames function to organise experience and guide action 'by simplifying or condensing aspects of "the world out there" but in ways that are intended to mobilise potential adherents and constituents, to garner bystander support, and to demobilise opponents' (Benford & Snow, 2000, p. 614). While I do not dismiss the descriptive and analytic utility of framing theory, the diffuse powers that transnational collectives of dissenters face increasingly problematise this process (Olausson, 2009; Schrock et al., 2004). Such diffusion of power is now common across the liberalised globe. While the dictator's delight in pasting his bust on every street corner ultimately portraits him as the head that must roll, the evicted Palestinians from *Sheikh Jarrah* are locked in an Israeli court fight over private property rights and Ottoman era documentation. That their opponents in court are *Nahalat Shimon International*, one of a number of US funded organisations that have explicit Zionist motivations to settle Jews in East Jerusalem, has no bearing on the proper proceedings of civil cases (Fendel, 2010; Ir Amim, 2009; OCHA, 2010; Reiter & Lehrs, 2010). Apportioning blame in *Sheikh Jarrah* is highly problematic and is just one particular instance of how dispossession has been advanced during this period of quiet.

However, the lack of unified diagnostic or prognostic does not preclude participation in protest, nor does it inhibit non-instrumental socialisation by the dissenters. Given that most protests are routine events, there is a limited need for tactical meetings and those that occur are not open to the dissenting masses. Being 'normal' people, dissenters spend much of their week tending to the ordinary needs of living, the quotidian affairs. In doing so, a complex of intersecting personal networks and structural momenta produce a high degree of non-instrumental exchange as a matter of routine, hospitality, friendship and chance. A Rabbi, an Anarchist and an Arab walk into a bar is not a joke, the bar just happens to be *Uganda*. This is what Stewart (2007) calls the 'ordinary affects' of life, the unceasing and unremarkable encounters which make up most of our days. The residents of *Sheikh Jarrah* invite activists to join them in breaking the Ramadan fast for *Eid al-Fitr*. Vered visits a hospital in West Jerusalem to be with the family she knows from *Bel'in*. She has not seen them in almost a year and their young son is seriously ill. A Jewish-American activist falls in love and marries a Palestinian in the West Bank. Mia returns from Finland for two weeks and we go for coffee where an (other) anthropologist friend of hers joins us. I am asked if I can collect someone's cat from the vet in West Jerusalem and bring it to Bethlehem. Introductions are made at dinner parties and particular 'bi-lingual' schools become places for dissenters to send their children. If all this direct and indirect sociality, structure, specialisation, leisure activity exchange and contestation existed within a village or neighbourhood there would not be much compunction about using the term community.

Is the colloquial use of 'community' just shorthand for dissent's capacity to produce social capital – 'ties that are based on mutual trust and mutual recognition [that] do not necessarily imply the presence of collective identity' (Diani, 1997, p. 129). To what extent is collective identity essential to the notion of community? Indeed, how and why should we be talking about community at all? In the last section, I discuss the historical understanding of this concept in social science and its contemporary reformulations. I suggest that what links the various interpretations, practices, purposes and interests is the shared feeling that something is wrong. To use Nate Silver's term *Wrong* is the affective signal which cuts through the discursive noise and is what motivates the disparate individuals to come together (Silver, 2012). The consequent emplaced sociality of this political tourism, structured by the famous protest performances and the intervals of ordinary living, follow and create pathways of dissent sociality that are often devoid of strategic content. In the small and severely constrained landscape of the Israeli–Palestinian conflict, the daily reality of military occupation creates inescapable avenues along which dissenters are compelled to travel. When one chooses to attend the performances of dissent and follow the pathways that lead from one to another the faces and places encountered become familiar, shared and sometimes intimate. Is this what we might call community?

What is community?

'There's a left-wing community in Tel Aviv, but not here in Jerusalem'

Vered Amit points out that the historical practice of ethnography has reinforced a correlation between place and community, in effect employing location as the unit of analysis rather than the object of research (Amit & Rapport, 2002). Anthropology took its time in coming to understand that their cultural isolates were not timeless units of utopian sociality. In the 1950s, Max Gluckman and the Manchester School confirmed that 'tribal' life was neither harmonious nor isolated. Gender, generation, blood lines and indeed any facet of a social structure as much shaped dissent as it did order (Epstein, 1969; Gluckman 1955, 1958; Mitchell, 1969; Turner, 1957, 1967). Some time passed before this observation was applied to that great community of modernity, the Nation. Gellner and Anderson were amongst the first to unpick the historical contingency and the mechanisms through which national communities had come to be imagined in the minds of their members (Anderson, 1991; Gellner, 1983, 1994). The later turn to transnational studies has further problematised traditional concepts of belonging and also questioned the role that academia has played in reproducing the notion of nation as the natural representation of modernity (Appadurai, 2008; Beck, 2005; Wimmer & Glick-Schiller, 2002).

If communities need not be constructed from harmonious outgrowths of concrete social bonds and face-to-face relationships, then what are they? There is insufficient space to fully address this debate here, but the transnational turn has led to a reformulation of the concept in various ways. Studies on migration, business and finance, trade agreements, tourism, scientists, elites and more now talk of transnational communities in which 'place' is of secondary importance or less. Instead we have communities of practice, episteme, purpose or interest which are based on shared convictions, values, expertise, goals or socio-political visions. What most authors agree on is a sense of *belonging* emerging from mutual interaction, a common project and/or imagined identity and the active involvement of some of its members (Basch, Glick-Schiller, & Blanc, 1994; Djelic & Quack, 2010a; Hannerz, 1992; Levitt, 2001; Mayntz, 2010; Metiu, 2010; Morgan, 2001; Morgan & Kubo, 2010). Despite the perceived explosion in transnationalism 'approaches that dominate the study of globalization direct attention selectively to markets, organizations, and networks, neglecting other kinds of social collectives extending beyond national boundaries, such as communities' (Mayntz, 2010, p. 64). Though some authors are now beginning to critically apply the term to transnational socialites (Dobusch & Quack, 2010; Mariussen, 2010; Metiu, 2010), its general absence limits our understanding of the both role and impact of novel community formations in the studies of social protest and the wider discussion of how and when community is produced.

How is community?

Amit uses the term community to distinguish a collective connection that is not merely or even primarily instrumental. This excludes for example members of a workforce if they engage only through formal roles. However, when co-workers begin to meet for coffee, lunch conversations or go bowling together some of them may come to feel part of a community.

> Most of our experiences of communality arise similarly out of more or less limited interactions afforded by a variety of circumstantial associations, with our neighbours, the parents of children at our children's school, or team-mates, fellow students, club members, conference-goers and more. (Amit & Rapport, 2002, pp. 58–59)

This sense of belonging, through quotidian and banal interaction which Amit calls *consociation,* emerges first through eye-contact, recognition, then being able to put names to faces, telling stories about mutually shared experiences, and in some cases leading to friendship, intimacy, love or lasting animosity. An example is Dyck's observation of the construction of community sentiment in suburban Canada through the consociation practices of parents supporting their children at track and field days. At these weekly events parents shared the purposes and practices of positive child rearing, leading to formal identification as a 'track parent with reference to a person's history of co-participation with others in happenings' (Dyck, 2002, p. 116). Repeated presence at and participation in track days, entailing casual social interactions and a growing intimacy with both people and behavioural norms, can lead to one being identified with – and feeling as part of – a community. Even more limited, less formal and indirect familiarities are produced through the proclivities of our daily routines. Over time we begin to recognise others, at shops, bus stops or our favourite bars. By regular movement through spaces we learn the rhythms of the lives of people whom we do not know. For Wallman (1998) recognising and occasionally being recognised by others in these 'traffic relations' also fosters a sense of belonging, without the need for direct interpersonal relationships or substantial exchange. Implicit in Wallman's analysis is the awareness that community imagination comfortably accommodates an affinity to others whom we shall never meet. This understanding is of course in line with Anderson's (1991) formulation of national belonging and also evokes 'a wider set of social potentials that exist for a specified population' (Pink, 2008, p. 171). However, the community of dissent, which passes through Israel and Palestine, is a rather ambiguous population to specify. Due to its diffuse and dispersed constituency, in which 'belonging may or may not be recognized, interpreted, responded to and felt' (Amit in Rapport & Amit 2012b), and because of its non-traditional modes this population is not well imagined as a community along its transnational dimension, either by observers or practitioners.

Communities of practice, purpose, interest and affect

All the community processes outlined above are apparent if one spends a few months at sites of dissent such as *Sheikh Jarrah*, *Beit Ummar* or *Kikar Paris*. Authors have being re-imagining the concept of community in the face of such novel socialities and perhaps we could call the transnational populace that pass through these performances a community of practice, purpose, interest or episteme. While the popular committee protests do share a mode of practice in non-violent or more properly 'unarmed' resistance, practice alone would exclude the professional contingency of journalists, legal experts, fund raisers and NGO assistance that have such crucial and engaged roles. The purposes of protest performances are well stated in the local dimension; resisting evictions, dispossession, restriction, ending the occupation, etc. However, there is no consensus on the greater purpose of the network of protests, as Nilli admitted 'we are fighting for different things'. Perhaps, we can better imagine this transnational dissent as producing a community of interest or episteme. However, interest too 'must be understood in a very general sense to avoid misinterpretation' (Mayntz, 2010, p. 66), whereas episteme has more generally been applied to communities of 'professionals with recognized expertise and competence in a particular domain' (Haas, 1992, p. 3). We can say though, that even while practices, purposes interests and episteme are differentially constructed and constrained, everyone from the Palestinian waiting at the checkpoint, to a Rabbi for Human Rights, the Anarchist blocking a bulldozer, the UN report compiler, the fact finding Christian or Fasel who wants his house back, all share the feeling that something is wrong there.

This feeling is not of secondary importance, nor is it a mindless reaction. It is a sophisticated, pervasive and often astute process by which we perceive, understand and judge our world. This model of affect follows from the work of neuroscientist Antonio Damasio who sees emotions as describing the relationship between the organism and the environment. Emotion is not the result of higher cognitive process, it is not the by-product of a rational actor designed to prepare them for fight or flight. It is a 'wordless knowledge' which informs our understanding of the world and the actions of others independent of conscience discursive critique (Damasio, 1997, 2000). Jesse Prinz expands on this to propose that emotion is a form of perception and that feelings of *Right* or *Wrong* are an embodied judgement on an act or a behaviour subjectively apprehended which constitutes the essence of morality. Feeling that something is wrong is what tells us that a moral precept has been transgressed (Prinz, 1997, 2004, 2007).

There is of course no universal Right or Wrong which we all access. Wrong is a cultural construct and we cannot doubt that those advocating a 'Greater Israel' through the expansion of settlements feel this to be the Right thing, but all transnational dissenters be they foreign or local come to the scheduled sites of protest because they feel something is wrong. They may arrive there by different paths but they have all become moral actors. Palestinians who have lived for generations under both banal and violent expressions of military occupation have little reason to judge their lot as somehow legitimate. Many Israeli dissenters have had to overcome nationally promoted sentiments of Right and Wrong and both they and the Internationals are no doubt also being acculturated in some way by the emergent 'moral entrepreneurs' of GCS (Beck, 2005).

Given that the feeling that something is wrong is the basis of any moral judgement and precedes cognitive formulation, the need for a unifying framing is not proven for collective mobilisation. Regardless of its origin or object of attribution, what resonates with all is the sense of wrong and this is enough to sustain dissent and overcome discursive complexity, ideological tension and post-modern obfuscation of oppression. Driven by the ambiguous certainty of wrongness, these people move through and come to share the established and emergent physical spaces in which first faces and places become familiar and then possibly loved or loathed in concrete relationships. Yet, others in the dispersed population equally engaged by this sense of wrongness pass by unmet in the bustling commerce of dissent. It not only apposite and analytically useful to conceive of dissent in Israeli and Palestine as producing community on the basis of a sheared sense of wrong, it is in many ways a more concrete and inclusive unit of analysis than the practices, purposes and interests.

Conclusion: imagining the unimagined

It would be wrong to ignore the impediments that this community faces. It is certainly not a peaceful 'place' to be and is the object of systematic derision, oppression, incarceration and occasionally violent death. Its national fragmentation is highly problematic. Despite being ideal candidates for cosmopolitan identity, the mobile, affluent and urbane Israelis find it particularly hard to subordinate nationalist identity and their role as the oppressor. Palestinians in the occupied territories have an impeded capacity for movement and which restricts their opportunity for non-instrumental activities; you cannot simply go for coffee in Jerusalem. The Israeli and Palestinian constituents are not only a minority in the surrounding populations, they are dispersed across a dozen or more performances which mostly happen at the same time on Friday or Saturday, thus diminishing their visible extent. Though the Internationals bring much needed vigour to activities, their framings and actions sometimes unintentionally offend both Palestinians and Israelis. For this they are mostly forgiven but their high turnover diminishes the sense of permanence of the community. The *professionalisation* of dissent and service provision by NGOs is also open to accusations of profiteering or 'normalisation' (Allen, 2013; Nakhleh, 2012). Finally, it cannot be said that there has been much material success in terms of ending the occupation, and few Palestinians or Israelis speak of hope.

Communal divisions, costly misunderstandings, a fast and fluid turnover of people and institutional dysfunction are perhaps inevitable in transnational communities, indeed we have come to expect as much from their traditional counterparts. However, such issues will inevitably play out through framing processes and novel negotiations in the unfolding global civil structures. A lack of instrumental progress or hope and subsequent burnout and despair are perhaps the most difficult and most important issues to address, and not just for pro-Palestinian activism. Many other contemporary social issues requiring major structural realignment, such as the global capital system, military-industrialism, patriarchal power and so on, will not be overcome quickly and will be opposed by resource rich embedded interests within those structures. If as academics we recognise that community is 'good to think with' we can still critically approach the ambiguities of its instances in terms of scale, duration, mediation, formalisation and so forth (Rapport & Amit, 2012b). Perhaps more relevant to the performance of dissent, given that community is traditionally evoked to express and harness social capacity and a sense of permanence, its appropriation by academia may also assist its practitioners in re-imagining the extent and potential of their own novel social formations. The knowledge that from within GCS distributed communities emerge, interact and provide a legitimate sense of belonging may assist dissenters in imaging their capacity to endure what may be many years of striving to put the obvious wrongs of the world to right.

Notes

1. The term pro-Palestinian is technically problematic in that it may not be a central rational for some dissenters and because it falsely connotes 'anti-Israeli' stances in other quarters. However, its colloquial power is sufficient to describe many of the undefined sentiments discussed in this piece.
2. Ecumenical Accompaniment Programme in Palestine and Israel. A programme of international observers developed by the World Council of Churches in 2001.
3. Di LaKibush (Hebrew) meaning End the Occupation. This is written on each black-hand placard in one of three languages, Hebrew, Arabic or English.
4. An Arabic name for a major gateway on the Old City walls. Also known as *Sar Schem* (Schem Gate) in Hebrew or Damascus Gate in English.
5. Shabbat (Hebrew) runs from sundown on Friday evening till sundown on Saturday evening. Most commercial venues in the Jewish west of the city and all public transport stops. Private cars become a premium at this high point of the weekly protest cycle.
6. In the West Bank since the Oslo accords, the Palestinian Authority nominally administers civil and security matters in Area A and civil matters in Area B. Israel administers security in Area B and both civil and security matters in Area C.

References

Allen, L. (2013). *The rise and fall of human rights: Cynicism and politics in occupied Palestine*. Stanford, CA: Stanford University Press.

Al Saafin, L. (2012, July 10). How obsession with 'nonviolence' harms the Palestinian cause. *The Electronic Intifada*. Retrieved from http://electronicintifada.net/content/how-obsession-nonviolence-harms-palestinian-cause/11482

Amit, V., & Rapport, N. (2002). *The trouble with community: Anthropological reflections on movement, identity and collectivity*. London: Pluto.

Anderson, B. R. O. (1991). *Imagined communities: Reflections on the origin and spread of nationalism* (2nd ed.). London: Verso.

Anheier, H., & Katz, H. (Eds.). (2004). *Network approaches to Global Civil Society. In Global Civil Society 2004–2005*. London: Sage, pp. 206–221. Retrieved from http://www2.lse.ac.uk/internationalDevelopment/research/CSHS/civilSociety/yearBook/contentsPages/2004-2005.aspx

Appadurai, A. (2008). *Modernity at large: Cultural dimensions of globalization*. London: University of Minnesota Press.

Basch, L. G., Glick-Schiller, N., & Blanc, C. S. (1994). *Nations unbound: Transnational projects, postcolonial predicaments, and deterritorialized nation-states*. London: Routledge.

Beck, U. (2005). *Power in the global age : A new global political economy*. Cambridge: Polity.

Benford, R. D., & Snow, D. A. (2000). Framing processes and social movements: An overview and assessment. *Annual Review of Sociology, 26*(1), 611–639. doi:10.1146/annurev.soc.26.1.611

Bennett, W. L., & Segerberg, A. (2011). Digital media and the personalization of collective action. *Information, Communication & Society, 14*(6), 770–799. doi:10.1080/1369118X.2011.579141

Berezin, M. (1999). Political belonging: Emotion, nation and identity in fascist Italy. In G. Steinmetz (Ed.), *State/Culture: State-formation after the cultural turn* (pp. 355–377). London: Cornell University Press.

Berezin, M. (2001). Emotions and political identity: Mobilizing affection for the polity. In J. Goodwin, J. M. Jasper, & F. Polletta (Eds.), *Passionate politics: Emotions and social movements* (pp. 83–98). London: University of Chicago Press.

Bevington, D., & Dixon, C. (2005). Movement-relevant theory: Rethinking social movement scholarship and activism. *Social Movement Studies, 4*(3), 185–208. doi:10.1080/14742830500329838

Billig, M. (1995). *Banal nationalism*. London: Sage.

Borah, P. (2011). Conceptual issues in framing theory: A systematic examination of a Decade's literature. *Journal of Communication, 61*(2), 246–263. doi:10.1111/j.1460-2466.2011.01539.x

Dalai Lama. (n.d.). The Global Community | The Office of His Holiness The Dalai Lama. Retrieved February 8, 2013, from http://www.dalailama.com/messages/world-peace/the-global-community

Damasio, A. R. (1997). Deciding advantageously before knowing the advantageous strategy. *Science, 275* (5304), 1293–1295.

Damasio, A. R. (2000). *The feeling of what happens: Body, emotion and the making of consciousness*. London: Vintage.

Diani, M. (1997). Social movements and social capital: A network perspective on movement outcomes. *Mobilization: An International Quarterly, 2*(2), 129–147.

Djelic, M.-L., & Quack, S. (Eds.). (2010a). *Transnational communities: Shaping global governance*. Cambridge: Cambridge University Press.

Djelic, M.-L., & Quack, S. (2010b). Transnational communities and governance. In M. Djelic & Quack (Eds.), *Transnational communities: Shaping global governance* (pp. 26–63). Cambridge: Cambridge University Press.

Dobusch, L., & Quack, S. (2010). Epistemic communities and social movements: Transnational dynamics in the case of creative commons. In M.-L. Djelic & S. Quack (Eds.), *Transnational communities: Shaping global economic governance* (pp. 262–288). Cambridge: Cambridge University Press.

Durkheim, É. (1912). *The elementary forms of religious life*. (K. E. Fields, Trans.) (1995th ed.). New York: Free Press.

Dyck, N. (2002). Have you been to Hayward field? Childrens's sport and the construction of community in suburban Canada. In V. Amit (Ed.), *Realising communities: Concepts, social relationships and sentiments* (pp. 105–123). London & New York: Routledge.

Epstein, A. L. (1969). Gossip, norms and social network. In J. C. Mitchell (Ed.), *Social networks in urban situations: Analyses of personal relationships in Central African towns* (pp. 117–127). Manchester: Manchester University Press.

Fendel, H. (2010, March 25). Benny Elon: Sheikh Jarrah is critical. *Arutz 7 Israel National News*. Retrieved December 31, 2012, from http://www.israelnationalnews.com/News/News.aspx/136723

Fog Olwig, K. (2002). The ethnographic field revisited: Towards a study of common and not so common fields of belonging. In V. Amit (Ed.), *Realising communities: Concepts, social relationships and sentiments* (pp. 124–145). London & New York: Routledge.

Gellner, E. (1983). *Nations and nationalism*. Ithaca, NY: Cornell University Press.

Gellner, E. (1994). *Encounters with nationalism*. Oxford: Blackwell.

Gluckman, M. (1955). *Custom and conflict in Africa*. Oxford: Blackwell.

Gluckman, M. (1958). *Analysis of a social situation in modern Zululand*. Manchester: Manchester University Press.

Goffman, E. (1974). *Frame analysis: An essay on the organization of experience*. Cambridge: Harvard University Press.

Goodwin, J., & Jasper, J. M. (2004). *Rethinking social movements: Structure, meaning and emotion*. Oxford: Rowman & Littlefield.

Goodwin, J., Jasper, J. M., & Polletta, F. (2001). *Passionate politics: Emotions and social movements.* London: University of Chicago Press.

Gould, D. (2004). Passionate political processes: Bringing emotions back into the study of social movements'. In J. Goodwin & J. M. Jasper (Eds.), *Rethinking social movements: Structure, meaning and emotion* (pp. 124–145). Oxford: Rowman & Littlefield.

Haas, P. M. (1992). Introduction: Epistemic communities and international policy coordination. *International Organization, 46*(01), 1–35. doi:10.1017/S0020818300001442

Hannerz, U. (1992). *Cultural complexity: Studies in the social organization of meaning.* New York, NY: Columbia University Press.

Ir Amim. (2009). *Evictions and settlement plans in Sheikh Jarrah: The case of Shimon HaTzadik. Ir Amir.* Retrieved from http://www.ir-amim.org.il/Eng/_Uploads/dbsAttachedFiles/SheikhJarrahEngnew.pdf

Jasper, J. M. (2011). Emotions and social movements: Twenty years of theory and research. *Annual Review of Sociology, 37,* 285–303.

Jean-Klein, I. (2003). Into committees, out of the house? Familiar forms in the organization of Palestinian committee activism during the first Intifada. *American Ethnologist, 30*(4), 556–577.

Juris, J. S. (2008). *Networking futures: The movements against corporate globalization.* Durham, NC: Duke University Press.

Keane, J. (2003). *Global civil society?* Cambridge: Cambridge University Press.

Korten, D. C., Perlas, N., & Shiva, V. (2002, November 20). *Global civil society: The path ahead.* Retrieved November 25, 2012, from http://www.davidkorten.org/global-civil-society

Landy, D. (2011). *Jewish identity and Palestinian rights: Diaspora jewish opposition to Israel.* London: Zed Books.

Levitt, P. (2001). *The transnational villagers.* Berkeley: University of California Press.

Mariussen, A. (2010). Global warming, transnational communities, and economic entrepreneurship: The case of carbon capture and storage (CCS). In M.-L. Djelic & S. Quack (Eds.), *Transnational communities: Shaping global economic governance* (pp. 370–390). Cambridge: Cambridge University Press.

Mayntz, R. (2010). Global structures: Markets, organizations, networks – and communities? In M.-L. Djelic & S. Quack (Eds.), *Transnational communities: Shaping global economic governance* (pp. 64–83). Cambridge: Cambridge University Press.

Metiu, A. (2010). Gift-giving, transnational communities, and skill building in developing countries: The case of free/open source software. In M.-L. Djelic & S. Quack (Eds.), *Transnational communities: Shaping global economic governance* (pp. 233–261). Cambridge: Cambridge University Press.

Mitchell, J. C. (1969). The concept and use of social networks. In J. C. Mitchell (Ed.), *Social networks in urban situations: Analyses of personal relationships in Central African towns* (pp. 1–50). Manchester: Manchester University Press ND.

Morgan, G. (2001). Transnational communities and business systems. *Global Networks, 1*(2), 113–130. doi:10.1111/1471-0374.00008

Morgan, G., & Kubo, I. (2010). Private equity in Japan: Global finance markets and transnational communities. In M.-L. Djelic & S. Quack (Eds.), *Transnational communities: Shaping global economic governance* (pp. 163–185). Cambridge: Cambridge University Press.

Nakhleh, K. (2012). *Globalized Palestine: The national sell-out of a Homeland.* Trenton, NJ: Red Sea Press.

Nepstad, S. E. (2004). *Convictions of the soul.* New York, NY: Oxford University Press.

Nepstad, S. E., & Smith, C. (2001). The social structure of moral outrage in recruitment to the U.S. Central American peace movement. In J. Goodwin, J. M. Jasper, & F. Polletta (Eds.), *Passionate politics: Emotions and social movements* (pp. 158–174). Chicago & London: University of Chicago Press.

OCHA. (2010, October 1). The case of Sheikh Jarrah – Israeli settlers' activities in Palestinian neighbourhoods – OCHA report (12 October 2010). *United Nations: Office for the Coordination of Humanitarian Affairs occupied Palestinian territory.* Retrieved December 31, 2012, from http://unispal.un.org/UNISPAL.NSF/0/16BCBEE7EBF67D5F852577BA004C06F1

Olausson, U. (2009). Global warming–global responsibility? Media frames of collective action and scientific certainty. *Public Understanding of Science, 18*(4), 421–436. doi:10.1177/0963662507081242

Pink, S. (2008). Re-thinking contemporary activism: From community to emplaced sociality. *Ethnos, 73*(2), 163–188. doi:10.1080/00141840802180355

Prinz, J. J. (1997). *Perceptual cognition: An essay on the semantics of thought.* Chicago: University of Chicago, Department of Philosophy.

Prinz, J. J. (2004). *Gut reactions: A perceptual theory of emotions.* Oxford: Oxford University Press.

Prinz, J. J. (2007). *The emotional construction of morals.* Oxford: Oxford University Press.

Rapport, N., & Amit, V. (2012a). *Community, cosmopolitanism and the problem of human commonality (anthropology, culture and society)* (Kindle.). London: Pluto Press.

Rapport, N., & Amit, V. (2012b). Communities as 'good to think with'. In *Community, cosmopolitanism and the problem of human commonality (anthropology, culture and society)* (Kindle, Chapter 1, Section 'affect/belonging'.). London: Pluto Press. Retrieved from http://www.amazon.com/Community-Cosmopolitanism-Commonality-Anthropology-ebook/dp/B00885RZZ2/ref=tmm_kin_title_0

Reiter, Y., & Lehrs, L. (2010). *The Sheikh Jarrah affair: The strategic implications of Jewish settlement in an Arab neighborhood in East Jerusalem*. The Jerusalem Institute for Israel Studies. Retrieved from http://jiis.org/?cmd=publication.7&act=read&id=584

Risley, A. (2012). Rejoinder. In J. Goodwin (Ed.), *Contention in context: Political opportunities and the emergence of protest*. Stanford, CA: Stanford University Press.

Schrock, D., Holden, D., & Reid, L. (2004). Creating emotional resonance: Interpersonal emotion work and motivational framing in a transgender community. *Social Problems, 51*, 61–81.

Silver, N. (2012). *The signal and the noise: Why so many predictions fail-but some don't*. New York, NY: Penguin Group US.

Stewart, K. (2007). *Ordinary affects* (Kindle.). Durham, NC: Duke University Press.

Turner, V. (1957). *Schism and continuity in an African society: A study of Ndembu village life*. Manchester: Manchester University Press ND.

Turner, V. (1967). *The forest of symbols: aspects of Ndembu ritual*. New York, NY: Cornell University Press.

Turner, V. (1988). *The anthropology of performance*. New York, NY: PAJ Publications.

Wallman, S. (1998). New identities and the local factor – or when is home in town a good move? In N. Rapport & A. Dawson (Eds.), *Migrants of identity: Perceptions of home in a world of movement* (pp. 181–205). Oxford: Berg.

Warren, M. R. (2010). *Fire in the heart: How white activists embrace racial justice*. Oxford: Oxford University Press.

Wimmer, A., & Glick-Schiller, N. (2002). Methodological nationalism and beyond: Nation-state building, migration and the social sciences. *Global Networks, 2*(4), 301–443.

Why the psychology of collective action requires qualitative transformation as well as quantitative change

Andrew G. Livingstone

Psychology, University of Exeter, Washington Singer Labs, Exeter, UK

The argument of this paper is that social psychological models of collective action do not (and cannot) adequately explain social change and collective action through models based on shared variance between variables. Over and above the questions of *why* and *how* collective action and social change occur, such models do not adequately address the question of *when* they occur: at what point on a measure of perceived illegitimacy – or any other predictor – does a person decide that enough is enough, and at what point do shared grievances transform into mass protest? Instead, it is argued that the transition from inaction to action at the level of both the individual and the group is better conceptualised as a qualitative transformation. A key agenda for the social psychology of collective action should therefore be to conceptualise the link between quantitative variation in predictors of action and the actual emergence of action.

Relatively few phenomena are that orderly or well behaved; on the contrary, the world is full of sudden transformations and unpredictable divergences. (Zeeman, 1976, p. 65)

The 'transformation of quantity to quality' defends a systems-based view of change that translates incremental inputs into alterations of state. (Gould, 1987, p. 154)

The aim of this paper is to critically consider whether social psychological models of collective action adequately explain the *emergence* of collective action and protest. Its core argument is that these models, to the extent that they focus on shared variance between variables, underplay the qualitative transformations involved when people decide as individuals and communities that enough is enough. That is, as with any action, there is a *point at which* it emerges, both at the level of the individual and at the collective level of a community or social movement. In other words, the emergence of action involves a transformation of *form*; a transition that involves dis-continuous change as one acts by signing a petition, attending a rally or smashing a window, rather than doing nothing or doing something else. The question posed in this article is whether social psychological models sufficiently address this aspect of collective action – that is, can they tell us something about the point at which protest emerges?

While it touches upon a number of different perspectives and academic disciplines, the initial impetus for this article actually came from media coverage of collective action, and particularly the way in which journalists so frequently employ metaphors of heat and temperature when describing collective action and mass events. This is especially so when these events involve physical confrontation and violence. Accordingly, tensions between groups 'simmer' before 'boiling over'; anger 'explodes'; violence 'erupts'; and riots are 'sparked'. Correspondingly, tensions 'cool' as the likelihood of confrontation dissipates. The metaphor is also extended into discussions of the underlying structural, economic, cultural, political and historical conditions of conflict, which turn a region or a situation into a 'powder keg' or a 'tinderbox', ready to burn or explode should someone be so careless or cruel as to 'light the fuse'.

Social psychological predictors of collective action

As a social psychologist with a dedicated interest in understanding the causes and consequences of collective action, it is tempting to dismiss these journalistic tropes as the clichéd language of individuals who have little grasp of (or worse, no inclination to grasp) the complexity, meaning and *explicability* of social action (Bassel, 2012; Philo & Berry, 2004). This is especially so in view of the recent proliferation of research into the social psychological predictors of collective action, which has advanced our understanding of the factors that lead people to engage in protest. Much of this work draws on classic theories in intergroup relations which emphasise the role of perceiving our group as being relatively deprived (relative deprivation theory; Crosby, 1976; Walker & Mann, 1987; Walker & Smith 2002) or as having lower status (social identity theory; Tajfel & Turner, 1979) compared to a relevant out-group. Importantly, this disadvantage must be appraised in terms of group memberships and social identification, rather than in terms of interpersonal comparison. That is, our relatively deprived position must be fraternal, rather than egoistic (Crosby, 1976).

When group-level social comparison does reveal a deficit, a number of factors help to determine whether we seek to engage in action that will rectify it. For example, partaking in collective action is more likely when we subjectively *identify* with the group in question (Kelly, 1993; Simon et al., 1998). This is especially so when the identity relates to a specific social movement rather than the more abstract social category (Simon et al., 1998), and when the identity has been 'politicised' (Simon & Klandermans, 2001). Other appraisals of the nature of the status difference are also important, not least of all in terms of whether it is perceived as fair or unjust (see Van Zomeren, Postmes, & Spears, 2008). Thus, researchers drawing on social identity theory have emphasised the importance of the perceived illegitimacy of an in-group's low status (e.g. Bettencourt, Charlton, Dorr, & Hume, 2001; Ellemers, Wilke, & Van Knippenberg, 1993), while relative deprivation theory emphasises the importance of felt entitlement as a driver of action against one's relative deprivation (Crosby, 1976).

While legitimacy and entitlement reflect a sense that collective action is *proper* or *appropriate*, other factors relate to whether such action is seen as *possible*. Relevant concepts here include the perceived stability of status differences from social identity theory (Ellemers et al., 1993; Tajfel & Turner, 1979), and the perceived feasibility of challenges to inequality from relative deprivation theory (Crosby, 1976; Walker & Smith, 2002). Within models of collective action, a sense of collective (as opposed to individual) efficacy has been found to increase collective action tendencies (see Van Zomeren et al., 2008, for a review), while research on the elaborated social identity model of crowd behaviour (Reicher, 1996) has highlighted the importance of experiences of empowerment in collective behaviour, both as a dynamic outcome of participation in collective action and as a driver of future participation (Drury & Reicher, 1999, 2005).

In addition to drawing on classic theories of intergroup behaviour, social psychological models of collective action have also provided a fresh take on predominant 'rationalist' accounts of motives for collective action participation, based on cost–benefit calculations (see Olson, 1965). Klandermans (1997) differentiates between a *reward* motive for collective action participation, reflecting the expected value and cost of participation for the individual, and a *social* motive for participation. This social motive is conceptualised in terms of the expected reactions of important others (family and friends) to one's participation – a distinct set of concerns to those based on individual utility.

Finally, the development of intergroup emotion theory (Smith, 1993; see Iyer & Leach, 2008 for a review) has further stimulated the integration of emotion into social psychological theories of collective action (see also Runciman, 1966). Drawing on appraisal theories of emotion (e.g. Lazarus, 1991), various studies have shown how different appraisals of a context give rise to particular emotions. Appraising one's in-group's disadvantage as illegitimate thus gives rise to anger (Van Zomeren, Spears, Fischer, & Leach, 2004), while appraising an in-group's past actions as illegitimate can give rise to collective guilt or shame (Iyer, Schmader, & Lickel, 2007). These group-based emotions in turn influence specific action intentions: for example, anger predicts a desire to engage in collective action (Van Zomeren et al., 2004), shame predicts a desire to withdraw from a conflict (Iyer et al., 2007) and contempt predicts an orientation towards more radical or illegal forms of protest (Tausch et al., 2011). Other emotions shape collective action by *inhibiting* tendencies towards protest. These inhibitory emotions include both negative emotions such as fear (Miller, Cronin, Garcia, & Branscombe, 2009) and positive emotions such as admiration (Sweetman, Spears, Livingstone, & Manstead, 2013).

Temperature gauge? Quantifying collective action

Of particular relevance to the present argument is that most of the developments described above have, with some exceptions (e.g. Drury and Reicher, 1999, 2005), involved methods and data that are amenable to quantitative analyses. This has numerous benefits, not least of all in allowing complex models to be tested, and the contribution of individual factors to be pinpointed. The result is that we have a sense not only of the range of factors that matter in predicting collective action, but also of their relative predictive value when taking other factors into account.

It is helpful to illustrate this in relation to perceived illegitimacy, one of the most prominent factors in models of collective action (see Jost & Major, 2001). Many studies have found a direct association between illegitimacy perceptions and collective action tendencies (e.g. Ellemers et al., 1993; Livingstone, Spears, Manstead, & Bruder, 2009). As noted above, illegitimacy is also the main appraisal which has been found to produce intergroup anger, which in turn predicts collective action tendencies and behaviour (Mackie, Devos, & Smith, 2000; Van Zomeren et al., 2004). Other research has examined how the strength of the link between illegitimacy and anger also depends on other concurrent appraisals, such as a perceived threat to one's in-group's identity (Livingstone et al., 2009).

Quantifying illegitimacy has also allowed its role across a large number of studies to be assessed. Van Zomeren et al.'s (2008) meta-analysis found support for their social identity model of collective action (SIMCA), in which illegitimacy is rooted in social identity, and plays a distinct predictive role to that played by collective efficacy. Moreover, as is clear in the model illustrated in Figure 1, this quantitative synthesis allows specific effect sizes to be estimated for each link in the model, providing a clear indication of the *magnitude* of the association between illegitimacy and its antecedents and consequences. When used to predict similarly measured outcomes such as collective action tendencies, a continuous measure of illegitimacy (or any construct) enables us to gauge whether it is a statistically significant predictor of the outcome, the magnitude of its effect (e.g. the effect of a unit increase in illegitimacy on collective action tendencies) and the amount of variance in the outcome that is explained by illegitimacy.

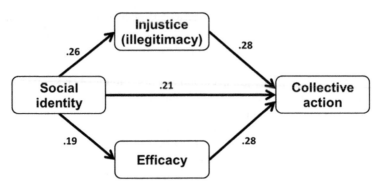

Figure 1.   Van Zomeren et al.'s (2008) social identity model of collective action. The path weights are standardised effect sizes estimated from their meta-analysis.

Quantitative change and qualitative transformation

On the basis of this brief review, it is tempting to assert that social psychological models have done a very good job of explaining collective action, especially relative to lay characterisations of protest and collective conflict as abrupt, out-of-nowhere eruptions of frustration. From here on, however, I want to suggest that there is another sense in which these models have *not* done such a good job at explaining collective action.

The issue here is that the statistical association between illegitimacy and intentions to protest (for example) begs a number of other questions about the emergence of collective action. Not least of these is that of *how much* illegitimacy is required for a person to go from abstaining to engaging in an act of protest. At what point on a scale of illegitimacy would a person go from doing nothing to doing something? When is a unit increase in perceived illegitimacy *enough* to instigate an act of protest? The same question can be asked in relation to genuinely collective behaviours: At what point in their emerging sense of injustice does a community or nascent social movement go from not acting to acting? The more general point is that for any collective action – and indeed, for any intentional act at all – there is *a point at which* it emerges, when an individual goes from doing nothing to doing something, or shifts from doing one thing to doing something else. Likewise, the development and behaviour of social movements and less structured groups involve not just variance in their collective action intentions and behaviour, but the transition from not acting to acting, and transitions between different types and targets of action.

These points also echo the apparent abruptness with which events such as the recent revolutions in Tunisia, Egypt and Libya, or the riots in England in 2011 developed. These events were clearly precipitated by much longer term structural factors, coupled with the preparedness of activist individuals and networks – however loosely constituted and otherwise invisible to outsiders – to seize opportunities to act (Reicher & Stott, 2011). The psychological factors discussed above – collective identity; disadvantage; illegitimacy; emerging efficacy; and emotions – are also quite clearly central to explaining such events. Nevertheless, to frame an explanation of such events in terms of high levels of illegitimacy, or any other variable or combination of variables, is to dodge other important questions: Why *there*? Why *then*?

The key argument of this paper is therefore that social psychological models of collective action in one sense offer compelling explanations for collective action and protest, but in another sense explain little about the actual *emergence* of action. That is, they say little about when *qualitative*, discontinuous change occurs in the outcome. The very fact of the transition between inaction and action (or vice versa) indicates that such discontinuous change is a fundamental feature of collective action both at the level of the individual and the group, yet the relationship between this change and underlying psychological variables has largely been ignored in favour of analyses that focus on explaining quantitative variance in measures of collective action (a point that echoes the more general limitations of 'arbitrary metrics' – measures whose meaning is unclear in terms of *absolute* levels of a variable – in psychology; Blanton & Jaccard, 2006). In short, at some point on our scales of illegitimacy or any other predictor, something *happens*.

It is probably useful at this point to be clear about what this argument is *not*. For one thing, it is not a simple call for greater statistical sophistication, at least not in and of itself (the potential contribution of complex modelling will be discussed further below; see Smith & Conrey, 2007). This is important because it could be countered that quantitative analyses of collective action are more nuanced and sophisticated than the sketch presented here. One might argue, for example, that the link between perceived illegitimacy and collective action can be more fully articulated through examining moderation (interaction) effects, nonlinear effects and effects on behavioural outcomes rather than measured intentions to engage in protest. However, far from addressing the issue of how quantitative variation translates into qualitative transformations in outcomes, these practices in and of themselves only recapitulate it in different terms. For example, one might specify that the linear effect of illegitimacy (or whatever) might be different depending on another variable (e.g. Ellemers et al., 1993; Livingstone et al., 2009; Tajfel & Turner, 1979; Turner & Brown, 1978), but this again fails to identify the *point at which* action emerges on any of the simple regression slopes that could be drawn. Likewise, a curvilinear effect simply suggests that the effect of a unit change in a predictor is different at different levels of itself, producing increasingly or decreasingly large quantitative change in the outcome without specification of *where* on the outcome scale (or indeed, the predictor scale) action might be expected to emerge.

Lastly, while behavioural measures, such as whether or not a participant signed a petition (e.g. Sweetman et al., 2013), are something of a gold standard when it comes to gauging outcomes, their relation to predictors is usually indicated by an odds ratio which indicates the *probability* that an individual falls into one category or another (i.e. whether they signed the petition or not). An odds ratio can thus indicate the likelihood that an individual will engage in a behaviour following a unit increase in a predictor (see Tabachnik & Fidell, 2012), but not *how much* of that predictor is necessary to engender a *shift* from one outcome category to another – that is, to go from not signing a petition to signing a petition, or from performing a legal act of protest to performing an illegal act of protest.

If statistical sophistication does not provide an easy way to address the relationship between quantitative change and qualitative transformation, it is because the issue is as much a question of theory as it is a question of method. That is, the roots of the issue lie in conceptual treatments of collective action which do not pay sufficient attention to the *points of transition* involved in the phenomena that interest us. It should be made clear at this stage that the problem is not inherent to the use of the statistical tests discussed above. In fact, they could all be used to meaningfully help in identifying the point(s) at which transitions to and between action occur. The key issue, as I will discuss in more detail below, is the willingness to conceptualise and to try to identify points of transition in the first place, and to try to relate them to underlying predictors such as perceptions of illegitimacy.

Quantitative change and qualitative transformation beyond social psychology

Whatever the reason for the failure to address the emergence of collective action in terms of a transition or qualitative change in form, a particularly striking thing about that failure is just how *unusual* social psychology is among academic disciplines in neglecting the link between quantitative change and qualitative transformation. Turning first to the 'hard' sciences, a simple example is the notion of *phase transitions* between states of matter as a function of temperature. To state the obvious, substances not only get warmer or cooler: at certain points on the temperature scale, unit changes in temperature result in qualitative transformation as the substance boils, melts or freezes.

Taking the freezing process from a micro- to a macro-level, climate change theory has also posited that qualitative transformation can occur in the climate as a result of quantitative unit changes in an input or inputs. Specifically, some theorists have suggested that climate change cycles occur because the equilibrium between positive (cooling) and negative (warming) feedback effects is altered by changes in the planet's pattern of orbit (e.g. Milankovitch, 1941). The result is that at some point, a unit change in the planet's orbit (however that is quantified) means that ice spread not only increases, but acquires a *self-sustaining momentum* even in the absence of change in the input (i.e. the pattern of orbit) – the ice-albedo feedback effect (Cubasch & Cess, 1990).

The idea that large-scale transformations in phenomena can be understood in terms of disturbed equilibria between competing forces can also be found in other fields such as evolutionary biology. The theory of punctuated equilibria (Eldredge & Gould, 1972; Gould & Eldredge, 1977) posits that evolution is characterised less by smooth, incremental change, and more by long periods of stasis punctuated by short, rapid bursts through which 'branching' – the emergence of new species – occurs. This pattern, according to the theory, reflects the negation of opposing pressures during periods of stasis (equilibrium) and the breaking of that equilibrium during periods of rapid change. At a higher level still, science itself has been characterised by Kuhn (1996) as developing not through steady incremental gains but through periods of stability followed by rapid periods of revolution – so-called paradigm shifts.

Attempts to address sharp, qualitative change in the form of our objects of study are thus quite apparent in the 'hard' or physical sciences. Turning in the opposite direction from the vantage point of social psychology, it is also apparent that social sciences are marked by efforts to address such transformations. The notion of a 'tipping point' is a prime example. Although popularised as a metaphor for understanding the rapid social transmission of ideas and trends (see Gladwell, 2000), tipping points were initially conceptualised as a point at which a (small) input change leads to a change in process with self-sustaining momentum, and transformative outcomes – even in the absence of further changes in input. As a concrete example, tipping points were invoked by scholars such as Grodzins (1958) and Schelling (1971) to understand the dynamics of racial (de)segregation in housing in the USA. The utility of the tipping point analysis was in identifying that so-called white flight did not just increase as a function of the number of black families moving into a predominantly white neighbourhood. Rather, according to Schelling, there was a point at which one additional black family moving into the neighbourhood would trigger a process that ultimately led to complete racial segregation as white families moved out of the area, *irrespective* of whether more black families moved in.

Turning closer to the topic of this special issue, the idea that there is a point at which transformative outcomes start to emerge has also characterised a number of approaches to the study of collective action. A case in point is the development of threshold models (Granovetter, 1978) which attempt to model the point at which individuals choose to perform a behaviour in the collective interest, as a dynamic function of the number of others performing the behaviour in a particular context. Again, the implication is that there is *a point at which* individuals start to act. Similar points can be made in relation to other sociologically oriented theories of collective action, such as critical mass theory (Marwell & Oliver, 1993) or the processes of 'frame alignment' emphasised within framing theory (Benford & Snow, 2000).

Even within social psychology itself, the issue of qualitative transformation – such as sudden 'jumps' in the occurrence of behaviours of interest – has been broached. For example, Scherer

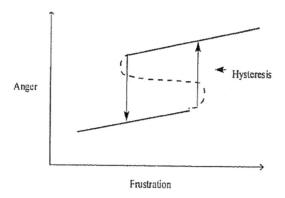

Figure 2.   Scherer's (2000) illustration of hysteresis in the relationship between anger and frustration. The dotted portion of the curve is 'inaccessible', in that no actual observations occur on it. The arrows represent points at which there is a 'jump' (sharp increase or decrease) in anger as a function of frustration.

(2000) has argued that the link between specific emotions and their underlying appraisals is neither straightforward nor linear. Instead, Scherer (2000) argues, an important aspect of emotional phenomena such as the relationship between anger and frustration is instead that 'with increasing frustration there may be a point where anger will, in a dramatic fashion, jump to a considerably higher level rather than continue to increase in a linear fashion' (p. 89).

In order to explain (or at least to appropriately describe) this aspect of the phenomenology of emotions such as anger, Scherer suggests that the relationship between appraisals and emotions can be represented by a particular type of nonlinear curve characterised by *hysteresis* – a concept that constitutes a key element of catastrophe theory (Thom, 1975; Zeeman, 1976), discussed further below. Figure 2 provides an example of such a function in the case of the frustration–anger relationship. As Scherer (2000) suggests, 'whereas a linear function would predict steadily rising anger with increasing frustration, the hysteresis function, containing a folded-back, nonaccessible region, suggests that the intensity of anger will change abruptly for specific degrees of frustration' (pp. 88–89).

Clarifications

It should be made clear at this juncture that in very briefly reviewing the various theories above, there is no claim that all (or any) of them are necessarily *right*. Indeed, many have been subjected to sustained critique and remain controversial in their fields. But independently of their specific *explanatory* value, their value in the present context is quite simply that in their different ways, they directly address a fundamental feature of the phenomena under study: the existence of points of transition or qualitative change in form, and their relationship to incremental quantitative variation in inputs.

Another point to make clear here is that in arguing for the need to study points of qualitative transformation in order to adequately explain collective action, it is not the case that this should necessarily supersede or replace the linear, quantitative, shared variance approaches reviewed at the beginning of this article. More generally, it is not a question of competing perspectives or levels of analysis. This should be quite evident from the range of approaches covered above, each of which is underpinned by the quantification of inputs and (statistical) analysis of their relation – linear or otherwise – to the object of study. The point is that in doing so, they also recognise the existence of, and are theoretically concerned with, points of transition in those phenomena and their relationship to quantitative change in the inputs. In relation to collective action, the message is not that analyses based on shared variance are somehow misguided or necessarily of limited value. Rather, it is that such analyses signal a preoccupation with the question of *why* collective action occurs, and that the challenge they face is to address the question of *when* it happens, as a function of explanatory factors. While it was argued earlier in this article that interactive, nonlinear and/or behavioural effects are not the answer, it should be clear that they are very much *part* of the answer – just not in and of themselves.

The transformation of quantity to quality in collective action: setting an agenda

Having disparaged the journalistic cliché of heat metaphors at the outset of this paper, there is perhaps now a case for admitting that the implicit equation of the emergence of protest with a phase transition signals (unwittingly, for sure) an important blind spot in the social psychology of collective action. In doing so, it also sets the challenge of addressing that blind spot. So how can the study of collective action address this challenge? I have no intention of trying to offer a confident answer to this question here. Instead, the aim of the remainder of this article is simply to offer some thoughts on how to at least go about asking the right sorts of questions.

Sticking for the moment with the applicability of heat metaphors to collective action, it might be tempting to treat the emergence of action in the individual and in groups as a simple phase transition that occurs at identifiable points on measures of illegitimacy, efficacy, anger, etc. In short, can such measures be used as thermometers to indicate the 'boiling point' of an individual or a society? Unfortunately, the shift from inaction to action or from one action to another is unlikely to be tied to specific points on our measurement scales, or at least not straightforwardly. The issue here is that even for something as inanimate as water, the relationship between its boiling point and temperature is variable, contingent on factors such as atmospheric pressure. In the case of a psychological construct such as illegitimacy, its contingency on other variables is profound (Livingstone et al., 2009; Van Zomeren et al., 2008). Added to this is the fact that we are agentic and sense-making beings, and always *interpret* and *react* to self-report measures. The very act of trying to measure an individual's subjective sense of illegitimacy can thus lead to unexpected and highly varied responses, further muddying the link between any specific point on the scale and specific outcomes (see Blanton & Jaccard, 2006).

A more fruitful approach may be to draw more general conceptual guidelines from other approaches that have addressed the quantity–quality transition. For example, as noted above, the hysteresis concept employed by Scherer (2000) in relation to emotions is a key element of catastrophe theory (Thom, 1975; Zeeman, 1976). As the quote from Zeeman (1976) at the beginning of this article indicates, this mathematical approach was concerned with mapping precisely the sorts of transitions discussed here. Mapping these transformations as a function of underlying variation in predictors involves, in the simplest instance, the specification of a *bifurcation set* or *cusp*, such as the beginning of the fold-back curves in Figure 2. This represents the threshold(s) at which transformations occur. According to Zeeman, this provides a way of reconciling the observations that sometimes behaviour varies smoothly as a function of underlying predictors, but also sometimes undergoes sudden change. Importantly, more complex arrays of bifurcation sets can be produced as the number of inputs rises, modelling *multiple* points of transition that can occur depending on the specific levels of the inputs.

Outside of the mathematical complexity of catastrophe theory, the principle that can be extracted for present purposes is actually quite simple: that no matter how quantitatively complex or nuanced our model of inputs may be, its utility is only as great as our concurrent description of the nature of the phenomena we seek to explain – including acknowledgement of its sudden transformations as well as its smooth variation. That is, we need to have a grasp of the form of the behaviour surface (the forms that protest behaviour and collective action may take, including the nature of their emergence), as well as the underlying variables that shape it (the underlying control surface, in catastrophe theory terms). As Aubin (2004) puts it, the goal of catastrophe theory 'was to understand natural phenomena by approaching them directly' (p. 98), rather than beginning with the underlying inputs and inferring the form of phenomena from them (a one-way street to reductionism in Thom's, 1975, view). In short, there is value in starting with a fuller and franker characterisation of collective action and protest – when it happens, what happens, when it does not happen and where it all happens (or does not happen) – and working backwards to develop an adequate (descriptive) model of *the phenomena as they exist*, in addition to the hypothetico-deductive process that leads us to start with theoretical principles and work forward.

It is worth noting at this point that several researchers have begun to advocate complex modelling techniques developed in relation to theories of complex/dynamic systems (e.g. Thagard & Nerb, 2002), such as agent-based modelling (e.g. Smith & Conrey, 2007). At a basic level, such techniques allow complex interactions between large numbers of autonomous agents within an environment – and their interactions *with* their environment – to be modelled over time. As these advocates point out, this has major advantages over what Smith and Conrey (2007) term variable-based modelling (the more traditional covariance-based approach described briefly above), including that it allows the incorporation of qualitative effects, such as a threshold point at which an individual agent switches behaviour.

Approaches such as agent-based modelling clearly show the availability of analytic techniques that can help to address the issues raised thus far in this paper, signalling that theories of collective action that do directly address qualitative transformations are not placed beyond the bounds of quantitative analysis. Indeed, agent-based modelling is championed as a tool of theory *development*, in the sense that it allows examination of dynamics and outcomes that emerge over time given a specific set of parameters. That is, it is an inductive enterprise that is shaped by the assumptions and descriptions that are used to define the parameters of a model, for example, through the production of cognitive–affective maps (Thagard, 2010; see Schröder & Thagard, 2013, for an example). There is therefore a significant caveat to the potential value of complex modelling techniques when it comes to accounting for the points of transition identified here: the quality of such models is only as good as the quality of the inputs, in terms of measurement and in terms of conceptualisation and description (see Bonanbeau, 2002). Indeed, the development of appropriate inputs and parameters within such models can involve drawing on embedded, 'thick' descriptions of phenomena using techniques such as participant observation and interviews, or detailed descriptive surveys. This again leaves us with important conceptual and descriptive work to do regarding the nature of collective action and protest, and the place of qualitative transformation within them.

As a starting point, it is worth noting that the principle that quantitative variation translates into qualitative transformation is also recognisable in strands of philosophy, and particularly as a principle of Hegel's (1969) dialectical reasoning, later developed by Engels as the second principle of dialectical materialism. The utility of the principle of quantity-into-quality in explaining social change is tied to another of the principles of dialectics, one which resonates with a number of the scientific and social scientific approaches mentioned above. The principle is that any object of study – say, the climate, or the relationship between different individuals or between different groups – is best conceptualised as a system or process that consists of a set of opposing forces. Stability or stasis in that system therefore does not necessarily indicate the *absence* of factors that would precipitate change, such as the perceptions of illegitimacy that might instigate collective action (see Stewart, Leach, & Pratto, 2013). Rather, these factors are neutralised by countervailing forces; for example, emotions such as fear (Miller et al., 2009), or practical barriers to collective organisation or expression (Klandermans, 1997). The reason that the accumulation of quantitative changes can lead to qualitative transformations – when people act on their perceived illegitimacy – is that at a certain point, the quantitative change breaks the equilibrium between the opposing forces, allowing abrupt change to occur in the system as one force suddenly overwhelms the other, at least until new, countervailing forces emerge in response to the abrupt change. This philosophy of change is applied quite directly in the theory of punctuated equilibria, as noted earlier. In fact, while primarily concerned with questions within evolutionary biology, the quote from Gould (1987) at the beginning of this article offers an agenda for studying change that should resonate with collective action researchers, as part of 'a holistic vision that views change as interaction among components of complete systems, and sees the components themselves not as *a priori* entities, but as both products and inputs to the system' (p. 154).

A practical agenda for the social psychology of collective action

In this final section, I want to take these principles forward into a slightly more practical research agenda. The first point relates to how external forces, such as an event that evokes a sense of illegitimacy and anger, not only affect the intra-psychic world of individuals who form a 'mobilisation potential' (Klandermans, 1997), but also affect how individuals relate to and interact with one another. Accordingly, an increasing amount of research in social psychology is acknowledging that communication between individuals is crucial to understanding the way in which collective action pans out (Livingstone, Spears, Manstead, Bruder, & Shepherd, 2011; Smith & Postmes, 2011; Thomas, McGarty, & Mavor, 2009; Van Zomeren, Leach, & Spears, 2012; Van Zomeren et al., 2004). Importantly, a shared sense of social identity not only *shapes* our orientations to one another through initial definitions of 'us' and 'them', but in turn *changes* as a result of communication as people engage in shared meaning-making.

While the importance of communication in this dynamic is increasingly being addressed, it is also important to acknowledge that one of the barriers to genuinely shared representations and coordinated action is that precipitating events *happen to and are experienced differently by different individuals*. This is true even in dramatic and intense events such as a police baton charge against a group of protestors: not everyone will be hit, and even those who do get hit will vary in whether they have had previous experiences of such events, or whether it is a shockingly new experience. At the same point in time, many others a short distance away will not even be aware that a baton charge has begun (Stott, Adang, Livingstone, & Schreiber, 2007). The result is that a 'given' event can create *asymmetries* in the experiences and understandings of people who are involved. The extent to which particular points of transition into action are reached – the point at which one flees in fear, or collectively resists – will therefore be a function of whether shared representations and identity emerge *in situ* that both explain and provide a basis for acting in that context. As research on crowd behaviour has shown, the emergence of particular forms of action – a qualitative change in the nature of a collective's behaviour – is unlikely in the absence of shared identity and representations; but can emerge dramatically when such shared representations do develop (Drury & Reicher, 1999, 2005). Thus, the emergence of action is tied to *transformations in self-definition*. Consequently, getting a handle on the emergence of action requires conceptualising and studying identity as a *process* that is dynamically related to unfolding events, not just as a discrete, abstracted input or output.

The preceding discussion also makes it clear that the emergence of collective action, both at the level of the individual and the group, is a process that is embedded within wider, ongoing intergroup relations. This being the case, and in light of the review of catastrophe theory above, the second suggestion is to develop a psychology of *key events or points* in a dynamic – what may be termed points of phase transition – as well as of more abstracted perceptions over time. The importance of specific events is clearly acknowledged in many studies of collective action, both as precipitating factors that instigate appraisals and emotions (e.g. Iyer et al., 2007), or as intervening factors that affect appraisals and emotions across different time points (Tausch et al., 2011). However psychological impactful these events may be, they are nevertheless still treated as something of a black box whose specific *dynamic* and *content* are not an object of study in itself. What is it about the specific event – materially, temporally and psychologically – that saw people shift from inaction to action, or between different forms of action? Put more simply, what actually *happened*?

The importance of such an enterprise is brought into focus by another principle that has been central to research on crowd behaviour (e.g. Drury et al., 1999): That one group's actions *create specific material contexts* within which another group can (re)act, facilitating or inhibiting actions that may have or have not occurred otherwise (see also Kriesi, 2007). As Reicher and Stott (2011) have argued in relation to the riots in England in 2011, more abstracted psychological predictors such as illegitimacy, threat, anger and so forth are clearly necessary for the transition to action at an individual and a collective level, but understanding *when* and *how* that happens also requires a focus on how specific events, such as the nature of a police intervention in a particular situation, open up the material possibilities for these worldviews to be enacted.

Conclusion

In simple terms, the aim of this paper has been to signal an important blind spot in social psychological models of collective action and to provide some impetus towards addressing this shortfall. There were three aspects to this. The first was a recognition that the emergence of collective action (or any action) involves discontinuous change or transition as well as smooth, continuous variation, and that this is not sufficiently acknowledged in analyses that solely focus on shared variance between predictors and collective action outcomes. The second was to draw out the principles that (1) transitions *can* conceivably be mapped on to underlying quantitative change, but only if those transitions are fully acknowledged and appropriately conceptualised; and (2) that an appropriate conceptualisation of such transformations involves seeing social change as a process or system composed of opposing forces that at any point may negate (producing stability) or overwhelm (producing sharp change) one another (see Smith & Conrey, 2007; Stewart et al., 2013). The third step was to advocate a social psychology of points of transition, that is, the study of *in situ* moments of change within and between individuals, and between interacting groups. Hopefully these straightforward, incremental changes in theory and practice can edge us towards understanding the transformative change that characterises the world around us.

Acknowledgements

I am grateful to Colin W. Leach for his thoughtful comments on an earlier draft of this paper, and to two anonymous reviewers for their comments.

References

Aubin, D. (2004). Forms of explanations in the catastrophe theory of René Thom: Topology, morphogenesis, and structuralism. In M. N. Wise (Ed.), *Growing explanations: Historical perspective on the sciences of complexity* (pp. 95–130). Durham, NC: Duke University Press.

Bassel, L. (2012). *Media and the riots: A call for action*. London: Citizen Journalism Educational Trust and The-Latest.com

Benford, R. D., & Snow, D. A. (2000). Framing processes and social movements: An overview and assessment. *Annual Review of Sociology, 26*, 11–39.

Bettencourt, B., Charlton, K., Dorr, N., & Hume, D. L. (2001). Status differences and in-group bias: A meta-analytic examination of the effects of status stability, status legitimacy, and group permeability. *Psychological Bulletin, 127*, 520–542.

Blanton, H., & Jaccard, J. (2006). Arbitrary metrics in psychology. *American Psychologist, 61*, 27–41.

Bonanbeau, E. (2002). Agent-based modeling: Methods and techniques for simulating human systems. *Proceedings of the National Academy of Sciences of the United States of America, 99*, 7280–7287.

Crosby, F. J. (1976). A model of egotistical relative deprivation. *Psychological Review, 83*, 85–113.

Cubasch, U., & Cess, R. D. (1990). Processes and modelling. In J. T. Houghton, G. J. Jenkins, & J. J. Ephraums (Eds.), *Climate change: The IPCC scientific assessment, Intergovernmental Panel on Climate Change (IPCC)* (pp. 69–91). Cambridge: Cambridge University Press.

Drury, J., & Reicher, S. (1999). The intergroup dynamics of collective empowerment: Substantiating the social identity model of crowd behaviour. *Group Processes and Intergroup Relations, 2*, 1–22.

Drury, J., & Reicher, S. (2005). Explaining enduring empowerment: A comparative study of collective action and psychological outcomes. *European Journal of Social Psychology, 35*, 35–58.

Eldredge, N., & Gould, S. J. (1972). Punctuated equilibria: An alternative to phyletic gradualism. In T. J. M. Schopf (Ed.), *Models in paleobiology* (pp. 82–115). San Francisco, CA: Freeman, Cooper.

Ellemers, N., Wilke, H., & Van-Knippenberg, A. (1993). Effects of the legitimacy of low group or individual status on individual and collective status-enhancement strategies. *Journal of Personality and Social Psychology, 64*, 766–778.

Gladwell, M. (2000). *The tipping point: How little things can make a big difference*. New York, NY: Little Brown.

Gould, S. J. (1987). *An urchin in the storm: Essays about books and ideas*. London: W. W. Norton.

Gould, S. J., & Eldredge, N. (1977). Punctuated equilibria: The tempo and mode of evolution reconsidered. *Paleobiology, 3*, 115–151.

Granovetter, M. (1978). Threshold models of collective behavior. *American Journal of Sociology, 83*, 1420–1443.

Grodzins, M. M. (1958). *The metropolitan area as a racial problem*. Pittsburgh, PA: University of Pittsburgh Press.

Hegel, G. W. F. (1969). *The science of logic* (A. V. Miller, Trans). London: Allen & Unwin.

Iyer, A., & Leach, C. W. (2008). Emotion in inter-group relations. *European Review of Social Psychology, 19*, 86–125.

Iyer, A., Schmader, T., & Lickel, B. (2007). Why individuals protest the perceived transgressions of their country: The role of anger, shame, and guilt. *Personality and Social Psychology Bulletin, 33*, 572–587.

Jost, J. T., & Major, B. (2001). *The psychology of legitimacy: Emerging perspectives on ideology, justice, and intergroup relations*. Cambridge: Cambridge University Press.

Kelly, C. (1993). Group identification, intergroup perceptions and collective action. *European Review of Social Psychology, 4*, 59–83.

Klandermans, B. (1997). *The social psychology of protest*. Oxford: Basil Blackwell.

Kriesi, H. (2007). Political context and opportunity. In D. A. Snow, S. A. Soule, & H. Kriesi (Eds.), *The Blackwell companion to social movements* (pp. 67–90). Oxford: Blackwell.

Kuhn, T. L. (1996). *The structure of scientific revolutions* (3rd ed.). London: The University of Chicago Press.

Lazarus, R. S. (1991). *Emotion and adaptation*. Oxford: Oxford University Press.

Livingstone, A. G., Spears, R., Manstead, A. S. R., & Bruder, M. (2009). Illegitimacy and identity threat in (inter)action: Predicting intergroup orientations among minority group members. *British Journal of Social Psychology, 48*, 755–775.

Livingstone, A. G., Spears, R., Manstead, A. S. R., Bruder, M., & Shepherd, L. (2011). We feel, therefore we are: Emotion as a basis for self-categorization and social action. *Emotion, 11*, 754–767.

Mackie, D. M., Devos, T., & Smith, E. R. (2000). Intergroup emotions: Explaining offensive action tendencies in an intergroup context. *Journal of Personality and Social Psychology, 79*, 602–616.

Marwell, G., & Oliver, P. E. (1993). *The critical mass in collective action: A micro-social theory.* New York: Cambridge University Press.

Milankovitch, M. M. (1941). *Canon of insolation and the ice age problem.* Belgrade: Königlich Serbische Academie. English translation by the Israel Program for Scientific Translations.

Miller, D. A., Cronin, T., Garcia, A. L., & Branscombe, N. B. (2009). The relative impact of anger and efficacy on collective action is affected by feelings of fear. *Group Processes and Intergroup Relations, 12,* 445–462.

Olson, M. (1965). *The logic of collective action: Public goods and the theory of groups.* Cambridge, MA: Harvard University Press.

Philo, G., & Berry, M. (2004). *Bad news from Israel.* London: Pluto Press.

Reicher, S., & Stott, C. (2011). *Mad mobs and Englishmen? Myths and realities of the 2011 riots.* London: Constable and Robinson.

Reicher, S. D. (1996). 'The Battle of Westminster': Developing the social identity model of crowd behaviour in order to explain the initiation and development of collective conflict. *European Journal of Social Psychology, 26,* 115–134.

Runciman, W. G. (1966). *Relative deprivation and social justice: A study of attitudes to social inequality in twentieth-century England.* Berkeley: University of California Press.

Schelling, T. (1971). Dynamic models of segregation. *Journal of Mathematical Sociology, 1,* 143–86.

Scherer, K. R. (2000). Emotions as episodes of subsystem synchronization driven by nonlinear appraisal processes. In M. D. Lewis & I. Granic (Eds.), *Emotion, development, and self-organization: Dynamic systems approaches to emotional development* (pp. 70–99). Cambridge: Cambridge University Press.

Schröder, T., & Thagard, P. (2013). The affective meanings of automatic social behaviors: Three mechanisms that explain priming. *Psychological Review, 120,* 255–280.

Simon, B., & Klandermans, B. (2001). Politicized collective identity: A social–psychological analysis. *American Psychologist, 56,* 319–331.

Simon, B., Loewy, M., Sturmer, S., Weber, U., Freytag, P., Habig, C., … Spahlinger, P. (1998). Collective identification and social movement participation. *Journal of Personality and Social Psychology, 74,* 646–658.

Smith, E. R. (1993). Social identity and social emotions: Toward new conceptualizations of prejudice. In D. M. Mackie & D. L. Hamilton (Eds.), *Affect, cognition, and stereotyping: Interactive processes in group perception* (pp. 297–315). San Diego, CA: Academic Press.

Smith, E. R., & Conrey, F. R. (2007). Agent-based modeling: A new approach for theory building in social psychology. *Personality and Social Psychology Review, 11,* 87–104.

Smith, L. G. E., & Postmes, T. (2011). The power of talk: Developing discriminatory group norms through discussion. *British Journal of Social Psychology, 50,* 193–215.

Stewart, A. L., Leach, C. W., & Pratto, F. (2013). *What constitutes social change? Conceptualizations, critiques, and new directions.* University of Connecticut. Unpublished manuscript.

Stott, C., Adang, O., Livingstone, A., & Schreiber, M. (2007). Variability in the collective behaviour of England fans at Euro2004: Policing, intergroup relations, identity and social change. *European Journal of Social Psychology, 37,* 75–100.

Sweetman, J. P., Spears, R., Livingstone, A. G., & Manstead, A. S. R. (2013). Admiration regulates social hierarchy: Antecedents, dispositions, and effects on intergroup behavior. *Journal of Experimental Social Psychology, 49,* 534–542.

Tabachnik, B. G., & Fidell, L. S. (2012). *Using multivariate statistics* (6th ed.). London: Pearson.

Tajfel, H., & Turner, J. C. (1979). An integrative theory of intergroup conflict. In W. G. Austin & S. Worchel (Eds.), *The social psychology of intergroup relations* (pp. 33–47). Monterey, CA: Brooks-Cole.

Tausch, N., Becker, J., Spears, R., Christ, O., Saab, R., Sing, P., & Siddiqui, P. (2011). Explaining radical group behavior: Developing emotion and efficacy routes to normative and non-normative collective action. *Journal of Personality and Social Psychology, 101,* 129–148.

Thagard, P. (2010). EMPATHICA: A computer support system with visual representations for cognitive-affective mapping. In K. McGregor (Ed.), *Proceedings of the workshop on visual reasoning and representation* (pp. 79–81). Menlo Park, CA: AAAI Press.

Thagard, P., & Nerb, J. (2002). Emotional gestalts: Appraisal, change, and the dynamics of affect. *Personality and Social Psychology Review, 6,* 274–282.

Thom, R. (1975). *Structural stability and morphogenesis.* London: Benjamin.

Thomas, E. F., McGarty, C., & Mavor, K. I. (2009). Aligning identities, emotions, and beliefs to create \commitment to sustainable social and political action. *Personality and Social Psychology Review, 13,* 194–218.

Turner, J. C., & Brown, R. (1978). Social status, cognitive alternatives and intergroup relations. In H. Tajfel (Ed.), *Differentiation between social groups: Studies in the social psychology of intergroup relations* (pp. 201–234). London: Academic Press.

Van Zomeren, M., Leach, C. W., & Spears, R. (2012). Protesters as 'Passionate Economists': A dynamic dual pathway model of approach coping with collective disadvantage. *Personality and Social Psychology Review, 16*, 180–198.

Van Zomeren, M., Postmes, T., & Spears, R. (2008). Toward an integrative social identity model of collective action: A quantitative research synthesis of three socio-psychological perspectives. *Psychological Bulletin, 134*, 504–535.

Van Zomeren, M., Spears, R., Fischer, A. H., & Leach, C. (2004). Put your money where your mouth is! Explaining collective action tendencies through group-based anger and group efficacy. *Journal of Personality and Social Psychology, 87*, 649–664.

Walker, I., & Mann, L. (1987). Unemployment, relative deprivation, and social protest. *Personality and Social Psychology Bulletin, 13*, 275–283.

WalkerI., & SmithH. (Eds.). (2002). *Relative deprivation: Specification, development, and integration.* New York, NY: Cambridge University Press.

Zeeman, E. C. (1976). Catastrophe theory. *Scientific American, 234*, 65–70, 75–83.

Index

Note: Page numbers in *italics* represent *tables*
Page numbers in **bold** represent **figures**
Page numbers followed by 'n' refer to notes

For Product Safety Concerns and Information please contact our EU
representative GPSR@taylorandfrancis.com Taylor & Francis Verlag GmbH,
Kaufingerstraße 24, 80331 München, Germany

Batch number: 08158490

Printed by Printforce, the Netherlands